D0482602

About Island Press

Since 1984, the nonprofit organization Island Press has been stimulating, shaping, and communicating ideas that are essential for solving environmental problems worldwide. With more than 1,000 titles in print and some 30 new releases each year, we are the nation's leading publisher on environmental issues. We identify innovative thinkers and emerging trends in the environmental field. We work with world-renowned experts and authors to develop cross-disciplinary solutions to environmental challenges.

Island Press designs and executes educational campaigns in conjunction with our authors to communicate their critical messages in print, in person, and online using the latest technologies, innovative programs, and the media. Our goal is to reach targeted audiences—scientists, policymakers, environmental advocates, urban planners, the media, and concerned citizens—with information that can be used to create the framework for long-term ecological health and human well-being.

Island Press gratefully acknowledges major support of our work by The Agua Fund, The Andrew W. Mellon Foundation, The Bobolink Foundation, The Curtis and Edith Munson Foundation, Forrest C. and Frances H. Lattner Foundation, The JPB Foundation, The Kresge Foundation, The Oram Foundation, Inc., The Overbrook Foundation, The S.D. Bechtel, Jr. Foundation, The Summit Charitable Foundation, Inc., and many other generous supporters.

Biting the Hands that Feed Us

Biting the Hands that Feed Us

How Fewer, Smarter Laws Would Make Our Food System More Sustainable

Baylen J. Linnekin

Washington | Covelo | London

Library of Congress Control Number: 2016938036

Printed on recycled, acid-free paper

Manufactured in the United States of America
10 9 8 7 6 5 4 3 2 1

Keywords: agriculture, beef, dietary guidelines, FDA, food, food freedom, food law, food safety, food waste, foraging, FSMA, Good Samaritan laws, organic farming, raw milk, standard of identity, sustainability, ugly fruit, USDA.

Contents

Foreword

Few consumers realize the law's impact on our ability to produce and access certain foods. But food is a heavily regulated field—safety rules control the production and sale of food, labeling laws regulate the information that must, may, and may not appear on a package, and zoning ordinances restrict where food may be grown and where and when it may be sold. These examples are just the tip of the iceberg.

Recently, consumers have begun to recognize the significance of these laws and have started examining the policy decisions surrounding them. For some, this is due to changing eating habits, such as the growing interest in purchasing foods that were produced more sustainably, or products prepared without the use of certain ingredients. Others may have come into contact with this system when their favorite farm or dairy was forced to shutter its doors, not because its products were unsafe but because of the crushing burden of complying with regulations. *Biting the Hands that Feed Us* provides a groundbreaking account of this flawed system. Baylen Linnekin skillfully examines laws at various levels of government that, despite good intentions, operate in ways that make the food we produce and consume less sustainable, rather than more so.

I first met Baylen at a food law conference at Northeastern Law School in January 2011, where he spoke about current and historical food safety laws that, paradoxically, have made our food supply less safe.

I could see immediately that Baylen possesses a genuine curiosity about the consequences of our system of food regulation, and that he brings a necessary critical perspective to the discussion. He is a gifted storyteller, weaving together historical facts, personal anecdotes, and legal explications in a way that makes this field compelling to a broad audience.

Baylen and I bonded over a shared frustration with the many laws that privilege large, industrial food producers at the expense of small, nonconventional food producers. These laws can stifle opportunity, even as their benefits are dubious or at least unproven. Examples of these contradictions are rife, and many are recounted in this book. They include USDA rules that require the use of nitrates or nitrites in the production of salumi, even though small-scale production does not necessitate such additives for safety. [p. 2] (What is salumi, you may ask? Read on to find out!) Or FDA on-farm requirements that could force small and large farmers alike to spend thousands of dollars to comply—rules that, as you'll learn, "won't put a stop to foodborne illness, but . . . threatened to put an end to sustainable farming." [p. 27] There are even laws that make it impossible for people to grow and consume their own food, such as city ordinances that prohibit growing vegetables in a front yard. [p. 148]

Another crucial issue that I'm sure will incense readers concerns laws that cause the waste of healthy, wholesome food. Forty percent of the food produced in the United States goes to waste. For each pound of food wasted, we waste all of the energy, water, and other resources that went into producing that food, causing a tremendous environmental impact. Yet many laws either cause us to waste food or make wasting it the easy decision. *Biting the Hands that Feed Us* includes several maddening examples, such as the fruit and vegetable grading standards sanctioned by the U.S. Department of Agriculture. Grading is based on the visual appearance of produce rather than on its safety, healthfulness, or flavor, yet it dictates the purchasing decisions of most retailers. Stores refuse to buy apples that are not graded "fancy" or carrots not graded "U.S. No. 1." [p. 126] As Baylen describes, these grading standards are among many senseless rules that lead us to waste more food and have a less sustainable food system.

Baylen has a strong orientation toward "food freedom," or the idea that individuals should have the right to grow, buy, and consume the foods of their choice. Indeed, he is recognized as a national leader in the food freedom movement. Supporting the food freedom agenda generally means limiting the government's role in the food supply. Indeed, as Baylen shows, "the continued growth of the nation's food rules has not made for a more sustainable food system." [p. 194] In this book, he outlines his litmus test for how food regulations can and should be adapted to foster sustainability—by eliminating rules that promote unsustainable outcomes and those that prohibit sustainable practices. While I would not always prescribe the same policy solutions as he does, I see great value in learning about these failed regulations and engaging in robust debate about potential solutions. Baylen's ease in relaying these compelling and frustrating stories demonstrates the absurdities in our current approach to regulating the food system and establishes the pressing need for reform. Though the structure of such reform is subject to debate, *Biting the Hands that Feed Us* provides the catalyst to stimulate this vital discourse.

In addition to shining a light on the many food laws that do not support sustainability, *Biting the Hands that Feed Us* presents readers with a call to action. Throughout the book, you will see how citizen outrage and organizing has helped halt legislation or influenced agency decisions. Such organizing led to (i) an FDA reversal of its spent-grain rules that, if enacted, would have made it nearly impossible for breweries to continue their age-old practice of donating spent grains for use as animal feed [p. 31], and (ii) FDA's decision to rewrite its rules implementing the Food Safety Modernization Act (FSMA) after citizen pushback about the potential effects on small farms. [p. 28] Food is personal, which makes this topic approachable, especially when described in Baylen's clear and straightforward manner. People know what they like to eat, how they like to eat it, and where they like to buy it. Baylen shows that when regulations thwart those choices, individuals can affect policy decisions if they make their voices heard.

Biting the Hands that Feed Us presents fascinating illustrations of food laws gone wrong, showcasing Baylen's knowledge of the legal issues and ability to convey their relevance to everyday eating. This book is written in his unique, witty, and insightful voice, and will both inspire readers to understand these struggles and empower them to take action.

—Emily Broad Leib, assistant clinical professor of law, director of the Harvard Food Law and Policy Clinic, and deputy director of the Center for Health Law and Policy Innovation, Harvard Law School

Preface

In this book, I take a fresh look at many of the things that are wrong with America's food system—specifically, rules that hinder sustainable food practices and promote unsustainable ones—and propose much-needed changes. The book's focus on ways that government rules hamper sustainability may be a new one for many readers. But its recommendation that the solution to many sustainability issues in the food realm is *fewer* rules—rather than more—is likely to strike most readers as new, unusual, and even a little unsettling. But I believe strongly that readers who truly want a more sustainable food system should—and will—embrace my arguments in favor of eliminating these bad rules. Consider, for example, that if rules senselessly shut out farmers who want to sell meats or produce at their local farmers market—as you'll learn, they very often do—then those rules are broken. They're not serving farmers or consumers. Instead, they're what's biting the hands that feed us. The correct response isn't to build new rules on top of the old, dysfunctional ones. Rather, it's to throw out the broken rules. As I argue throughout this book, we need to remove the shackles that bind America's food system to ensure a more sustainable food future. Notably, although I believe many food rules hamper sustainability, this is not a book about eliminating all rules that govern food. I support many food rules and suspect readers will agree with my arguments in favor of those rules, which I describe throughout the book and in greater detail in chapter 5.

I think you'll see that I want many of the same things that other supporters of sustainable food want. Unlike some writers, though, I see laws and regulations as frequent barriers to sustainability. Simply piling on more and more rules, as commentators often suggest, isn't going to solve many of the problems with our food system. Instead, doing so will exacerbate these problems. The alternative I propose is this: I think it's easier, smarter, more just, and less costly to remove all of the anti-sustainability regulations that helped get us into this mess in the first place. People waste food, for example. But as you'll see in chapter 3 of this book, oftentimes that's because rules mandate that they do so, or make it more difficult or expensive for them not to do so. Eliminate the rules that promote food waste, and we'll see it decrease dramatically.

My journey to write this book has taken several years. In law school, about ten years ago, I decided that I would make food law my life's work. Delving deep into the past and present of many terrible food laws during my academic studies while also tending an organic garden plot in Washington, D.C.'s oldest and largest victory garden, in the city's Glover Park neighborhood—coupled with my long-standing interest in civil liberties—perhaps made that focus inevitable. After graduating in 2009, I moved to Fayetteville, Arkansas, where I spent the year studying for a master of laws degree in agricultural and food law. Once I moved back to the District, I put the degree to good use by starting a nonprofit group, Keep Food Legal, that worked to promote the idea that people have the right to make their own food choices.

Since that time, I've written hundreds of online columns for *Reason*, a libertarian magazine, on the pervasive impact of many federal, state, and local food laws. Many of the columns I've written there and elsewhere—including at outlets such as the *Boston Globe*, *Huffington Post*, *New York Post*, *Baltimore Sun*, and *Playboy*, and scholarly legal publications such as the *Wisconsin Law Review* and *Hastings Constitutional Law Quarterly*—have served to stimulate the ideas that form the basis of this book. Over the years, my writings have focused on topics as varied as cottage food laws, animal welfare, soda taxes, barbecue fumes, school lunches, food safety, GMOs, "ag gag" laws, urban agriculture, local meat processing, food trucks, dietary guidelines, raw milk, obesity, farm subsidies, food deserts, beer laws, food waste, and countless others. Along the way, I've been fortunate to have the opportunity to speak out on many of these same issues on MSNBC, HuffPost Live, Fox Business Network, numerous NPR affiliates, BBC Radio, and other radio shows and television channels, and have been quoted by leading news outlets such as the *Wall Street Journal*, *Washington Post*, *Los Angeles Times*, Reuters, and many others.

In recent years, I've also taught a variety of food-policy courses to undergraduate students at American University, my alma mater (both for my bachelor's and law degree). And I've taught a food law and policy seminar at George Mason University Law School for the past few years. The excellence of the students at both schools means I've been fortunate to have the opportunity to discuss many of the issues in this book with interesting—and interested—young adults. The location of these schools—both are situated in the Washington, D.C. area—also means that I've had the opportunity to tap into the area's vast network of experts to serve as guest lecturers in my classes. That list so far has included congressional staffers, journalists from publications such as *National Geographic*, the *Washington Post*, and *Politico*, and policy experts from the Humane Society of the United States, the Environmental Working Group, and many other nonprofits. And I've been able to take advantage of other unique resources in the area. For example, I've taken my undergraduate students on a tour of First Lady Michelle Obama's White House garden, and my law students to a farm-to-table restaurant and a local craft brewery.

I also speak regularly at many law schools and universities around the country. In winter 2014, I was invited by Yale Law School student organizers to take part in a workshop at Yale's annual environmental law conference, New Directions in Environmental Law. The workshop at which I presented focused on recent progress in environmentally sound food policies. Despite the focus of the workshop, I sounded an ominous tone. Progress was scant, I noted. So many federal, state, and local food rules were environmentally *unsound*, I told attendees, that there was perhaps more work that needs to be done than ever before. My remarks at that workshop served as an inspiration for many of the ideas that appear in this book. Around that same time, I also met with Emily Turner Davis, my editor at Island Press, to discuss some of these ideas. We'd had an initial conversation thanks to Prof. Michael T. Roberts, who leads UCLA Law School's Resnick Program on Food Law and Policy. Prof. Roberts had very kindly suggested that Emily speak with me about a book for Island Press. Without Michael and Emily, this book simply wouldn't exist. I'm grateful to both for seeing promise in me and in my ideas.

Later that same year, I was invited by Prof. Emily Broad Leib, who founded and leads Harvard Law School's pioneering Food Law and Policy Clinic, to moderate a panel on sustainable and humane meat production as part of a conference cosponsored by two student groups at the law school. The panel's focus on reducing regulatory barriers for sustainable meat producers was the impetus for me to begin to dig deeper into the implications of freeing the nation's sustainable livestock farmers from needlessly burdensome regulations, something I discuss at length in chapter 1 of this book. The panel, unintentional as the timing was, coincided with the U.S. Department of Agriculture's (USDA) controversial recall of millions of pounds of meat from a USDA-inspected meat processor in California, an issue I also discuss in some detail in chapter 1.

Since agreeing to write this book, I've had the opportunity to discuss many of the issues you'll read about here at conferences held at Duke Law School, University of Kentucky Law School, and Seattle University Law School, and in talks at the University of Chicago Law School, University of Idaho Law School, and many other law schools and other forums around the country. These conferences and lectures, the excellent questions and feedback I've received from students, faculty, and other audience members alike, and the inspiration I've taken from my fellow speakers have helped me to hone many of the arguments I make in this book.

I've also had the opportunity to play a small role in three legal cases I discuss in the book. The first is a recent Supreme Court case that centered on California raisins (yes, including the claymation ones from the 1980s). The second is a federal court case that centers on skim milk labeling and the First Amendment. The third case, also now in federal court and also focusing on the First Amendment, concerns restrictions on agricultural whistle-blowing. You'll learn much more about these cases in chapter 2.

This work—focused as it has been on so many different food-law issues—has helped me to better learn to look beyond the obvious. To take a fresh look, as I noted here earlier. Often, when it comes to food policy in this country, that's a skill that seems to be sorely lacking. Consider, for example, that even food laws that appear to have little or nothing to do with the environment can have truly unintended consequences for sustainability. Take the U.S. Food and Drug Administration's (FDA's) 2015 decision to ban partially hydrogenated oils that contain trans fat. These oils are typically found in processed foods such as frostings and coffee creamers that don't exactly form the cornerstone of any diet that might be pegged as grounded in sustainability.

Still, although the public health community, the media, and the public were generally receptive to the law, many rainforest and animal-welfare advocates worry about what exactly will replace partially hydrogenated oils in processed foods. "The biggest beneficiary of the demise of trans fat has been palm oil, which has seen a dramatic increase in demand as a result," says Paul Shapiro, vice president for farm animal protection with the Humane Society of the United States.[1] "Most of the palm oil in the world comes from Indonesia and Malaysia, typically from plantations now sitting on former rainforests." Those rainforests, Shapiro explains, are home to threatened populations of animals such as orangutans, Sumatran tigers, pygmy elephants, Sumatran rhinos, and clouded leopards, to name a few. When the FDA banned partially hydrogenated oils, it didn't consider the ban's impact on Sumatran tigers. Yet the future of the tiger and many of its fellow Indonesian and Malaysian rainforest dwellers is threatened today by the FDA's ban.

You'll learn about many, many other unintended consequences throughout this book. Most often, they're more direct than the connection between banning trans fats and harming rainforests and the creatures that live there. As you'll see, however well-meaning a law is, it can have dramatic unintended consequences. You'll also see that many laws appear not to be very well-meaning at all. Regardless of intent, you'll learn that laws that might seem "good" or "bad" often have a similar effect: they handcuff sustainable food producers, create tons of food waste, or even prohibit people like you from engaging in sustainable food practices at home.

Acknowledgments

Thanks to my parents for everything.

Thanks to my partner, Roxanne Alvarez, for her love and support.

I'm grateful to Emily Broad Leib for being a great collaborator, colleague, and friend, and for agreeing with me and disagreeing with me, depending on the issue, with equal aplomb.

Josh Galperin from Yale Law School, Margot J. Pollans from the Elisabeth Haub Law School, and Michael T. Roberts from UCLA Law School graciously contributed their valuable time and their expert opinions in reviewing the manuscript that became this book. The text was improved vastly thanks to their respective willingness to offer comments, suggestions, and edits, and to point me in the right direction in places where they saw I was headed elsewhere.

I'm grateful to a handful of law students around the country—busy people who are not known for their wealth of free time—who kindly offered to fact check chapters of the manuscript. Vytas Babusis, Rosemarie Hebner, Caleb Trotter, Aaron Voit, and my own former student, Kathleen Garman, helped make sure my facts checked out.

Thanks to my fantastic editor at Island Press, Emily Turner Davis, without whom this book wouldn't have been possible. Thanks, too, to everyone at Island Press.

Thanks to my alma mater, American University, and to George

Mason University Law School for allowing me to teach students how food, law, and policy intersect.

Thanks to the many people who supported my work with Keep Food Legal. I'm particularly grateful to Liz Williams and Nick Gillespie, who's also my editor at *Reason*, and to Jackson and Kristie Kuhl.

Thanks to Lewis Grossman and Susan Schneider for helping me find solid footing in food law and agricultural law, respectively, while I was a law student.

I'm grateful to my friends, colleagues, fellow editors and staffers, and faculty advisers at the *Administrative Law Review*.

Thanks to Joel Salatin, who has been and continues to be an inspiration.

Many, many smart people with interesting stories to tell were kind enough to speak with me in person, in sometimes-lengthy phone conversations, and in often-lengthy emails as I was writing this book. You have my gratitude, Mark DeNittis, Sara Nelson, Bill Marler, Donna Pacheco, Christophe Hille, Greg Visscher, Iso Rabins, Greg Van Ullen, Jason Foscolo, Justin Pearson, Thomas Massie, Maria Canelhas, Jay Hamburger, Sean Dimin, Madeleine Redfern, Ben Sargent, Michele Simon, Paul Shapiro, Nathan Rosenberg, Don Carr, Lynda Simkins, Trish Umbrell, Josh Tetrick, Tommy Daniel, Tyler Lindholm, Susan Walsh, Juliana Cohen, and William J. McCarthy.

Others with whom I'm fortunate to have discussed ideas that appear in this book include Dan Donahue, Graham Downey, Rob Hohne, Brad Bryan, Anthony Renzulli, Harold Singerman, Essa Penglase, Rachel Laudan, Pete Kennedy, Chellie Pingree, John Hendrickson, Michael Girard, Kristen Rudd, Jim Morrell, Tatiana Graf, Joe Donatelli, Leena Jayaswal, Ted Linnekin, Brooke Barron, Kristin Canty, Pete Shanafelt, Liz Reitzig, Karissa Orris, Dino Kraniotis, Michael Bachmann, Ari Bargil, Mahesha Subbaraman, Michael Bindas, Elizabeth Evans, Leland Smith, Jeff Stier, and Brittany, Seth, and Nate Peters.

Finally, thanks to all of the farmers, ranchers, chefs, fishermen, farmers market staff, entrepreneurs, gardeners, foragers, food Samaritans, lawyers, lawmakers, activists, and others whose valuable work appears in this book, and to all those in the United States and beyond whose work promotes the sorts of food rules (and resulting food system) this book envisions.

Introduction

Chef Mark DeNittis was a rising star in the Denver food community early in 2012. His artisanal salumeria, Il Mondo Vecchio, was still relatively new to the scene, but was already one of the hottest and most respected food businesses in the state.

With a partner, DeNittis had founded Il Mondo Vecchio as a tribute to the principles, traditions, and recipes he learned while growing up as a first generation Italian-American. The homage was explicit; Il Mondo Vecchio translates to "The Old World." As a traditional salumeria, Il Mondo Vecchio produced and sold a rich variety of Italian sausages and aged meats. Its products contained no artificial ingredients. In fact, the ingredient list was short on words. "Sea salt, meat, quality spices, and time," DeNittis told me in 2012.[1] Favorites, all crafted by DeNittis's hands, included guanciale, coppa, bresaola, culatello, capicola, pepperoni, and salami.[2]

Those hands worked magic. A *Denver Post* profile of Il Mondo Vecchio raved that its products had helped make Denver "a special place for Old World meats."[3] DeNittis won the Colorado Restaurant Association's 2012 Exceptional Newcomer Award, which recognizes "extraordinary contributions in the hospitality industry."[4] That same year, he was a finalist for Denver's Hottest Chef, awarded by the popular food website Eater.[5] Reviewers referred to Il Mondo Vecchio as "Denver's premier supplier of cured meats." Bravo, the television network that's home to *Top Chef*, called DeNittis the "Sausage King."

But it wasn't just its artisanal methods that set Il Mondo Vecchio apart. The company also sourced the ingredients that went into its products with the utmost care. Its salt came from an ancient seabed in nearby Utah. It sourced heritage pork from Boulder's Cure Organic Farm, a family business that also raises over one hundred types of certified-organic vegetables. Cure Farm markets its produce only within fifty miles of the farm and uses "biodynamic methods . . . to maintain and encourage natural diversity."[6]

It was difficult not to be impressed by Il Mondo Vecchio. "I think it would be hard to find a better example of a traditional, conscientious, sustainable, and local producer than Il Mondo Vecchio," I wrote in 2012.[7] Il Mondo Vecchio expanded its facilities thanks to growing demand for its products. DeNittis's partner launched a retail store to expand the business further.

But by Thanksgiving 2012, DeNittis was out of a job, forced to close Il Mondo Vecchio.[8] What had changed so quickly? Had demand plummeted? Had everyone in Denver suddenly become vegetarian?

Hardly. Instead, the government had come calling. The USDA, which inspects facilities such as Il Mondo Vecchio, told DeNittis he could no longer use those award-winning artisanal methods to make his salumi. USDA inspectors, who had always been present when food was being prepared, now claimed Il Mondo Vecchio's food was unsafe. The agency's decision came as a shock to DeNittis, he told me. Il Mondo Vecchio's website boasted that the company adhered "to Old World techniques of natural process while following New World regulations." USDA regulators and inspectors had always agreed. Always.

To say Mark DeNittis is a stickler for food safety would be putting it far too lightly. An independent lab tested every batch of food Il Mondo Vecchio produced for pathogens. The company kept diligent records of its testing. DeNittis had followed the USDA rules to the letter. He'd tested and tested and always passed those tests with flying colors. So what happened?

The USDA decided, arbitrarily, that Il Mondo Vecchio's production methods were no longer sufficient. The agency imposed on the company "additional requirements" designed to prevent pathogens such as salmonella from growing. Those new requirements meant Il Mondo Vecchio would have to add nitrates or nitrites—food preservatives—during the salumi-making process. Most dried meats today contain nitrates, nitrites, or both. These substances occur naturally in many places, including some green vegetables. Plenty of artisanal producers and commercial manufacturers alike use them. Culinary giants such as Michael Ruhlman cheer their use.[9] But Il Mondo Vecchio wasn't in business to sell most dried meats, and it was different from plenty of other artisanal producers. Just as using only heritage-breed pork from Cure Farms and sea salt from Utah were conscious decisions that were key to the mission of Il Mondo Vecchio, so too was the choice not to use nitrates or nitrites.

The USDA was now enforcing rules different from the ones DeNittis had followed diligently. Would a government agency just change its mind like that? It sounds ludicrous. There had to be more to the story, didn't there? There must have been some illness or bacteria or other food-safety demons lurking amid the sausage casings.

To be clear, had USDA inspectors found that harmful bacteria such as salmonella were present, then it would have made sense for the agency to shut down Il Mondo Vecchio until it cleaned up its act. Had its products sickened anyone, the USDA's actions would have been eminently reasonable. But neither of these things had happened. Ever. That wouldn't surprise anyone who knows DeNittis or his work. His products met the highest standards of safety and quality thanks not just to years spent perfecting his craft but also to a decade spent teaching the tools of the trade to others. In fact, before launching Il Mondo Vecchio, DeNittis had spent ten years on the faculty of Johnson & Wales University, a top choice for those looking to pursue a culinary career.[10] There, DeNittis oversaw the school's curriculum for butchering meat—a curriculum heavy on food safety. He served as a consultant to national groups such as the American Lamb Board. DeNittis had earned his chops—quite literally so. And only then did he leave his job at Johnson & Wales to open Il Mondo Vecchio.

Although he stressed Old World methods, DeNittis recognized that relying on tradition alone is no guarantee of quality. Ancient methods are no good if those methods sicken people. So DeNittis's attention to food safety was exacting and thoroughly modern. Photos of the artisan at work call to mind a germophobic government scientist—clad in a blue safety helmet, donning medical gloves and a mask, posing in front of gleaming stainless steel racks full of neatly organized, aging salumi.

How seriously did DeNittis take food safety at Il Mondo Vecchio? In addition to constant USDA inspection, Il Mondo Vecchio also established and executed a holistic food-safety regime. It had in place a requisite USDA Hazard Analysis and Critical Control Point (HACCP) program, followed Standard Sanitation Operation Procedures, implemented a Food Safety/Quality Assurance program, conducted regular food-safety audits and facilities inspections, followed Good Manufacturing Practices, carried out regular food-safety training, implemented an allergen control plan, and had all its labels preapproved by the USDA.[11] Such was the care Il Mondo Vecchio and DeNittis took to ensure their salumi was safe. But none of that mattered now.

In August 2012, according to DeNittis, a USDA inspector told him that though no test had found salmonella in Il Mondo Vecchio's foods, the agency was concerned with the "process" and "steps" he was taking to prevent salmonella.[12] In other words, the problem, in the USDA's estimation, wasn't that Il Mondo Vecchio's food contained any pathogens. It didn't. Instead, the agency was worried that Il Mondo Vecchio wasn't following a process the agency was now deciding to enforce. When the inspector returned with a regional USDA director later that month, says DeNittis, they barred Il Mondo Vecchio's perfectly safe, inspected food from being sold.

Even then, the USDA didn't come out and order Il Mondo Vecchio to close. Instead, the agency gave DeNittis a choice. He could continue to produce and sell salumi products under the Il Mondo Vecchio name. He'd just have to do so using processes (adding nitrates or nitrates) that were rare throughout much of the history of the Old World. To survive, Il Mondo Vecchio could keep its name, but it would have to use the methods of *Il Mondo Nuovo*. The only alternative was for the company to pay for a "challenge study" that, if successful, might force the USDA to go back to interpreting its rules as before. But challenge studies are time-consuming and costly, and have only a vague chance to succeed.

These were the options the USDA offered Il Mondo Vecchio. But they were no choices at all. Mark DeNittis wouldn't mislead his customers by using new-world methods under an old-world name. The company couldn't afford to halt its operations while spending thousands of dollars on a study that might or might not help sway the fickle minds at the USDA. A company founded on principles would stand on those principles. DeNittis closed Il Mondo Vecchio. Cure Farm's head, Paul Cure, told me ahead of Il Mondo Vecchio's closure that its exit would be "an enormous loss for the food community" in Denver.[13] And so it was.

Il Mondo Vecchio had done everything right. It used artisanal methods and sourced ingredients from sustainable suppliers. It captivated customers, peers, and the press alike. It won awards. It followed government rules and passed every government inspection. But all that hadn't been enough. Why? It turns out that the rules DeNittis had to follow—

the new ones that had closed Il Mondo Vecchio, and even the old ones that seemed to work just fine for a while—weren't created with artisanal producers in mind.

A large competitor that's producing bulk salumi and sausage for sale in stores across the country might find the USDA rules cost-effective and eminently reasonable. And if that large competitor ran into problems with regulators, spending several thousand dollars on a challenge study (or, more likely, a lobbyist or two) would be a drop in its profit bucket. That same large competitor would also likely think DeNittis crazy to buy expensive heritage pork and to avoid nitrates. Il Mondo Vecchio and its larger competitors were simply two very different business models. But USDA regulations treated tiny Il Mondo Vecchio and America's largest food companies exactly the same. Prof. Ken Albala, who teaches history at the University of the Pacific and makes his own salumi, explained the problem to me.

"The small producer, especially using traditional procedures for curing meat, simply does not have a chance—even when they take every precaution possible," Prof. Albala told me.[14] "The only solution is to go commando, do it yourself and stop buying mass produced salumi."

Certainly, there are consumers who are perfectly happy buying mass-produced salumi. Even if they've never used the word "salumi" in their lives—even if they have no idea what the word "salumi" *means*—they are awash in commercial options on each and every trip to the grocery. But what about those who want products like those Il Mondo Vecchio produced? What are their options? Going rogue, like Prof. Albala suggested, has some appeal in today's foodie culture. But is that really the best choice? The only choice?

If sustainably produced salumi were the only food that government rules made difficult to obtain, then Prof. Albala's appeal to "go commando" might be a call that's easy enough to heed. People who wanted products just like those Il Mondo Vecchio crafted could trek to the company's suppliers in Utah and Colorado and make their own at home. If only it were that simple.

It turns out that USDA salumi regulations are but one small set of rules in a sea of red tape that make growing, raising, buying, selling, and marketing a panoply of sustainably produced foods anywhere from difficult to impossible. Regulations like those that closed Il Mondo Vecchio aren't the exception. They're the rule—quite literally. And the USDA is not unique. Other federal agencies, including the FDA, as well as state and local agencies, have their own sets of rules that result in fewer and fewer sustainable food choices being available.

All told, there are thousands of federal, state, and local laws and regulations (what I'll refer to collectively as "rules" in this book) that restrict sustainable food. Often, they do so by making less sustainable choices the default position. Many times, as Mark DeNittis and Il Mondo Vecchio learned, that default position is the only permissible choice.

Even going commando, as Prof. Albala suggests, can run afoul of the rules. Many supporters of sustainable food were stunned when a Wisconsin state court ruled in a 2011 case that any person (in that case, a farmer) who owns a cow has no inherent right to drink milk from that cow.[15] Such a right, the court found in that case, which I discuss in chapter 4, exists only if government rules allow it. Meanwhile, in many cities and towns across America, homeowners have been fined for growing fruits and vegetables in their yards.[16] Some have even had their gardens ripped out by city employees for no other reason than because the rules don't allow it.[17]

Rules like these were uncommon in America prior to the New Deal era, a complex period that saw President Franklin D. Roosevelt attempt to manage the economy to lift the country out of the Great Depression and secure victory in World War II. One of the central tenets of the New Deal was the exercise of greater government control over the food supply.

There's perhaps no better-known example of this tight grip on the food supply than *Wickard v. Filburn*, a 1942 U.S. Supreme Court case that pitted an Ohio small farmer, Roscoe Filburn, against the USDA.[18] Filburn grew wheat on just over twenty acres. The USDA, which was trying to drive up the price of wheat as part of its economic recovery plan, said he could plant and sell only a little more than eleven acres' worth of wheat. Filburn sold the amount the federal government permitted, and kept another dozen or so acres worth of wheat he harvested. His family used the remainder to bake bread, feed their cattle and chickens, and save seeds.[19] The USDA fined Filburn for breaking agency rules. Filburn appealed his case all the way to the Supreme Court. The court sided with the USDA, ruling that the government could indeed bar him from growing wheat for use at home. The case set a precedent that's still followed by American courts to this day.

The decision in the *Filburn* case to bar a small farmer from growing wheat for use at home seems as bizarre as it is overzealous. But one tale of prevailing USDA attitudes at the time shines perhaps an even harsher light on just what the nation's smallest farmers were up against at the agency. Just two weeks before the Supreme Court heard arguments in the *Filburn* case in 1942, a *Time* magazine story discussed plans by First Lady Eleanor Roosevelt, the president's powerful and likable wife, to launch a victory garden on the White House grounds.[20] Victory gardens, patriotic plots for raising edible fruits and vegetables, were slowly popping up around the country as a response to wartime food shortages.[21]

"Mrs. Roosevelt planned to plant one on the White House grounds," *Time* reported, "if the Agriculture Department, skeptical of amateur farmers, decides that the soil is fertile enough to make a garden worthwhile."[22] That's right. The USDA, the agency responsible for guiding the nation's agricultural policy, was "skeptical of amateur farmers." And the agency had veto power over Mrs. Roosevelt's victory garden on the grounds of the White House.

In the end, Mrs. Roosevelt got her garden—though not until the next year. And while current First Lady Michelle Obama faced none of the same USDA hostility before launching her sustainable White House garden in 2009, regular Americans today often aren't so lucky.[23] Even if governments are no longer openly skeptical of amateur farmers and sustainable food entrepreneurs—though, as this book reveals, some still are—the rules they make and enforce still betray the same skepticism evidenced by President Roosevelt's USDA.

That's largely what this book is about. Too often, government rules and sustainability are at loggerheads. Many rules handcuff America's most sustainable farmers, producers, sellers, and consumers alike. And they often do so while favoring or even rewarding others whose practices are anything but sustainable.

In the following chapters, I'll provide stark examples of several types of rules, existing at various levels of government, that treat sustainability and its supporters with a combination of disdain, disrespect, and hostility. Chapter 1 discusses how many food-safety rules, such as those that forced Mark DeNittis and Il Mondo Vecchio out of business, bar people from using sustainable methods to grow, raise, produce, prepare, sell, and buy a variety of foods. You'll read about restrictions on artisanal cheesemakers and beer brewers of all sizes, and learn how FDA rules proposed under a law known as the Food Safety Modernization Act threatened to treat small farmers like manure and to treat manure—the lifeblood of organic fertilization and sustainable farming—as a toxin.

Chapter 2 discusses how many government rules favor—and even promote—large-scale food producers. The U.S. Farm Bill, which hands out billions of dollars in taxpayer subsidies every year to large farms that often raise monocultures of crops such as soy and corn, is one of the most pervasive examples. Chapter 3 reveals how many government rules promote food waste. You'll learn about a campaign in Portugal—one I've seen and tasted firsthand—to fight back against ridiculous European Union rules that constrain the sale of so-called "ugly" fruits and vegetables and that also promote food waste. Chapter 4 describes laws that prevent individuals from raising or obtaining sustainable food for themselves, their families, and their communities. Examples include government rules that bar people from keeping home gardens or raising egg-laying hens. You'll also learn about one of the most egregious illustrations of this phenomenon, seen in many cities around the country, in the form of rules that bar people from sharing food with the homeless and less fortunate.

Do these and other harmful rules that I catalog in the following chapters mean that rules are always bad? Absolutely not. I've already noted, for example, that the USDA would have been justified in cracking down on Il Mondo Vecchio had the company's food been found either to be harboring dangerous bacteria or, worse, to have sickened customers. The same would have been true had USDA inspectors found unsanitary conditions in the company's production facilities. Chapter 5 discusses good food rules, including why good food-safety rules are important. These good rules include those Il Mondo Vecchio had complied with: food-safety inspections and testing to ensure safe outcomes. The chapter also explores why I support rules like those that prohibit the "finning" of sharks.

But it's important not to confuse the fact that *some* rules are necessary and desirable with a blind faith in the ability of rules (and rule makers) to produce just and desirable outcomes. As this book demonstrates, rules often have negative consequences—intended or not. In 2012, for example, the nonprofit I led commissioned a report by Harvard Law School's Food Law and Policy Clinic looking into whether some farmers market regulations might be too strict. The clinic, the first in the nation to work solely on legal issues in the food realm, is staffed by law student attorneys and overseen by a clinical professor.[24] We asked the clinic to look into reports we'd been hearing out of Pennsylvania that new rules there could jeopardize food vendors at many farmers markets in the state. In particular, one rule would appear to require farmers to chill foods such as beef and poultry using costly generators and refrigerated trucks. Many farmers use ice, which costs very little, chills just as well, and doesn't generate air or noise pollution like that produced by a generator or refrigerated truck. For the small farmer, using ice to chill food often yields the best outcome. But it also might be her only cost-effective option for selling products at a farmers market and, indeed, for staying in business. What's more, in Pennsylvania, the option to chill meats using ice is the only option available for many of the state's Amish farmers—who generally use sustainable farming methods while eschewing modern technology such as generators and refrigerated trucks.

Thankfully, as the Harvard report described, many of the fears over the new Pennsylvania regulations turned out to be overstated.[25] But the news was not all good. In comparing Pennsylvania's farmers market rules with those in nine other U.S. states, the report revealed that several other states did have in place a variety of needlessly burdensome rules for farmers markets.[26] The report concluded with several recommendations to help loosen rules across the country and help America's farmers markets be more welcoming for small farmers.[27] As you'll learn in chapter 1, one state in particular is home to some particularly burdensome farmers market rules that are in need of change.

When real and potential problems like those posed in Pennsylvania arise in the food system, thoughtful writers such as Michael Pollan, author of *The Omnivore's Dilemma*, are often quick to sound the alarm. But the solutions Pollan and many others suggest regularly involve crafting more and stricter rules. Those FDA rules that could prevent many sustainable farmers from using manure to fertilize their organic crops? Pollan cheered on the law that would give rise to the proposed manure rule in a *New York Times* column in 2010, writing that the law would "greatly benefit consumers without harming small farmers or local food producers."[28] Remember, as you read the following chapters, that rules didn't help Mark DeNittis, Cure Farm, or their customers. They don't help people in many cities who want to share food with the homeless and less fortunate. And it's rules—not interloping deer and foxes—that will likely prevent you from growing tomatoes or raising a few hens in your yard.

Is there an alternative to the rule-heavy food system we have today? I believe there is. That's why I argue throughout this book that the only way to create a better food system is by having fewer rules in place to govern that system. Reducing the government's regulatory footprint would help sustainable food options—foods grown or produced using a set of practices that aspire to maximize the benefits of the food system while minimizing its negative impacts—to flourish. I also believe that this approach would foster a more just food system.

How would that work? I'll recommend two guiding principles to facilitate sustainable food options going forward. Briefly stated, the first principle is that federal, state, and local rules that promote unsustainable food system outcomes (such as food waste) should be jettisoned whenever possible. The second principle is that rules that prevent sustainable food system practices should also be eliminated whenever possible. The rules that remain—the good food rules—should require good outcomes (such as food that's free of harmful bacteria) rather than mandating a particular process or processes.

The idea that decreasing the number of rules can help foster a more just food system is at the heart of "food freedom"—a belief that individuals have a right to make their own food choices. Food freedom—which I define as the right to grow, raise, produce, buy, sell, share, cook, eat, and drink the foods of one's own choosing—is an increasingly popular rallying cry that's uniting longtime supporters of sustainable food with others who favor lowering the regulatory burden on farmers and other food producers. Throughout this book, you'll read about a loose and growing coalition of farmers, food entrepreneurs, advocates, lawyers, and others across the country who, like me, are fighting for food freedom from a variety of angles. You'll see how the food freedom movement is breaking down many traditional partisan and ideological barriers in Washington, D.C., a place that isn't exactly known these days as a bastion of cooperation and collegiality. One example of how food freedom is uniting Americans across these typical divides came recently, when Rep. Thomas Massie (R-KY), one of the more libertarian members of Congress, cosponsored a set of "food freedom" bills with Rep. Chellie Pingree (D-ME), a stalwart liberal member of the House.[29]

Rep. Pingree and Rep. Massie are both small farmers. Rep. Massie and his family raise grass-fed beef, fruits, and vegetables on a Kentucky farm, while Rep. Pingree raises goats, pigs, chickens, cows, and vegetables on an organic farm in Maine. They know better than anyone in Washington the burden that rules place on small farmers, food producers, and consumers. On this issue, Rep. Pingree and Rep. Massie—and a growing number of Americans—speak with one voice. My hope is that after you finish this book, if you haven't already done so, you'll add your voice to the chorus.

CHAPTER 1

Unsafe at Any Feed

IN 2013, CALIFORNIA'S STATE ASSEMBLY adopted a new law requiring chefs, bartenders, and virtually anyone in the state who prepares ready-to-eat food for customers to wear disposable latex gloves when handling that food.[1] The law was intended to improve food safety in restaurants, which—thanks largely to poor hand washing by some food preparers—is the source of many foodborne illnesses. At first, the bill was uncontroversial. In fact, it won unanimous approval in the legislature. More than forty other states have similar laws on the books.[2]

Its quiet passage might have been the last anyone heard of the glove law. But something extraordinary happened soon after the law took effect in January 2014. Many sushi chefs, who often use bare hands to prepare dishes, particularly ones made with rice that would stick to gloves and make sushi preparation impossible, revolted against the law.[3] They were joined by other chefs and bartenders—who found they would have to don a pair of disposable gloves to do something as simple as placing a sprig of parsley on a plate or squeezing a lime into a customer's mixed drink—across the state. Thousands signed petitions to repeal the law.[4]

What had spurred this loud and sudden outcry against a new law that had drawn the unanimous support of state legislators and is similar to one on the books in dozens of other states? First, most restaurateurs in California were completely unaware of the law until after it passed. Second, it turns out the food-safety justifications on which the glove law rested were deeply flawed. What's more, the negative unintended consequences of the law were just too much for chefs, foodies, and even—as it turned out—for legislators.[5]

Shortly after the law took effect, San Francisco food entrepreneur Iso Rabins, a foraging expert who you'll read about in greater detail in chapter 4 of this book, told me he was outraged by the law for several reasons. The law would create countless tons of unnecessary waste, thanks to the mandatory use of disposable gloves. What's more—astonishingly so, as Rabins told me—"studies show glove use actually increases overall bacteria, which makes more people sick."[6]

How could that be? "People who wear gloves are much less likely to change them than people are to wash their hands, and studies show that they can actually spread more bacteria when they (inevitably) rip, because of the sweat that pools beneath them during the work shift," Rabins said. He's right. The glove law was a food-safety law that actually *made food less safe*.[7] Research has indeed shown this to be true.

And then there's the problem of creating waste, something that goes against the very ethos of a sustainable food system. "Northern California especially is very concerned with sustainability," said chef Todd Davies, in comments to the *Marin Independent Journal*. "Why would we want to create more trash in a society that creates way too much trash anyway?"[8] Rules such as the glove law that promote waste are far too prevalent, and frequently promote wasting food itself, as you'll learn in chapter 3. Finally, the law's prohibition on letting chefs and bartenders prepare handmade food with their hands also skewed in favor of fast food and other institutional settings, where working with fresh food is less common. The law wouldn't hurt fast-food companies, which is perhaps one reason they—in partnership with federal, state, and local food-safety officials—supported it in the first place.[9] But sushi chefs, cocktail wizards, and others who handle food directly would be severely disadvantaged by the law.

The public outrage, petitions, and bad press quickly made the glove law's demise a foregone conclusion. Even Assemblyman Richard Pan, who had sponsored the glove law, had become a leading critic.[10] "Just wearing gloves alone is not necessarily going to make the food safer," he told KQED.[11] Shortly afterward, the same legislature that had unanimously adopted the law did something dramatic. They unanimously repealed it.[12] Still, despite the sensible repeal in California, similar laws are still on the books in most states. Health inspectors closed one New York City sushi restaurant in 2015 because its chefs refused to wear gloves.[13]

The story of California's glove law is troubling, but it's hardly unique. The very premise on which the glove law rested was defective. Proper hand washing makes food safer. Wearing gloves does not. The law didn't make food safer; it made food less safe. The glove law also created a host of undesirable results that—anticipated or not—would not have existed but for the law. It harmed sustainability efforts by promoting waste. It handcuffed food artisans. You'll see a similar pattern repeated again and again throughout this chapter, as I discuss many food-safety rules—often targeting the most sustainable food producers—that are adopted and enforced without regard either to their efficacy or to their unintended consequences.

More Rules, Safer Food?

In early 2011, President Obama signed the Food Safety Modernization Act (FSMA) into law.[14] The law, which drew far more support from Democrats in Congress than from their Republican colleagues, was intended to strengthen the nation's food-safety system and improve the overall safety of the foods Americans eat. FSMA supporters—a mix of food-safety advocates and big-business interests—hailed its passage as the most consequential update of the nation's food-safety laws in seventy-five years.

Although portions of FSMA apply to food produced abroad and to pet food, the two most important and far-reaching provisions pertain to domestic farmers and food producers. For farmers, the law requires the FDA, the federal agency in charge of enforcing the law, to "establish science-based minimum standards for the safe production and harvesting of fruits and vegetables." For other food producers—from makers of fresh pasta sauce to Greek yogurt—the law orders the FDA to require food manufacturers to have in place a written plan for preventing transmission of pathogens that could cause foodborne illness. FSMA—the acronym is pronounced *FIZZ-muh*—also contains a host of other provisions, a few no doubt long overdue. For example, the law gave the FDA, for the first time, the authority to order the mandatory recall of food found to be harboring pathogens.[15]

Some FSMA supporters are also longtime advocates of sustainable farming. Shortly before FSMA became law, as I noted in the introduction to this book, author Michael Pollan predicted that FSMA "promises to achieve several important food-safety objectives, greatly benefiting consumers without harming small farmers or local food producers."[16]

Since the law's passage, the FDA has been busy crafting specific rules to implement the law. FSMA, like many laws, requires that an agency (here, the FDA) first develop proposed rules and then seek out public opinion on those proposals before finalizing any rules. That process can take—and, indeed, has taken, in the case of FSMA—several years. One dramatic change that is supposed to occur under FSMA is that the law gives the FDA new powers to regulate food safety on the farm. Although the FDA has long had a role in policing food safety at egg-producing facilities, FSMA would effectively, for the first time, invite the FDA onto many of the nation's farms.

But even after supporters of sustainable farming such as Pollan hailed FSMA's ability to improve food safety without hurting small farms and local food producers, the reality of the law has proven to be quite different. Many FSMA rules proposed by the FDA since the law's passage have, in fact, been anathema to sustainable farming. Among other things, the proposed rules would mandate "minimum application intervals" of up to nine months on the use of manure, which is a key ingredient in soil health and organic farming.[17] They also proposed requiring costly inspection, maintenance, monitoring, testing, and treatment of irrigation water, even when such water is used to grow foods that are not eaten raw. The FDA has estimated FSMA will cost the average American small farm—which the rules defined as one with average annual food sales under $500,000—about $13,000 per year.[18] Those compliance costs could put many beginning and small famers and food entrepreneurs out of business.

The threat FSMA poses to small farmers and food producers in general, and to sustainable ones specifically, crystallized as members of the public responded to the law's requirement that the FDA seek out public opinion on its proposed FSMA rules. Farmers spoke of the existential threats the rules posed to them and their mindful, hard-earned livelihoods. Farmers market managers told of how the proposed rules could wreak havoc with their farmers and food entrepreneurs. Sustainability advocates lined up to oppose the measures. Health professionals predicted dire consequences if the proposed rules were adopted. Even everyday consumers spoke out—oftentimes in impassioned pleas—against the proposed rules.

Some of the most thoughtful and stinging criticism of FSMA came in a series of listening sessions the FDA sponsored across the country after releasing its proposed rules. At an FDA-sponsored listening session in

Oregon, for example, farmer Elizabeth Fujas told FDA officials about the sustainable farm she started with her husband more than three decades ago. The Fujases have been organic farmers since 1982. In 1985, they launched Rising Sun Farms, responding to what their website notes was "a discernable lack of organic foods" and a need to "provide healthy food utilizing the highest quality clean ingredients while supporting organic and sustainable agriculture." The couple later founded the Southern Oregon Farmers Market. Today, Rising Sun Farms sells produce, along with a variety of prepared foods, including tortas, spreads, and pestos. The company has received dozens of awards over the years—including a 1989 award as the most progressive farm in Oregon and a 2014 gold medal from the American Cheese Society—and, as Fujas noted, has been lauded by the Oregon Department of Agriculture.[19]

The story of Rising Sun Farms is one of humble beginnings. "We spent all of our savings on our farm . . . living in a small nomadic tent known as the yurt on our farm as we built our business," Fujas told the FDA.[20] The Fujases now own a 25,000 square-foot facility and employ more than thirty workers. Not surprisingly, given such growth, Rising Sun Farms has been ranked among the top 100 fastest growing private companies in Oregon by the *Portland Business Journal*[21] and among the top twenty-five women-owned businesses in Oregon.[22]

Rising Sun Farms appears to take food safety very seriously. In addition to obtaining a voluntary top-level food-safety certification, SQF Level 3, their operations are inspected by a third-party auditor, the U.S. military (which buys their products), the FDA, the Oregon Department of Agriculture, and their own quality assurance team. Their inspections, Fujas told the FDA at the listening session, have always produced "excellent" results.[23]

The Fujases appear to be doing everything a supporter of sustainable agriculture could want. But the proposed FSMA rules, Fujas said, "suggest many major new obligations for food businesses, including businesses like Rising Sun Farms, that have a long [history] of producing only safe food."[24] Fujas said although the proposed rules would prove onerous to her and Rising Sun Farms, they could prove devastating to many start-up food businesses. "The changes will have big impacts on start-up small food businesses like we were in 1984," she said. "In 1984 and even in 1991 it would have been overwhelming for us to make and pay for the staff, and the internal changes that FDA's suggesting that small food companies must make." Fujas told the FDA she worried about the impact of the rules on these businesses. "Your proposal will possibly put small food companies out of business and/or out of compliance," she said of the FSMA rules. "It will discourage anyone from starting a food manufacturing business, making our food supply more industrialized, and reducing economic benefits that small start-up businesses contribute to [the] local economy."[25]

Fujas wasn't the only one worried. Other listening sessions around the country echoed her concerns. At one session in Maine, potato farmer Jim Gerritsen told FDA officials that FSMA was a bad deal for small farmers like him. "I think you're trying to mold small, family farmers to an impossible ideal that will not work in Maine," said Gerritsen.[26] At another New England listening session, Will Allen of Vermont's Cedar Circle Farm, which bills itself as an "organic farm with a social mission [to] engage the community to develop and share practices that promote regenerative agriculture, good health, and a resource-rich environment," called FSMA "a corporate attempt to squash a movement in food."[27]

Fujas, Gerritsen, and Allen were joined by thousands of Americans who submitted comments to the FDA.[28] Commenters warned that the rules would severely curtail manure and compost use, require costly water testing for many crops that don't pose food-safety hazards, mandate fencing off of farms and potential destruction of wildlife habitat, impose costly new burdens, and curtail on-farm production of jams and other value-added farm products.

Everyday consumers wrote to the FDA in droves. "This unfairly targets organic farmers and will result in higher costs for organic eaters without any guarantee of safer products," wrote Kimberly Olsen, a self-described "eater." Erica Gruebler, a farmer and parent, wrote she was "deeply concerned about the impact that FDA's proposed rules under FSMA would have on my farm and business as well as my family."

Doctors and others in the medical community argued the supposed health protections offered by FSMA were no protections at all. "The FDA's approach to traditional farming methods, such as diversified livestock-crop farms, the use of working animals, and the use of biological soil amendments, is fundamentally flawed," wrote Joseph Kohn, MD. "The agency should not restrict these sustainable methods of farming without data showing an actual, verified increased rate of foodborne illness; the simple fact that these methods include diverse microbiological communities is not a sound scientific basis for restricting them." Many dietitians also spoke out against the proposed rules, voicing concerns that FSMA would drive up the price of fruits and vegetables for their clients and themselves. Dayna Green-Burgeson, a registered dietitian and organic farmer in California, cautioned that few small farmers in her state "make enough profit to bear the burden of any additional costly regulations." Ann Kucelin, a registered dietitian, worried about her family's ability to find healthy local food.

Around the country, many state and local farm bureaus, which represent the interests of local member farmers, also opposed the rules. For example, the Rhode Island Farm Bureau urged the FDA not to adopt the rules, which the group said will "drive a lot of farmers out of business." The Wisconsin Farmers Union likewise argued the "rules could potentially have devastating effects on small and medium-sized produce farmers."

Not surprisingly, those same small, sustainable farmers were among the new law's most vocal critics. Charles NovoGradac, a chestnut farmer for more than two decades, described how the proposed FSMA irrigation-testing rules could put him out of business. As NovoGradac described, chestnuts are harvested after they ripen and fall to the ground. Farmers work to gather them each day, and sell them in the shell. But applying FSMA rules to chestnuts would make it "impossible" to harvest and sell them, wrote NovoGradac. Though it may make sense to require water testing for fruits such as melons that are grown at ground level and eaten raw, the rules make no sense for tree fruits such as apples that are harvested directly from the tree or tree nuts such as chestnuts that are harvested in their natural, inedible shell and roasted before being eaten. "Unless there is an exemption, as we read the proposed regulations, chestnuts gathered from the ground can be used only if processed," NovoGradac said. "The tradition of roasting chestnuts on the open fire would become a thing of the past."

Donald and Rebecca Kretschmann, a husband-and-wife team in their mid-sixties who farm on eighty acres in western Pennsylvania, noted in their comments that their community-supported agriculture (CSA) service supplies fresh produce to more than one thousand families in the Pittsburgh area. "After decades operating a small family organic farm," the Kretschmanns wrote, "we seriously think that many small produce farms like ours might be forced to close, not for any production or marketing issue whatsoever." The Kretschmanns went on to list several flaws with FSMA, before opining that "on nearly every level this act is a misguided effort with disastrous consequences when applied wholesale to small farmers and especially for sustainable and organic farmers like ourselves." They cautioned that FSMA comes "just when the local, organic, and sustainable agriculture movements are transforming the food scene nationwide."

Another small farmer, Kyle Young, described his concerns about the FSMA provisions for fertilizing his fields. Young grows produce and raises alpacas and chickens. He uses the animal droppings as fertilizer, he noted, and rotates the chickens into his four garden plots, after he harvests his crops, to eat insect larvae and crop debris and to fertilize the fields for next year's harvest. This "mixed livestock and vegetable production," Young wrote, "provides a local, energy efficient, free, on farm source of high quality fertilizer." Young takes steps to ensure food safety, he wrote, including timing his rotation to ensure "plenty of time for thorough decomposition before crops are harvested" and washing of all produce and eggs. The possibility that FSMA would restrict these time-tested practices irks Young. "As a small farmer utilizing farming techniques that have been safely providing food for humans for the past 10,000 years," Young wrote, "I'm very concerned about new regulations being proposed to deal with foodborne illness."[29]

Many longtime advocates of sustainable agriculture around the country were also critical of the proposed rules. The National Sustainable Agriculture Coalition pointed to "substantial problems in the proposed regulations and the lasting impacts these regulations will have." Jen Dalton, of California's Mendocino County Food Policy Council, wrote that the proposed rules could "raise costs for farmers, food businesses, and consumers," "squash local food," and "undermine sustainability."

Although many consumers, small farmers, food entrepreneurs, nutritionists, doctors, and sustainability advocates spoke out against the proposed FSMA rules, those deeply involved in farmers markets—which bring together small farmers and consumers like no other institution—constituted a particularly vocal group of commenters. "As written, the proposed Food Safety Modernization Act rules will have dramatic negative consequences for my market and the farmers and customers who depend on it," wrote Margaret Norfleet Neff, manager of the Cobblestone Farmers Market in Winston-Salem, North Carolina. Neff noted the rules would target many low-risk, value-added foods, including pickles, baked goods, syrups, oils, jams, salsas, pralines, and sauces. These "big sellers," she said, "provide an important revenue stream that has become integral to the livelihood of our farmers." Roxanne Jungé, manager of Glenview Farmers Market in Illinois and a member of the board of directors of the Illinois Farmers Market Association and the Illinois State Department of Public Health Farmers Market Task Force, cautioned the FDA against imposing "unnecessary burdens on farmers who are already working against the odds to bring fresh fruits and vegetables to people who need them."

All told, these comments by farmers, farmers market supporters, dietitians and medical doctors, sustainability advocates, consumers, and others represent a devastating assessment of FSMA's potential impact. The astonishing thing about fears over FSMA's impact on sustainable farmers and other small food producers is that they arose even after Congress sought, in passing the law, to ensure that the law would *exempt* many small farmers. Senator Jon Tester (D-MT) and then-Senator Kay Hagan (D-NC) included amendments to the law that would do just that.[30] As Sen. Tester stated after the law's passage, the amendments would "protect family farmers and food producers from new federal regulations they can't afford and don't need."[31]

The Tester-Hagan amendment, as it's known, was intended to exempt small farmers with less than $500,000 in annual sales of food covered under FSMA, and who sell their food directly to consumers either within their own state or within a 275-mile radius of where the food was grown or raised.[32] Among the FDA's many missteps in proposing to implement the rule—which spurred many of the comments discussed in this chapter—the agency determined that the rule should apply to *total annual farm sales*, rather than only to sales of food covered under FSMA. That meant many small farms that were not intended to be subject to FSMA would now be forced to comply with the rules. It's suspicion over this FDA-led assault that spurred small farmers such as Will Allen of Vermont's Cedar Circle Farm to view FSMA as an attempt to squash the local-food movement.

Many of these arguments against FSMA might be less convincing if the rules the FDA proposed to implement the law would make food safer. But they won't. That's not because foodborne illness isn't a real problem. It is. The federal government estimates that pathogens tied to food kill 3,000 Americans and sicken another 48 million each year. According to the Centers for Disease Control and Prevention (CDC), the federal agency responsible for tracking foodborne illness, the agency has seen a general "downward trend in foodborne infections" in recent years.[33] That's good news. Rates of infection from salmonella have decreased, for example, while those from *Vibrio* have risen. And other pathogens, including listeria and *E. coli,* have shown no statistically significant increase or decrease. That's also good news. But FSMA won't make things much better—if at all. And this is a fact the FDA openly admits.

The final FSMA produce rule, released in November 2015, estimates that it will help in "averting approximately 331,964 illnesses per year" that are attributable to contaminated fruits and vegetables.[34] The final FSMA good manufacturing practice rule, released earlier last year, estimates that it applies to foods that are responsible for 903,000 out of the 48 million total U.S. cases of foodborne illness each year.[35] Together, that means the FDA's own estimates predict these rules could—if implemented to absolute perfection—reduce foodborne illnesses by a maximum of 1.23 million cases. That would represent just a 2.6 percent reduction in total foodborne illness cases. Again, this is the FDA's own best-case scenario for the impact of these two key rules.

The predicted improvements in food safety under these FSMA rules are so tiny because foods regulated by the FDA are responsible for a very small percentage of foodborne illnesses to begin with. For example, norovirus, which is caused largely by sick food handlers and improper hand washing, is responsible for nearly three out of every five cases of foodborne illness in the United States.[36] The FDA doesn't regulate food preparation or handling in the places where norovirus lurks: restaurants, hospitals, cruise ships, and individual homes. That job is left to states, counties, cities, and—in the case of your home—to you and your family. That means FSMA has absolutely no impact at all on the leading source of foodborne illness. The FDA also doesn't regulate beef, pork, poultry, and other meats that are responsible for another 22 percent of foodborne illnesses.[37] Instead, that's the job of the USDA's Food Safety and Inspection Service.

So FSMA doesn't cover the most common cause of foodborne illness in America, and doesn't cover meats, which together are responsible for 80 percent of all foodborne illness in America. That means that FDA regulations could prevent, at best, only one out of every five cases, or up to 9.6 million cases of foodborne illness. Yet the FDA estimates that the two key FSMA rules could—at best—only dent that figure by 1.23 million cases.

Whether the final impact of the key rules is a 1 or 2 percent drop in foodborne illness cases—or even if the drop is somehow 3 percent—that's an absurdly small return for a law that's been described by the FDA as the solution to what it calls the "largely preventable" problem of foodborne illness.[38] FSMA won't put a stop to foodborne illness, but it's threatened to put an end to sustainable farming. That's a point driven home by at least one attendee at an FDA FSMA listening session. "Though given the opportunity, no FDA representative would assert the proposed regulations would produce a statistical increase in food safety," noted Frank Lyall of the Yakima County Farm Bureau in sharply worded comments on the high burdens and small benefits of FSMA. "So on a wing and a prayer the FDA is willing to burden and perhaps deprive farmers of their livelihood, to satisfy a desire for evermore government control of agriculture, which takes place in a natural environment, not a factory. A natural environment dictates that a farmer may not have complete control, as farmers will strongly attest, over his production methods. Yet this rule will criminalize farmers, or more specifically smaller farmers."

Another reason FSMA's impact is so low is that the law requires only that all "high-risk domestic [food] facilities" be inspected within five years of the law's passage, and every three years afterward.[39] The agency considers several factors in determining what is or is not a "high-risk" facility, including whether the facility makes or stores known high-risk foods, whether those foods have previously been responsible for cases of foodborne illness, the severity of any such illnesses, and the facility's specific manufacturing processes.[40] Inspections are necessary to help ensure food safety. But given these factors, can the FDA really believe that two inspections of a "high-risk" facility every decade are going to prevent or reduce foodborne illness? And just what amounts from those inspections? Not much. "Even when it does uncover health violations at food-processing plants, the FDA takes enforcement action in only about half of the cases and almost never imposes fines," wrote noted food journalist and author Barry Estabrook in a 2012 *Mother Jones* article.[41]

The FDA's proposed FSMA rules would have devastated many of the nation's sustainable food producers, all while making American consumers and our food little or no more safe. In large part thanks to the concerns of those farmers and food producers, farmers market managers, sustainability advocates, health professionals, and everyday consumers, the FDA was forced to revise the proposed FSMA rules, which the agency finalized at the end of 2015.[42] This was a tremendous victory for those around the country who want to see rules that foster a more sustainable food system.

On their face, the final rules eliminated some of the more burdensome fruit and vegetable rules and exempted many farms from FSMA's registration and process-oriented rules that govern retail food establishments. In the final rule establishing produce standards, for example, the FDA chose to exempt "produce that is rarely consumed raw" (like beans and chestnuts) from many FSMA rules.[43] The agency also removed its proposed manure rule, eliminating the nine-month waiting period the agency had proposed to implement before permitting farmers to apply some manure. Although these and other changes are positive steps, it's unclear if some of these changes, including the manure rule, represent just a small victory in what could be a much longer fight. That's because the agency also stated in the final rules that this solution may be only a temporary one. The final rule simply "defer[s] FDA's decision," it writes, while the agency studies the issue of manure application. In other words, future manure restrictions just like the one the FDA had proposed are definitely not off the table. In fact, just as I was completing my final edits to this book, the FDA announced that the agency was looking into the possibility of new manure restrictions.[44]

So where does this leave us? Does the tenuous rollback of the worst parts of the proposed FSMA rules and the fragile victory for sustainability supporters mean we and our food are less safe? After all, mere sustainability—in a vacuum—is no guarantee of food safety. Leading food-safety attorney Bill Marler reminded me that he represented a family whose son died from eating organic, grass-fed beef. Marler is skeptical that grass-fed beef—or any other putatively sustainable food—is inherently safer to consume than the grain-fed alternative. Marler has built an impressive record using litigation to ensure that food made by producers of all types and sizes is safe. When their products sicken or kill people, Marler has sued burger giants such as Jack in the Box and beverage makers such as Odwalla, and he's sued raw milk producers and the aforementioned grass-fed beef farmer. I have a tremendous amount of respect for Marler and his work. If someone produces food that causes illness or death, they—and their business—should pay a steep price. Marler ensures they pay that price. In fact, I believe he and other leading food-safety attorneys, along with public watchdogs, have played as important a role—if not a more important one—in keeping American eaters safe as have the FDA and USDA. "I think you overstate my usefulness," Marler told me modestly.[45] But even Marler, a noted FSMA supporter, acknowledges that food-safety rules often "benefit large scale producers and are a bar to entry to small scale producers." He'd like to see rules that are far more scalable, based on the size of the food producer. But, he told me, "Safety should not take a back seat for any reason." I couldn't agree more—even if we'll agree to disagree on the merits of FSMA.

Marler is right to acknowledge that food-safety rules are often skewed in favor of large producers. I admire his zeal in targeting food-safety violators of all sizes. The FDA could benefit from studying—and, indeed, emulating—these qualities. Instead, the agency appears completely willing to put countless sustainable farmers and food producers out of business for what may amount—at best—to a tiny uptick in overall food safety. At worst, in some cases agency rules can be counterproductive—making people and food less safe. Unfortunately, as you're about to learn, when it comes to other FDA rules, and rules made by a host of different federal, state, and local agencies, this foolhardy approach is often the norm.

Needlessly Fighting Over Beer & Cheese

In 2013, I attended the Craft Brewers Conference, an annual event in Washington, D.C., that brings together craft beer fans, experts, and brewers from around the country. I went to sample the beer, sure, but also to learn about the sorts of regulatory challenges that smaller brewers were facing at the time. During the question-and-answer session that followed an excellent lecture on beer regulations by a top beverage-industry lawyer, several brewers complained they'd been visited by "clueless" FDA inspectors who "should know what they're talking about" but appeared not to. One of the complaints aired by the brewers, which I wrote about at the time, was that an FDA inspector had suggested that they refrigerate grain before using it to brew beer.[46] Because refrigerated grains can become musty and pick up odors that can be passed on to—and, hence, ruin—beer, brewers never, ever refrigerate fresh grains. This has always been the case. All the brewers knew this. Bill Butcher, founder of Port City Brewing Company, which won small brewery of the year at 2015's Great American Beer Fest, confirmed this during a tour he gave me and my George Mason University Law School students that same year. Yet this fact had struck the FDA inspector both as entirely new information and a potential food-safety violation.

The lawyer delivering the lecture that day, Art DeCelle, who had served previously as general counsel for the Beer Institute, which represents several of the country's largest brewers, cautioned those in the room that FSMA would only increase the FDA's role in regulating breweries of all sizes. Given their recent experiences with FDA inspectors, this wasn't something the brewers wanted to hear. But DeCelle's warning turned out to be prophetic.

Later that same year, the FDA proposed an outrageous rule for dealing not with fresh grains but with those grains that had already been used to brew beer. So-called "spent grains," literally "spent" because they've been used as part of the process of brewing beer, have been used by farmers to feed livestock from prehistoric times through the present day. "The 'grains,' or exhausted mash, is sold to dairymen to feed cows," reads one American text from 1878.[47] Nowadays, in addition to selling them, many breweries donate their spent grains to farmers free of charge. This wonderful, synergistic relationship has helped reduce landfill costs for brewers and feed costs for farmers. It's also helped prevent literally tons of "food waste," a term that refers to the roughly 40 percent of our food that is not eaten or otherwise put to use and which ends up in landfills, often needlessly. I'll talk plenty about rules that promote food waste in chapter 3. But my focus with spent grains here is not on food waste but with how the FDA's overzealous and inane attempt to make the food supply safer by imposing meaningless new rules for farmers and brewers almost cost them—and us—dearly.

The FDA's proposed rules for spent grains, which were part of the agency's larger FSMA rules, likely would have required breweries of all sizes to dry and package their wet spent grains, to register with the agency as pet-food manufacturers, and to meet agency regulations for the manufacture of pet food. Brewers of all sizes—from tiny nano-breweries to the country's largest brewers—were dumbfounded by the proposed rule. The Beer Institute told the FDA the proposed rule was "based on the flawed and erroneous assumption" that breweries' intended customers are named Bessie, Spot, and Fido. "The goal of brewing is not to manufacture beer and animal feed simultaneously," the group wrote, in tersely worded comments that conveyed many brewers' thinly veiled disdain for the rule. "The goal of brewing is to manufacture beer."[48]

What exactly were the food-safety issues the FDA claimed spent grains posed? Much to the chagrin of those who were to be governed by the rule, the FDA never identified any. This was something brewers and farmers alike were quick to point out. "To our knowledge, there has never been a case of animals or humans becoming ill or harmed from consuming spent brewing grains or eating products from the animals who consume them," said Natalie Cilurzo of Russian River Brewing Company, in comments to the Huffington Post. "These proposed FDA rules appear to be a solution looking for a problem."[49]

The Brewers Association, a membership organization that represents America's craft brewers, and the Beer Institute, which represents the country's largest beer makers, both voiced spirited objections to the proposed spent-grains rules. The Brewers Association told the FDA there was an "absence of reports of illness or death among humans or animals associated with the handling and use of spent grains" and accused the agency of "attempting to provide a solution to something that isn't a problem and hasn't been for the thousands of years brewers have been feeding spent grain to animals."[50] The FDA admitted the regulations weren't a response to any problem. "We don't know of any problems," said Daniel McChesney, director of surveillance and compliance with the FDA's Center for Veterinary Medicine, which—as the center's very name suggests—should never have anything at all to do with regulating breweries. "But we're trying to get to a preventative mode."[51]

Although the proposed rule likely couldn't prevent food-safety problems from arising in places where no such issues have ever existed, it most certainly could create a host of unwanted new problems for farmers and brewers. It is these problems the rules weren't intended to create but which would arise just the same—"unintended consequences," as they're known—that show the proposed rule's dramatic potential negative impact. The spent-grains rule, in addition to creating mountains of food waste, would have taken money out of the hands of brewers and farmers of all sizes and, ultimately, would have raised the price every American pays for beer and food.[52]

Estimates of the costs associated with the proposed spent-grain rules across the food chain were staggering. The average brewer would be forced to spend nearly $14 *million* per year, the Associated Press reported, to comply with the rules.[53] Brewers would be forced to pass the extra costs on to farmers, who—you guessed it—would in turn be forced to charge consumers more for foods such as milk that come from dairy cows fed the spent grains.[54] Many farmers estimated that—without access to brewers' spent grains—their feed costs could rise by hundreds of dollars per day.[55] Brewmaster Christian Ettinger, of Hopworks, a zero-waste brewery in Portland, Oregon, that is a model of sustainability and has sent more than 750 tons of spent grains to a local organic dairy farmer, said the spent-grains rule would result in "higher prices for dairy, for meat and definitely higher prices for beer."[56]

The fact that a small urban brewery such as Hopworks is sending hundreds of *tons* of spent grains to farmers shows how large and vital the trade in spent grains is in this country. Sure enough, the amount of spent grains produced in this country is staggering. The Beer Institute says that U.S. brewers of all sizes produce nearly 3 million tons of spent grains a year.[57] Nearly all of it changes hands from brewers to farmers and ranchers each year. That's a remarkable partnership for promoting sustainability.

Large breweries produce—and sell or donate to farmers—much of those spent grains. They're also leaders in sustainability efforts. MillerCoors, for example, sells or donates nearly 100 percent of its spent grains.[58] Both it and Budweiser have been active in providing farmers with spent grains since the 1800s. It's largely thanks to these big breweries that nearly 8 percent of the nation's dairy cattle feed comes from spent grains, according to Beer Institute data. But smaller brewers are also key contributors and, perhaps more importantly, are probably more reliant on these relationships with local farmers. New Glarus Brewing in Wisconsin, for example, donates about 2,000 tons of spent grains per year to a local dairy farmer. Oregon Natural Meats (ONM), located just outside Eugene, appeals to supporters of sustainability and local food by partnering with local craft brewer Ninkasi Brewing Company. ONM's cattle eat more than 11 million pounds of Ninkasi spent grains each year. The ONM website features a constantly updating ticker that shows the number of pounds of spent grains the company has "upcycled" since 2009. That number stood at nearly 70 million total pounds at last check.[59]

Brewers and farmers have relied on each other for millennia. Each has benefited from the relationship, as have meat eaters, beer drinkers, livestock, and the environment. The FDA rules would have upset this beneficial, delicate, and tasty balance. As the Brewers Association argued, the proposed rules would harm "brewers looking to create local sustainable ties and close loops within their communities."

One company that's undoubtedly helping close that loop is Achadinha Cheese Company in Petaluma, California. The small dairy farm, run by the husband-and-wife team of Jim and Donna Pacheco, raises a variety of animals, including goats, cows, and chickens, and is known for its goat cheese. Jim's family has been making cheese for three generations. Achadinha obtains several tons of spent grains each week from Bear Republic Brewing Company in nearby Healdsburg and Russian River Brewing Company in Santa Rosa. The goats feast on a steady diet of alfalfa, spent grains, and (when drought strikes, as it has) hay. "The brewers grain is slightly fermented," Donna Pacheco told me, "which means that it is much easier to digest for the girls."[60]

The fact that Achadinha pastures its goats and buys spent grains from a brewery is just the beginning of the sustainability loop. In addition to selling cheese at about sixty farmers markets within a two-hour drive of their farm, the Pachecos also sell their cheese to a variety of local restaurants. One of those restaurants is Bear Republic's brewpub, which uses Achadinha goat cheese in its artisanal cheese and charcuterie sampler. So the spent grains from Bear Republic's beermaking process feed the Achadinha goats that make the cheese that's served with the beer back at the brewery. That's lovely, delicious, and a great example of a sustainability loop. But could the loop survive? Donna Pacheco said the FDA's proposed spent-grain rules, coupled with California's ongoing drought, could be a death knell. "The FDA requirements are going to make it more and more difficult for small companies to stay in business," Pacheco told me. "We are a small family farm struggling to provide a future in agriculture for our children. The grain is a healthy way for us to keep going."

Faced with this onslaught of opposition, the FDA dramatically reversed course in September 2014. The agency announced it would not treat spent grains like industrial waste and require breweries to be regulated as pet-food makers. FDA deputy commissioner Michael Taylor said in a statement that "redundant animal feed standards that would impose costs without adding value for food or feed safety . . . would not make common sense, and we're not going to do it." At the same time, Taylor cynically claimed the agency *would never* have done the very things it had proposed to do, things that caused brewers, farmers, cheesemakers, consumers, and others such consternation and that required countless hours and dollars to respond to in written comments (which were often drafted by costly attorneys). Taylor chalked the spent grains issue up as nothing more than a big misunderstanding—or "misperception"—and said, of imposing restrictions on spent grains, "it was never our intent to do so."[61]

Intent or not—and, absent any evidence to the contrary, I believe the former to be true—it's difficult to overestimate the negative impact such a rule would have. "Every brewer in Seattle that I know of has a relationship with a farmer to dispose of spent grain," Sara Nelson, co-owner of Seattle's Fremont Brewing Company, told me.[62] Nelson also applauded the Brewers Association for its lobbying efforts, and said they helped avoid "millions more tons of organic 'waste' clogging up landfills, inflating brewers' utility bills, and eliminating a no-cost source of animal food for local farmers." Thankfully, the proposed spent-grain rule appears dead. But Nelson said she and her fellow brewers remain vigilant. They have good reason. The FDA's pronouncement was not final. The agency is still pondering how it will treat spent grains.

Although sustainable brewers and farmers are wise to be skeptical that the proposed spent-grains rule was nothing more than the public "misperception" the FDA's Taylor painted it to be, those same brewers and farmers aren't the only ones suspicious of FDA rules. Readers who aren't yet skeptical of the FDA's judgment when it comes to food safety and sustainability need look no further than how another, completely unrelated agency rule would have affected cheesemakers, including Achadinha. That's because, just months before Achadinha and others faced dire consequences from the FDA's proposed spent-grain rules, the very same agency had dreamed up a completely unrelated way to endanger the livelihoods of artisanal cheesemakers.

The cheese crisis first arose in the wake of a letter the FDA sent to a New York cheesemaker in 2014. The agency letter declared that the use of wooden shelves "for cheese ripening does not conform to [agency good manufacturing] requirements."[63] This was news—*bad news*—for the artisanal cheese community. Wooden shelves have been used to age and ripen cheese for as long as cheese has been made. The FDA had never raised any concerns over the practice before. Although large food companies today often age their cheese on plastic or stainless steel surfaces, traditional and artisanal makers typically use wooden planks to ripen cheese. "Well over half the cheese that is being made and consumed in the U.S. is aged on wood boards," the American Cheese Society's Greg O'Neill told the *Burlington Free Press*.[64] According to O'Neill, most imported cheeses, including Parmesan and Gruyere, are also ripened on wooden boards.

"The very pillar that we built our niche business on is the ability to age our cheese on wood planks, an art that has been practiced in Europe for thousands of years," Wisconsin cheesemaker Chris Roelli told Cheese Underground, the website that broke the news about the FDA letter in June 2014.[65] Roelli, a fourth-generation, award-winning Wisconsin certified Master Cheesemaker, knows of what he speaks. But now the agency was telling Roelli and other cheesemakers that this ancient practice was not permitted. Not only that, but the letter went on to say the practice *had never been permitted* under FDA rules.

As with the spent-grains rule, prohibiting the use of wooden boards would have had existential consequences for cheesemakers, consumers, and cheese itself. Mateo Kehler of Jasper Hill Farm in Greensboro, Vermont, told the *Burlington Free Press* that it would cost him more than $20 million to swap out his wooden planks.[66] Yancey's Fancy, an artisanal cheesemaker located in upstate New York, ripens several cheeses, including its Gouda, on wooden boards. According to a *Buffalo News* report, the company was planning to invest more than $20 million to open a new facility, expand its existing plant, and hire dozens of new workers in the economically challenged Buffalo area. Its plans hinged in part on "developing at least four new cheese varieties that would rely on wooden boards for ripening."[67] Back in Wisconsin, an artisanal cheesemaker echoed the sentiments of many in his community, worrying that the FDA crackdown could serve to ban many styles of cheese entirely. "Wooden boards are so important for so many flavors of cheese," said Ken Monteleone of Fromagination Artisanal Cheeses, in remarks to WKOW.[68] "Without this process many of our favorite cheeses would cease to exist." Achadinha's Donna Pacheco, another who ripens cheese on wood, echoed Monteleone. "There's no way I could make this cheese without having my shelves," she told her local CBS affiliate.

There's plenty of confusion about just *why* the FDA chose to crack down on cheeses ripened on wooden boards. Although the agency's letter in early 2014 informed stunned cheesemakers that the FDA had always barred the use of wooden planks, other reports indicated that the agency's aggressive new stance under FSMA was to blame. The agency refuted those claims. In any case, the FDA said it targeted wood because wood surfaces can't be cleaned adequately, and that this lack of cleaning can foster listeria, a potentially deadly bacterium. Indeed, the impetus for the FDA's action was an agency finding of listeria contamination at a New York cheesemaker that had been using wooden planks to ripen cheese.[69] To be clear, the FDA and other government agencies should do what they can to keep listeria out of the food supply. Halting these specific New York cheese sales and imposing subsequent punitive measures on the cheesemaker was the right call by the FDA. And stainless steel is—at least superficially—easier to clean than wood. That's why the FDA suggested ripening cheese on stainless steel, or maybe using plastic wrap. But there's a good body of research that shows ripening cheese on wood is at least as safe as it is on stainless steel, possibly because wood can have natural antimicrobial traits. But does that make it safe?

"Wood is a perfectly safe surface," said Nora Weiser, executive director of the American Cheese Society, which represents artisanal cheesemakers, to the *New York Times*.[70] In fact, the porousness of wood may make it *safer* than stainless steel. Award-winning cheesemaker David Major told the *Burlington Free Press* that aging some cheeses on a non-wood surface could prevent the cheese from developing a protective rind, meaning "the cheese would turn into a bacteria-laden mush."[71] That's the opposite of what cheesemakers, consumers, and food-safety advocates want. "I can tell you conclusively there's no scientific reason to ban wood in cheesemaking," University of Vermont professor Catherine Donnelly, a food microbiologist and expert on cheese safety, told the *Free Press*.[72] "Mold ripened cheese[s] need wood to live and develop in a natural health[y] way," Achadinha's Donna Pacheco told me.[73] Bacteria is not the enemy. *Dangerous* bacteria is. "We need bacteria" to make cheese, she said. Given all this, it's no surprise that about 1,000 members of the American Cheese Society ripen some of their cheeses on wood.

If the FDA's attack on wood-ripened cheeses shares much with the agency's proposed spent-grains rule, the tremendous backlash against both rules is also strikingly similar. So it's perhaps no surprise that the FDA changed course on its stance against ripening cheese on wooden planks. Tellingly, the statement announcing the reversal began much like the agency's flip flop on spent grains. "Recently, you may have heard some concerns suggesting the FDA has taken steps to end the long-standing practice in the cheesemaking industry of using wooden boards to age cheese," the agency announced to cheesemakers who had not just *heard* concerns but had voiced them forcefully. "To be clear, we have not [banned] and are not prohibiting or banning the long-standing practice of using wood shelving in artisanal cheese."[74] The June 2014 FDA statement went on to declare that the wording used in the letter sent to cheesemakers earlier in the year—the one that declared that ripening cheese on wooden planks was not and never had been permitted—"may have appeared more definitive than it should have, in light of the agency's actual practices on this issue."[75]

Still, despite this seeming clarity, artisanal cheesemakers still have reason to be concerned. The agency's clarification stated its historic concerns "about whether wood meets [agency food safety] requirement[s]" and asked cheesemakers and others "to share any data or evidence they have gathered related to safety and the use of wood surfaces." It said that FDA officials "have not and are not" taking action against ripening cheese on wood. But it did not say the agency *will not* take such action. As with the FSMA manure rules, this sounds little like an agency that has backed down and very much like one that has chosen to gather more evidence before renewing its war on cheesemakers.

Rep. Peter Welch (D-VT), who was perhaps the most outspoken congressional critic of the FDA's attack on artisanal cheese, sees it this same way. That's why he introduced a bipartisan amendment to an appropriations bill that would prevent the FDA from banning the practice. His language was appropriately dire. "Artisan cheese makers cannot afford to live with this threat to their livelihoods caused by regulatory ambiguity at the FDA," said Rep. Welch in an angry press release posted at his House of Representatives website.[76] Rep. Welch had reason to be mad. In March 2014, an FDA official had responded to an inquiry he made, stating unambiguously in an email to the congressman that the agency's position was that "wooden shelves for the storing or aging of cheeses . . . are not permitted and never have been [permitted]." In June, they completely reversed course. "The FDA's right hand doesn't know what its left hand is doing," Rep. Welch tweeted after the FDA reversed itself. "Which FDA should cheese makers listen to?" he wondered. Rep. Welch also took to Twitter to share the hashtag #SaveOurCheese, so as to convey the gravity of the situation.[77] Despite gaining support, Rep. Welch's amendment to prohibit the FDA from banning the use of wooden planks to age cheese failed to make it into law. As a result, the specter of a crackdown on the practice—much like the attack on spent grains—still looms over the artisanal cheese industry.

If you're like me, you see the trio of FDA actions I've discussed so far in this chapter—FSMA's potential impact on small, organic, and sustainable farmers; the proposed spent-grains rule; and the agency's crackdown on artisanal cheese makers—as bullets needlessly fired at but so far dodged by sustainable food producers and their customers and supporters. Maybe you see these examples as evidence that the FDA is simply testing the limits of the public's tolerance for increased rules, and that sustainable food producers—with the public's help—were strong enough to beat back the impending rules. Maybe you think the agency claim to have backed down when confronted with the ire of sustainable farmers, brewers, and cheesemakers is proof that the public's voice really matters, or that this is simply evidence that the regulatory process is working.

But is it really working? It didn't work for Mark DeNittis, whose sustainable salumeria Il Mondo Vecchio—as you learned earlier in this book—was put out of business by USDA rules. Good guys like DeNittis don't always—or even *often*—win when facing crushing new regulations. Of all the food producers in America I've spoken with while writing this book, none is confident that their business can thrive in the face of stricter food-safety rules. Not one. And none have thought the regulatory hurdles they've faced would make their food safer. Still, as difficult as produce farmers, small food entrepreneurs, brewers, and cheesemakers have had it, they're not even the most threatened classes of food producers. In fact, of all the people I've spoken with, none is more concerned about their future than small meat producers.

America's Slaughterhouse Mess

When Americans grumble about how our food system is broken, the slaughter and processing of farm animals are often at the heart of their critiques. One hundred years ago, Upton Sinclair's damning novel, *The*

Jungle, exposed many gruesome and unsanitary practices in the food system of his day. A host of important federal food-safety regulations, including mandatory inspections, soon followed.

But that was hardly the end of the story. Instead, attention to livestock slaughter has only grown in recent years. In 2014, for example, I moderated a panel at Harvard Law School on sustainable meat production as part of a conference called "The Meat We Eat." The conference was cosponsored by two Harvard Law student groups—the Food Law Society, the first of many similar student groups that have popped up at law schools around the country in recent years, and the Student Animal Legal Defense Fund. The title of my panel—"Reducing Legal Barriers, Empowering Consumers, and Creating Pathways for Sustainably and Humanely Raised Meat"—nicely encapsulates the obstacles that many farmers, consumers, and others face in their efforts to sell, buy, and eat the type of meat they want. Many of these obstacles are the result of a mandatory food-safety inspection system, administered by the USDA, that is deeply flawed.

Today's USDA food-safety rules require that agency inspectors be present at a facility every day that meat is processed. In 2007, though, stunning reports emerged that USDA inspectors had failed to inspect hundreds of plants regularly, as required, for thirty years.[78] Although the agency's failure to inspect hundreds of facilities regularly for three decades is outrageous, even that fact doesn't illustrate the broken state of the agency's food-safety rules quite as well as does the closure of a Petaluma, California slaughterhouse in 2014. That year, the USDA suddenly forced Rancho Feeding Corporation—the only USDA-approved slaughterhouse in Northern California—to close. An agency investigation indicated the facility had illegally processed cattle that were suffering from cancer.[79]

The presence of cancerous meat led the USDA to order the recall of 8.7 million pounds of beef processed by Rancho.[80] The agency was clearly justified in taking any cancerous meat—which was disgusting at best and which could pose food-safety problems at worst—out of the food supply. By also ordering the recall of millions of pounds of beef that was entirely wholesome, though, the agency was throwing out the baby with the bathwater. Worse still, as I'll explain, the USDA's own food-safety rules were largely to blame for the agency's decision to order the destruction of perfectly good meat.

One morning in 2009, when I was living in Fayetteville, Arkansas, where I was studying agricultural and food law, I jogged by a pair of cattle dining on grass in a fenced pasture a couple blocks from my apartment. As I slowed down to take a look at them, I noticed some flyers attached to the fencing along the roadside. I stopped running and grabbed a flyer. Sure enough, these cattle—or parts of them, at least—would soon be for sale in fifty-pound boxes. After I finished my jog, I called the phone number on the flyers. Another phone call, a few emails, and a week or two later, I was the proud owner of a box of steaks and other cuts raised by Tommy Daniel, a recently retired professor of crop, soil, and environmental sciences at the University of Arkansas.

You'd think that these cattle, raised lovingly and openly in a pasture a block from the main intersection in a college town, might be spared the indignity of enduring a road trip to meet their end at a far-off processing plant. They'd be killed locally and sold to people like me. You'd be wrong. Though Prof. Daniel's cows lived out their days in a pasture only two blocks from my home, that fact hides the journey they—and animals like them around the country—face if they're to become dinner. Prof. Daniel had to send his cows *only* sixty miles to be slaughtered. Other farmers—and their livestock—aren't so lucky. USDA rules often force small, sustainable farmers to ship animals hundreds of miles away—even out of state—to be slaughtered and processed alongside animals that were raised without the same care. That's because USDA rules unnaturally amalgamate animals from farmers and ranchers of all types and sizes—from cattle raised on the smallest grass-fed beef farm to those raised on the nation's largest confined animal feeding operations (CAFOs)—into many of the same USDA-approved slaughterhouses. This is largely true because rules are uncaring, and because there simply aren't enough slaughterhouses to meet demand.

There are more than 800 federally inspected slaughterhouses in the United States, according to recent USDA data. Another 1,800 are operated by states or are "custom" slaughterhouses—where sales are severely restricted to prohibit, for example, sales to grocers. But figures showing a proliferation of custom slaughterhouses are misleading. The thirteen largest U.S. cattle slaughterhouses account for 56 percent of all cattle killed in this country. The figures are similar for hogs (twelve plants account for 57 percent of all slaughters) and other livestock. Commercial plants processed 47.3 billion pounds of red meat (including cattle, pork, sheep, and other hooved animals) in 2014.[81]

USDA requirements for slaughterhouses the agency inspects are part of the problem. They're so complex that the agency itself funded a report in 2012 for the purpose of establishing "a streamlined regulatory proposal that could be carried forward in future years to make the USDA inspection system less onerous to smaller facilities that could perceivably be built or utilized in more small local communities." That sounds great. But the report writers concluded that their mission was damn near futile. "After the numerous conversations and meetings, it became apparent that no one with the USDA or . . . working as professionals within the meat industry," they write, "believe[s] that streamlining regulations will ever occur."[82]

Despite this dire conclusion, small farmers do have some choices for operating outside of the USDA system. But these choices come with serious drawbacks. A 2013 report by the Spokane, Washington, *Spokesman-Review* detailed the problem. Farmers and ranchers are free to use slaughterhouses that are not inspected by the USDA. But meat from animals slaughtered there "must be sold to the consumer before it is butchered." That means consumers must buy cow, not beef. And they often have to buy hundreds of pounds at a time. "Since a steer yields about 400 pounds of meat, that's often too much for a single family," reported the *Spokesman-Review*. "Several families can go together to purchase an animal, but that's more hassle for the rancher. And it doesn't address the needs of individuals who just want to purchase a few steaks or some ground chuck."[83]

This helps explain why on-farm slaughter accounted for just 93.4 million pounds of red meat—or a paltry 0.2 percent of meat slaughtered commercially. This figure includes mobile slaughterhouses, vehicles that travel to farms to slaughter livestock without forcing them to undergo the discomfort and stress required by lengthy travel. All of this helps explain why Rancho was the only independent USDA-inspected slaughterhouse in all of Northern California in 2014. It also explains why most small cattle farmers are forced to use USDA facilities and pass up the local slaughterhouse. Some even literally drive by the latter on their way to the former. "I'm a beef farmer myself," Rep. Thomas Massie (R-KY) told me in 2015, "and when I take my animals to be processed, I drive past a custom facility three miles from my house and travel three hours to a USDA facility."[84]

How did we get to this point? As the *Washington Post* reported in 2010, the "processing, marketing and distribution networks that once made small farming viable . . . disintegrated in the last 30 years as U.S. agriculture went through a dramatic consolidation."[85] This dramatic decline has occurred even as "demand for pasture-raised niche meats is soaring," reported *USA Today* that same year.[86] In other words, the demand for niche meats is rising fast, but supply is being suppressed artificially by the lack of slaughterhouses.

These problems aren't just evident with cattle and pig slaughter. Consider poultry. Small farmers can slaughter up to 20,000 of their own chickens in a year. And if you're raising and slaughtering that many birds, chances are you can justify the cost of investing in your own processing facility. But very small operations can't afford to do so. And that hurts the smallest poultry farmers, because slaughterhouses are often difficult to find. For example, Massachusetts lacks a USDA-approved poultry slaughter facility.[87]

The impact of limiting where animals can be slaughtered has real-world consequences beyond mere inconvenience, including the Rancho recall. The USDA's mandatory recall ensnared not only cancerous cattle processed from (and by) a few bad actors but also that of every other producer who'd had an animal slaughtered in the Rancho plant in the past year—out of what the *San Francisco Chronicle* termed "an abundance of caution . . . to make sure none of the cancerous meat commingled with healthful beef."[88] That includes cattle sent to Rancho by celebrated grass-fed farmer Bill Niman, who told the *Chronicle* that he's out almost $400,000 even though the hundreds of his cattle that Rancho slaughtered were cancer-free and he could prove to the USDA that those cattle were not commingled with the diseased meat.[89] Niman's wife, Nicolette, an environmental law attorney and author of the book *Righteous Porkchop*, penned an excellent *New York Times* op-ed lamenting the recall as an overbroad reaction akin to chopping down hundreds of different orchards thanks to one bad apple. "The Agriculture Department's tools for safeguarding the nation's meat supply are blunt and clumsy instruments, especially when dealing with independent farmers," she wrote.[90] These USDA policies aren't just stupid—they're also reckless. And the alleged "abundance of caution" the department claims to be exercising now—after the fact—is entirely the result of its own recklessness.

The Rancho recall is part of a much larger problem that's existed for decades in the USDA inspection process. That program is a bad one for small, sustainable farmers and consumers. As you'll learn in chapter 5, the USDA inspection program is now under fire from a bipartisan group of lawmakers in Congress who support small farmers, including some, such as Rep. Massie, who are themselves small farmers. As you'll learn, Rep. Massie, a Republican, and Democratic colleagues such as Rep. Chellie Pingree (D-ME) and Jared Polis (D-CO), have cosponsored a bill that would permit farmers to expand options for selling meat locally that's been processed by local slaughterhouses.

Although USDA food-safety rules make selling sustainably raised meat a tough slog, you're about to learn that state and local food-safety rules are often no less complicated. Food-safety rules that govern the sale of fruits and vegetables, meats and cheeses, and other foods you buy at farmers markets and other local outlets can make doing business difficult—or impossible—for local farmers.

Farmers Market Restrictions

"We had an issue last year at one of our farmers markets where one of our bagged lettuces was considered a processed food," Lynda Simkins of Natick Community Organic Farm (NCOF) in Natick, Massachusetts, told me by phone in summer 2015.[91] Simkins has been executive director of NCOF for thirty-five years. The nonprofit, certified-organic farm, located just outside Boston, is dedicated to "humane animal care, sustainability in life style, and living in an environmentally friendly manner."[92] I first learned about NCOF several years ago, after calling to buy a gift certificate for my sister, who lives nearby. When I visited my sister later that year, we were given a great tour of NCOF by farm administrator Trish Umbrell. My sister, who loves to knit, turned the gift certificate I gave her into some yarn spun from the wool of some of NCOF's sheep.

NCOF's history and sustainability bona fides are impressive. Records indicate the land on which it is located has been farmed since at least the early 1700s. The farm has been certified organic since 1975. Composting is the rule on the farm. And 40 percent of the farm's power is generated by its solar panels, which it says helps eliminate 6.7 tons of carbon dioxide each year. NCOF raises and sells a variety of organic vegetables, fruits, eggs, turkey, beef, chicken, goat, lamb, mutton, and pork. They also sell maple syrup, which is cooked down in their sugar shack from syrup obtained by tapping local trees. They don't grade the syrup they make, Simkins told me, because she thinks the maple syrup grading system—which is based solely on color, rather than quality—is a joke.[93]

The idea that rules can be a joke brings us back to the idea that bagged lettuce is a processed food. NCOF sold its lettuce at a farmers market in nearby Newton, where the lettuce rule was enforced at the behest of the city's health department, Simkins said. Interestingly, the city's farmers market rules don't refer to lettuce specifically. The rules don't offer much clarity for a farmer, either, stating only that "[p]rocessed foods may be sold" and that fruits and vegetables "may be sold by the bunch, piece, container, or weight."[94]

"If we'd just sold the lettuce with the stalk on," Simkins told me, "we wouldn't have a problem. But because we cut off the stalk, it was considered 'processed.'" A lettuce stalk, while theoretically edible, is bitter. Most consumers never even see one, because most farmers cut it off, knowing that consumers won't eat it. And lettuce is often sold bagged. Bizarrely, Newton's bag rule didn't apply to celery, which, Simkins said, can be cut, bagged, and sold at the same farmers market free from any complaints about it being a "processed" food. Newton's lettuce requirements may stem from the state's own food-safety guidance for cut and uncut produce, which declares that fresh, uncut produce "can be displayed in the open air" but that "[a]ll food products, with the exception of uncut produce, require protection while on display."[95] Because NCOF put the lettuce in a bag, the city may have considered the lettuce to be cut produce and, therefore, a processed food.

The implications of whether a food is or is not "processed" can carry tremendous weight. Fresh fruits and vegetables are not processed foods, which are generally understood—as the Massachusetts rules state—to be foods such as pies, jams, and candy. As a general rule, if a food is "made," then it's processed. If it's merely grown or raised, then it's not processed. But the state's current "interpretation" of what constitutes fruits and vegetables is that they be "uncut." Does that make lettuce sold without the stalk "processed"? Does removing the inedible part of a plant—a stalk or roots or a disfavored part, like carrot tops—make a food "processed"? If so, then state laws would require that sellers of all these "processed" fruits and vegetables at a farmers market comply with a host of additional rules, including additional licensing and inspection requirements.

Ultimately, NCOF opted out of selling lettuce—or anything else at farmers markets. They chose instead to sell through their own CSA service—selling directly to subscribers. Although it wasn't the lettuce rule specifically that drove NCOF away, the CSA was just easier, Umbrell told me.[96] Given that Newton is just one of more than 300 cities and towns in Massachusetts, it's easy to see why many farmers prefer the CSA route. "Each town regulates its own farmers markets," Simkins said of the state of farmers market rules in Massachusetts. The state established its own model rules for farmers markets—which Newton's rules mostly reflect—but whether cities and towns follow them is up to those cities and towns. Whereas Newton focused far too much attention on lettuce, other cities across the state may have their own predilections. A farmer wanting to sell in more than one city or town has to learn the intricacies of each new set of rules. Because the way rules are applied often appears arbitrary and might not be reflected in the actual rules on the books—for example, a farmer would have no idea that rules might treat lettuce and celery and carrots so differently—it can be far easier for a small farm like NCOF to forego farmers markets altogether.

Who benefits when farmers are too overwhelmed by rules to take part in a market meant to benefit them and consumers? Do farmers and consumers benefit from food-safety rules that treat fresh produce as a processed food? Unfortunately, Newton's quirky rules for its farmers markets are hardly unique. Other cities around the country have similar rules for their farmers markets that make it difficult for small farmers and others to sell their products to eager consumers.

In 2011, New York State's agriculture department banned cheese vendors from slicing cheeses—for everything from customer sampling to weighing out desired portions—at all farmers markets in the state.[97] As in Massachusetts, the threat of "processed food" was to blame. In New York, the ban arose when the agriculture department applied an existing permit law to cheese slicing.[98] "Slicing cheese at a farmers' market, under [New York's] way of thinking, is food processing," said Jonathan White, of New Jersey's Bobolink Dairy, which produces a variety of artisanal cheeses from its grass-fed herds.[99] Just like in Massachusetts, because the state suddenly viewed slicing cheese as "processing" it, cheese sellers would need a separate food-processing license. That license requires a separate on-site building with a sink and water heater. One artisanal cheesemaker was fined $600 for failing to comply with the law. As I noted in an article I wrote at the time, the mission of New York State's agriculture department "is to foster a more competitive food and agriculture industry in New York State that benefits producers and consumers alike."[100] It was difficult to see how this rule, which by all accounts hurt producers and consumers alike, was achieving the agency's mission. Others agreed, and the state faced a tremendous backlash before reversing course and exempting cheese from the onerous rules.[101]

Still, New York's cheese-sampling laws aren't unique. Minnesota lifted a statewide ban on sampling cheese only in 2014.[102] One farmer I spoke with in California during the course of writing this book said the state appears to be tightening its rules for sampling cheese. Crushing and unnecessary food-safety rules such as these that target farmers markets spurred me, in 2011, to work with Harvard Law School's Food Law and Policy Clinic on the report—which I discussed briefly in the introduction to this book—examining whether farmers market regulations in this country are needlessly strict. The need for the report, as I noted in the introduction—was spurred by concerns I was hearing in Pennsylvania that a new state law could wreak havoc with the state's popular farmers markets.

"A Pennsylvania law that went into effect in January places new restrictions on farmers' market vendors, mandating licenses and inspections, detailed package labeling, and cleaning equipment including, in some cases, portable sinks," the *Philadelphia Inquirer* reported in 2011.[103] The *Inquirer* noted that farmers and market managers throughout the state were frustrated by the new rules, and that some farmers were choosing to scale back their offerings instead of attempting to comply with the new rules. Compliance costs were one major hurdle. Portable sinks can cost up to $1,500. Even worse, some markets were requiring farmers to use high-priced motorized cooling equipment such as generators and refrigerated trucks—rather than ice chests, which are equally effective and cost just a few dollars—to keep food chilled. These barriers were insurmountable for many small farmers.

The Harvard clinic's report, issued in 2012, was far-reaching. It examined not just Pennsylvania's new law, but also farmers market laws in nine other U.S. states—California, Illinois, Massachusetts, Michigan, New Jersey, New York, Ohio, Oregon, and Vermont. It was the first such report to compare farmers market regulations in a cross-section of states around the country. Report coauthors Nathan Rosenberg, then a law student, and Prof. Emily Broad Leib, who directs the law clinic, looked at Pennsylvania's rules from top to bottom.[104] They spoke with farmers market managers, farmers, state officials, and other stakeholders throughout Pennsylvania and across the country. The report contained a great deal of good news. By the time it was issued in 2012, public outcry over Pennsylvania's rules had forced the state to clarify and soften its stance in several key areas. For example, Pennsylvania was one of a handful of states studied that prohibits local governments from enacting their own, stricter requirements for farmers markets. Newton's lettuce rule, for example, would likely be barred if the city were located in Pennsylvania. And that state, like every state studied, opted to permit vendors to use lower-cost alternatives to commercial sinks (such as hand sanitizers) and mechanized refrigeration (such as ice chests). This meant Pennsylvania's rules were, in most cases, no stricter than those in other states.

But the report also cautioned that there was much work to be done to avoid imposing crushing burdens on small farmers. The report noted "many sustainable agriculture and local food system proponents agree that . . . overbearing food safety regulations [can] have the negative impact of suppressing the direct sales market."[105] To foster an environment in which that market can thrive, the report recommended easing local health department burdens on farmers markets, working closely with organizations that represent small farmers when governments draft any new rules for farmers markets, and auditing existing state rules that apply to farmers markets to ensure they're as lean as they can be while still promoting food safety.

Most importantly, the report recommended replacing rules that mandate specific *processes* with ones that mandate specific *outcomes* (what the report refers to as "results"). What does that mean? Mandating *processes* refers, for example, to rules that tell a farmer she must use a generator or a refrigerated vehicle to keep her beef and pork chilled below 40 degrees Fahrenheit. That's the temperature food scientists generally recognize as the maximum safe temperature for inhibiting the growth of bacteria and preventing foodborne illness linked to such growth.[106] Mandating good *outcomes*, on the other hand, refers to rules that simply tell a farmer she must ~~use a generator or a refrigerated vehicle to~~ keep her beef and pork chilled at or below 40°F. The results—the outcomes—are the same. A farmer can choose to keep her food below the 40°F "danger zone" by any reasonable method at her disposal, including use of a generator, refrigerated vehicle, water ice, dry ice, or, on very cold days, the ambient temperature. The farmer is free to choose the method that's right for her. A larger farmer with more food to chill, more area to cool, and more income will probably choose mechanized methods. That's great. A smaller farmer with less food to chill, less area to cool, and less income will probably choose one of the less expensive options. That's also great. The law can and should ensure—regardless of process—that the farmer keeps food below 40°F. Each process is right for the farmer who uses it so long as it achieves that desired outcome. "States should look for places to refashion process-driven food safety laws and regulations into results-driven ones," the Harvard report concluded, "benefiting both the public and small farmers."[107]

You may notice that this isn't the first time I've called for a food-safety regulatory system that's based on good outcomes rather than narrowly defined processes. For example, I wrote earlier that if USDA inspectors had found harmful bacteria in Il Mondo Vecchio's meats, then the agency would have been justified in shutting down the company until it cleaned up its act. The government's food-safety authority rightly includes the power to demand good outcomes. But the USDA simply determined that even though Il Mondo Vecchio achieved the outcome the agency wanted 100 percent of the time, the agency would no longer approve of the process they used to achieve those perfect results. That makes no sense. Whether the issue is ripening cheese on wooden planks, sending spent grains to farmers, selling heads of lettuce at a farmers market, or keeping meats properly chilled, smaller, sustainable producers can coexist with larger competitors only if lawmakers and regulators acknowledge that there are different paths to safe food, that rules for large food producers might not work for small ones (and vice versa), and that the rules they make and enforce must ensure the viability of large and small producers alike.

Unfortunately, many food-safety regulators and advocates oppose the outcome-dependent approach to food safety I've just described. They also tend to be the ones who propose, support, make, and enforce the rules. In Mississippi, for example, process-dependent agriculture department rules mean that anyone selling meat, poultry, or other animal products at a farmers market or other venue must use a refrigerated truck to chill the food. Ice is out of the question. Even a portable generator isn't sufficient.

The Mississippi rules, implemented in 2002, state the desired outcome (keeping food outside of the temperature danger zone). They also dictate a very specific—and, for many, prohibitively expensive—process. The rules mandate that the sale of meat and poultry at farmers markets and all other temporary spaces "must be from a refrigerated vehicle and have a workable continuous mechanical refrigeration system or cold plate system approved by the department as the refrigeration source." The rules also define a refrigerated vehicle as "an insulated vehicle (truck or trailer) equipped and used as a refrigerator to transport fresh perishable or frozen products."[108] A clever farmer or lawyer might see some daylight in that language. But Mississippi isn't having it. In recent years, the agriculture department clarified that meat and poultry "must be sold from a refrigerated vehicle and not from a cooler contained in the vehicle."[109] A refrigerated truck can cost upwards of $80,000.

But it gets worse. The rules also apply to those who want to sell virtually any animal products at a farmers market in the state. The agriculture department requires eggs to be chilled "under mechanical refrigeration" at farmers markets. The rules even apply to cheeses, as rules posted by the Square Market in Batesville, located in Mississippi's impoverished Delta Region, make clear.[110] That market operates just one day each week, for just four hours. It's hard to imagine that a small farmer could justify leasing—never mind buying—a refrigerated vehicle for a few hours of selling cheese. Even if a farmer could justify the cost of leasing a refrigerated truck, the state also requires that the farmer first physically deliver the truck to have it inspected by the state and then to display the farm's name, address, and telephone number on the side of a rented truck. What's more, most farmers markets in the state, including the Batesville market, require a seller at a market both to reside locally and to raise or produce the foods they sell locally. Hence, a farmer must sell only her own foods, and resale of foods is not permitted. Although this sounds great in theory, in practice it means that opportunities for a farmer to partner with a butcher or other business owner who has access to a refrigerated truck, for example, are limited at best.

If these rules strike you as uncommonly harsh and burdensome, you're right. In fact, they don't exist in other states. Mississippi is the only warm-weather state—and likely the only state anywhere in the country—that requires someone bringing food such as meat to a farmer's market to use a refrigerated truck or trailer to chill the food. Odder still, the rules were adopted just three years after another Mississippi law was adopted that permitted the use of "ice or mechanical refrigeration" to chill meat, poultry, and other foods sold on roadsides.[111]

Not surprisingly, the state's rules have had a tremendously negative impact on the ability of smaller farmers to sell meat, poultry, and other animal products at farmers markets in the state. "If you go to Mississippi's farmers markets, grocery stores, or food co-ops, you're not going to see much, if any, local meat," said Nathan Rosenberg, the Harvard Law School student who coauthored the farmers market report, and who later spent a year working on local-food issues in Mississippi after earning his law degree. But Rosenberg, now a fellow with the nonprofit Natural Resources Defense Council, told me the lack of locally raised meat is not due to any dearth of willing suppliers. In Mississippi, maybe "dealers" is the better term. "Buying local meat in Mississippi is akin to buying drugs—you know someone that knows someone and they hook you up," he said.[112]

The fact that state rules force local poultry, beef, and pork sellers to act like methamphetamine dealers to succeed is such a concern that the issue dominated a 2013 Mississippi Food Policy Council meeting that centered on the state's refrigeration requirements. The meeting revealed that, as of 2013, only one refrigerated truck in the entire state had been issued the necessary permits to transport and sell products such as meat at farmers markets.[113] That's as shocking as it is absurd.

During the meeting, a state representative said that the agriculture department believes that a cooler filled with ice is inappropriate for chilling food because it "will not maintain a constant temperature" in the hot Mississippi summer. Although one attendee noted that the FDA suggests ice as one way to keep eggs safely chilled, Mississippi agricultural officials believe that "mechanical refrigeration is the safest way"—ergo, the only way—to do so.[114] But mechanical refrigeration is hardly foolproof. Reports out of several states, including Ohio and Indiana, indicate—pardon the pun—chilling flaws in the food-safety record of the refrigerated-food-transportation industry.[115] In 2014, Senator Sherrod Brown (D-OH) called for increased "monitoring of refrigerated food transportation" over concerns about deliveries of "spoiled food."[116] That doesn't mean that refrigerated food transportation is unsafe or ineffective. It just means that high-tech methods don't always trump low-tech ones.

"When I was researching the law," Rosenberg told me, of Mississippi's requirement, "I asked a food safety scientist if there was any advantage to a refrigerated truck over a cooler with ice or cold packs. I was surprised when he said that not only were refrigerated trucks not any better than coolers, but that they were actually less reliable: unlike coolers, refrigerated trucks suffer mechanical failures." The scientist touted cheaper means. "Coolers are cheap and reliable," Rosenberg said. "Refrigerated trucks are expensive and susceptible to mechanical failure. Yet Mississippi only allows the latter. It makes no sense."[117]

Mississippi is home to at least eighty-three farmers markets, according to USDA data.[118] The state has close to 3 million residents, 18,000 farms that raise cattle,[119] and about 12,000 total small farms.[120] Both supply and demand exist in the state. But the state's refrigeration rules don't permit the former to fulfill the latter. "Farmers market managers report a huge, largely unmet interest in local meat products," reads a blog post on the refrigeration rule by Delta Directions, a nonprofit consortium that promotes health and economic renewal in the Delta Region. But the rules mean that local meat producers are "almost entirely absent from farmers markets within Mississippi."[121]

Taking the Canadian Out of Canadian Bacon

From Colorado to Vermont, New York to California, Massachusetts to Mississippi, at the FDA and USDA, and in the halls of Congress, senseless food-safety rules have erected often-insurmountable obstacles for sustainable food producers. In most cases, they have done so without making Americans and the food we eat any safer. Unfortunately, the United States has not cornered the market on lousy food-safety rules such as these. Our neighbor to the north, Canada, has its own tangled web of inane, often-contradictory rules. Perhaps no story better illustrates Canada's abysmal view of sustainable food production than the saga of Clinton and Pamela Cavers of Harborside Farms. The couple's farm, which they've owned for nearly 30 years, is located about two hours southwest of Winnipeg, the capital of Manitoba, and about a fifteen-minute drive from Canada's border with North Dakota. Harborside Farms raises hormone- and antibiotic-free pigs, cattle, lamb, and goats on about 200 acres and produces and markets a variety of sausages, prosciutto, and other all-natural meat products. It raises Mulefoot and Berkshire pigs, both of which are better able to endure pasturing in Manitoba's colder weather.[122]

"Clinton and Pamela are committed to the principles of small, sustainable farming and have incorporated these principles into their farm production systems and their lifestyle," reads a laudatory 2011 Canadian government profile of Harborside Farms.[123] A Canadian Broadcast Corporation profile of Harborside called it a "poster child for the free-range movement, with ducks, chickens, goats, lambs and grass-fed cows doing their thing; the whole place operating under a chorus of clucks, grunts, snorts and moos."[124] The Cavers's meats and charcuterie were served in a growing number of Winnipeg's top restaurants. Then, in spring 2013, Harborside won the Great Manitoba Food Fight, a competition sponsored annually by the provincial government, for their prosciutto. The award came with $10,000 in prizes.[125]

"There are no walls when you walk into our meat shop so you can see exactly what we are doing and that is the way that we have the farm as well," Pamela Cavers proudly told the CBC.[126] By August 2013, though, Cavers might have wished for a wall. Late that month, inspectors from the same Manitoba government that had heaped praise on Harborside Farms arrived at its shop one day—accompanied by a Royal Canadian Mounted Police officer—and seized the farm's cured meats, condemning them as "unfit for human consumption." Inspectors seized all 350 pounds of Harborside's charcuterie—worth about $8,000—and fined the couple $1,200.[127]

The *Manitoba Co-operator* referred to the Cavers's plight as a "bureaucratic and regulatory maze" the couple had been forced to navigate. But for what reason? What pathogens had inspectors found? None whatsoever. "The meat products were not found to contain any foodborne, illness-causing pathogen," the *Co-operator* reported. "Rather, they were told they must comply with certain procedures and processes, as well as upgrade their facilities to ensure no such pathogens have a chance to develop."[128]

Clinton Cavers countered that he was using old-world methods, that the food wasn't found to be unsafe, and that he knew provincial inspectors were aware of his meat processing practices—which they now criticized—because he'd detailed those practices to those same inspectors. But the couple's requests for more information from the province fell on deaf ears. "They said they had no idea what to compare it to," Pamela Cavers told the *Winnipeg Free Press*, speaking about the couple's award-winning, old-world methods for making charcuterie, and officials' views on the topic. "They didn't even know what charcuterie was."[129] A chef who spoke to the *Free Press* characterized the plight of Harborside as representing something greater, namely of "artisanal production facilities [that] struggle to adapt to an ever-changing set of regulations intended for large factories." The charges against the Cavers—along with the $1,200 fine—were dropped in 2014 due to a technical problem with the ticket given to the couple on the day their shop was raided. "But new obstacles have arisen," the *Free Press* reported. "The province insists the Cavers must use nitrates in their charcuteries." But Pamela Cavers said Harborside won't use nitrates. "That goes against our whole ethic," she said.[130]

"When small scale producers have been sanctioned or impeded in developing new products by provincial health departments, the issue of 'food safety' is used to justify the actions of the regulators," wrote Sheldon Birnie, editor of the *Manitoba Eco-Journal*, in a 2015 article in *Briarpatch Magazine* that focused in part on the plight of the Cavers family. "However, you'd be hard-pressed to find a small-scale producer who doesn't value food safety as highly, or more high[ly] than industrial producers."[131]

If the outrageous experience of Harborside Farms sounds to you just like that of Mark DeNittis and Il Mondo Vecchio, and similar to those of every other process-stung sustainable food producer whose mindful production methods and safe outcomes seem to matter little to those who make and enforce many food-safety rules, then you're not alone. For sustainable food producers and consumers, this is a rallying cry. But many food-safety advocates seem relatively unconcerned about the plight of Il Mondo Vecchio and sustainable farmers, cheesemakers, farmers, brewers, farmers markets, and others affected by the tangled web of food-safety rules.

When asked in 2009 about "the push back from small and sustainable agriculture folks" against stricter food-safety regulations, Prof. Marion Nestle, a leading food-safety advocate, responded that rules are rules. "As for small farmers: I think everyone producing food—no exceptions—should be using science-based food safety procedures with testing," she told *Food Safety News*.[132] In a 2013 column—attempting to refute many of my criticisms of FSMA in a *Food Safety News* column I'd written—a pair of writers from the Center for Science in the Public Interest (CSPI), a nonprofit that helped usher in the law's passage, argued that "farmers and food producers of all sizes [should] celebrate passage of" the law. The CSPI authors argued that the "conscientious farmers and food producers Linnekin mentions [are] on the side of wanting regulation."[133] I believe each and every sustainable food producer, advocate, supporter, and consumer I've described in this chapter is exceedingly conscientious. I believe each cares about food safety. And I believe the great majority—me included—support some food-safety regulations. But they're not celebrating FSMA—or rules that require them to buy a refrigerated truck in order to sell a few steaks at a farmers market—and other senselessly strict food-safety rules. They're not celebrating rules that could force them out of business, all while making us and the food we eat no safer.

Science can and should be used to identify real food-safety problems. Like Prof. Nestle, I agree that mandatory testing is important. And using a particular, science-based process may make sense for many producers. But another process may be based on science that's just as good—or better—than a mandated process. In many cases—as you've seen with rules that require chefs to wear gloves while preparing food or propose to require cheesemakers to ripen cheese on stainless steel—there's good evidence that the mandated solutions are far less safe than existing practices. When rules aren't based on good science, and they outlaw existing safe practices, these rules can actually cause foodborne illness.

That's a real cost of bad rules. Another such cost is that bad rules such as these so often serve to hurt small, sustainably minded food businesses. As we've seen in this chapter, perpetual calls to ramp up food safety tie up sustainable food producers in a vicious cycle. Many of those food producers simply can't comply with rules written with large producers in mind. That means smaller food producers disappear, and bigger ones get bigger as a result. That consolidation, in turn, is often used to justify the need for more stringent regulations. The cycle loops back to where it began with calls for stricter regulations, which leads to more consolidation, which leads to calls for stricter regulations. It's a death spiral that is crushing small, local food producers.

The ugly truth is, in many cases, that may be the very point of food rules. Shortly after Congress passed FSMA in 2010, the *Wall Street Journal* editors noted the law was "not the first time big business has leveraged government to weigh down smaller competitors."[134] As you'll learn in the following chapter, government rules often promote big producers at the expense of smaller ones. And, as you've seen with the food-safety rules described in this chapter, the rules tend to trample sustainable food producers in the process.

CHAPTER 2

"Big Food" Bigger Thanks to "Big Government"

WHEN IT COMES TO CONSUMERS' food-buying decisions today, perhaps no single symbol is more powerful and influential than a seal confirming a food meets the USDA's definition of "organic." To consumers, the symbol means an assurance that an agricultural product such as beef or celery has been produced using only naturally occurring fertilizers, pesticides, and other inputs.[1] To producers, the USDA organic seal means higher costs, but also the opportunity to charge consumers more for that beef or celery.

USDA involvement in organic food is a recent development. Organic certification programs began in the early 1970s, when small producers using natural and sustainable farming methods in states such as Oregon and California banded together to establish minimum standards for themselves and their peers. Certifiers and the small farmers worked with states to pass laws supporting the standards.

Accusations of fraud surrounding organic foods led Congress to scrutinize the certification process. That led to passage, in 1990, of a law intended to set national organic standards. But rules that would enforce the law failed to materialize. In 1995, five years after the law's passage, a class-action lawsuit targeted alleged fraud by two organic food producers.[2] It wasn't until 2000 that the USDA ultimately began regulating organic food. But if the USDA's involvement in organic certification was intended to prevent fraud, its success has been a mixed bag.

Criticism of the USDA organic label has been particularly fierce from small and sustainable farmers, many of whom have argued that the agency has used its congressional mandate to water down the meaning of the term "organic" to the benefit of large agricultural producers—and to the detriment of the consumers and small farmers the law was intended to benefit. Meetings of the USDA's National Organic Standards Board, which establishes limits for which foods may earn the USDA organic seal, have become a "semi-annual ritual of controversy," the *Washington Post* reported in a 2015 article that focused on the possible addition of synthetic pesticides and additives to the list of substances that would be permissible to use while still earning the agency's organic label.[3]

Sure enough, controversies over the USDA organic label have flourished. In 2005, for example, a battle erupted over language in the USDA rules meant to shine a little sunlight on livestock. "A collection of organic dairy farmers have been taking aim at larger farms that also market their product as organic," ABC News reported. "The contention is that the larger farms have been taking advantage of vague wording in the U.S. Department of Agriculture's organic food guidelines and are housing cows in industrial-like facilities while selling their brand with the certified organic label."[4] The controversy hinged on language in the USDA organic rules that required dairy cows to have "access to pasture" for their milk to be certified as organic. Cows kept inside a CAFO might have "access" to a small pasture through, say, a single door. But the smaller farms argued that the CAFO cows spent nearly all of their time confined inside and rarely, if ever, actually *accessed* that pasture.

The organic rules have been the source of other controversies. In 2009, USDA employees urged the agency to ban some synthetic additives from organic baby formula. But they were overruled, reported the *Washington Post*, "after a USDA program manager was lobbied by the formula makers and overruled her staff." The report said the issue went to the heart of "the integrity of the federal organic label."[5] In 2013, access to pasture was again at issue, now thanks to proposed FDA rules that could force organic chickens to have limited or no access to pasture. Such a rule would "significantly and permanently weaken the integrity of the organic standards," said Mark Kastel of the Cornucopia Institute, a nonprofit that promotes "the ecological principles and economic wisdom underlying sustainable and organic agriculture."[6]

The Cornucopia Institute is one of the nation's strongest supporters of organic farming. But it's also been one of the leading critics of USDA organic standards, which the group argues have weakened small organic producers and caused dramatic consolidation within the organic food industry. "In 1995 there were 81 independent organic processing companies in the United States," the group wrote in 2014. "A decade later, Big Food had gobbled up all but 15 of them."[7] Today, the Cornucopia Institute is just one of many supporters of organically raised food that finds itself harshly criticizing the USDA's National Organic Program. Prof. Marion Nestle, author of the book *Food Politics*, is "a big fan of organics." She contrasts her support of organic food with the USDA's position, which, she says, reveals an agency that "do[es]n't like organics much."[8]

Recall that the USDA, during President Franklin Roosevelt's time, was "skeptical of amateur farmers." Today, the same agency feels the same way about organic food—or, at least, the food grown and raised by small organic farmers. So just what—and who—does the USDA *like*? To figure that out, we need look no further than the agency's actions.

"Big Government" (to use a term popular on the right) likes "Big Food" (to use a term popular on the left). When we do look further into the USDA's actions—first by investigating the issue of farm subsidies—it's difficult not to see that sustainable farmers and food producers rate somewhere between an annoyance and an adversary. Later on in this chapter, we'll also see that the USDA isn't alone in favoring large food producers over smaller, sustainable ones. State governments are also in on the act.

What's Wrong with Farm Subsidies?

Farm subsidies are a key part of the U.S. Farm Bill, a law typically renewed by Congress every five years. The purpose of farm subsidies is to "help farmers manage the risk inherent in farming," says the federal government's nonpartisan Government Accountability Office.[9] These subsidies have often taken the form of direct cash payments to farmers. In practice, farm subsidies have served to encourage many farmers to plant a few types of crops—particularly monocultures of corn and soy—and to plant more of those crops than consumers would otherwise purchase. Subsidies encourage these decisions largely without regard to land conservation, water pollution, or the types of food ingredients—such as high fructose corn syrup, the now-ubiquitous caloric sweetener—that those subsidies promote. With bipartisan support in Congress, subsidies require the USDA, which administers the various farm-subsidy programs created by lawmakers, to direct taxpayer funds to agricultural producers. Typically, subsidies have benefited wealthy, larger farmers who farm just a handful of crops and who should not—and, flatly, *do not*—need them to succeed.

History is not on the side of farm subsidies, which were the brainchild of Henry Wallace, while he served as President Franklin Roosevelt's USDA secretary. During the height of the Great Depression in the 1930s, Secretary Wallace pitched farm subsidies as "a temporary solution to deal with an emergency." That emergency—long since ended—was the Great Depression.[10] What's more, recall that this was the same USDA that was openly skeptical of amateur (read: small) farmers.

That farm subsidies were intended to be "temporary" has been lost on the farmers—and even nonfarmers—who have come to rely upon them in record amounts. In 2012, for example, America's farmers earned a record profit.[11] That same year, farm subsidies were at their second-highest level in history, just eclipsing 2011's total.[12] This gives a hollow ring to claims by some that subsidies are all that stands between the success of America's farmers, on the one hand, and financial ruin and food shortages on the other. In 2006, for example, an Arkansas farmer defended farm subsidies because, he said, they "keep American farms operating and provide a steady supply of food that is relatively inexpensive and wholesome."[13] His contention, therefore, is that without farm subsidies, America's farms would not be "operating," and that the nation's food supply would be something other than "steady."

Many large-scale farmers, farm-state politicians from both major political parties, and the USDA are the biggest proponents of farm subsidies. If the farmers who receive the cash, members of Congress, and the USDA support farm subsidies, it's also true that many outside of this powerful bloc—on both the left and right—oppose farm subsidies. In 2002, for example, left-leaning Nobel Prize–winning economist and *New York Times* columnist Paul Krugman referred to farm subsidies and the Farm Bill as a "grotesque" exercise.[14] The right-leaning Heritage Foundation agrees, calling farm subsidies "so poorly designed that they actually worsen the conditions they claim to solve."[15]

One key problem Krugman, the Heritage Foundation, and others note—and it's a big one—is that the farmers who receive subsidies don't need them. Consider, for example, that recipients often aren't even farmers. In recent years, recipients of farm subsidies have included a veritable who's who of celebrities, millionaires, and even billionaires, including Microsoft cofounder Paul Allen, investment guru Charles Schwab, and S. Truett Cathy, the late owner of Chick-Fil-A.[16] Multimillionaire New Jersey rockers Jon Bon Jovi and Bruce Springsteen both received farm subsidies in recent years.[17] Although he's known for leading the NBA in steals and earning millions of dollars in salary as Michael Jordan's championship sidekick, Hall of Famer Scottie Pippen has also deftly pulled in farm subsidies.[18]

Politicians from both major political parties have also benefited from farm subsidies—even while serving in Congress. And they know better than most how to game the system. This includes Democrats such as Rep. Robert Marion Berry (D-AR) and Sen. Blanche Lincoln (D-AR) and Republicans such as Rep. Michele Bachmann (R-MN). Rep. Bachmann "received $251,000 in farm payments between 1995 and 2006," reported *Politico*, while railing against the excesses of government programs.[19] Rep. Berry, the *Arkansas Leader* reported in 2006, received "more than $800,000 in subsidies for his family's farming operation over a nine-year period while he was in Washington and unable to oversee it." How did Rep. Berry receive subsidies while sitting in Congress, a thousand miles from his farm? "Berry is accused of signing over 25 percent of the stocks in his farm corporation to his son Mitchell Berry and 25 percent to Danny Sloate, the farm manager, to meet a federal requirement that 50 percent of the ownership of the farm corporation must be actively involved in the operation to be eligible for subsidies," the paper reported.[20]

The Environmental Working Group (EWG) is a Washington, D.C.-based nonprofit that has done yeoman's work on farm subsidies for years, providing the media and the public with resources for tracking the dramatic costs and recipients of farm subsidies. EWG's thorough analysis of USDA farm-subsidy data presents a powerful argument against the continued existence of those subsidies. For example, EWG noted that the USDA paid farmers a stunning amount—nearly $300 billion—in crop subsidies between 1995 and 2012. Nearly one-third of farmers in America—typically small and sustainable farmers—received no farm subsidies during that period. According to EWG, 10 percent of America's farmers collected 75 percent of all farm subsidies—a staggering $175 billion—from 1995 to 2012. The top 10 percent of farmers averaged more than $30,000 in subsidies annually, while the bottom 80 percent received $600 per year.[21]

Criticism of farm subsidies has reached a crescendo in recent years. In 2012, for example, the editorial board of the *Minneapolis Star-Tribune* called subsidized crop insurance a "boondoggle" that "throw[s] money at farmers, whether they need it or not."[22] National Public Radio (NPR) reported in 2013 that farm-subsidy programs give "money to farmers and land owners regardless of need or loss."[23] Ironically, one vocal critic of farm subsidies in recent years has been the Roosevelt Institute, which is dedicated to celebrating and carrying on the legacy of President Franklin Roosevelt—a legacy that includes establishing those same farm subsidies. "Those that qualify for these [subsidy] payments are mostly big commodity firms that grow such crops as corn, wheat, soy, and cotton, and they are paid regardless of crop prices," a Roosevelt Institute fellow wrote in 2012.[24] "A majority of these firms are large enough that with the recent rise in commodity prices and without a regulatory limit on how much they can produce, much of the government subsidy gets banked as extra profits."

The confounding economic costs of farm subsidies are readily apparent. But the environmental costs and other unintended consequences of farm subsidies, while not as obvious, are just as widespread. Partly as a result, Congress in recent years has changed the fundamental structure of farm subsidies, moving away from direct payments to farmers and instead focusing its dollars on subsidizing farmers' purchases of crop insurance, which insures farmers against loss.[25] The subsidies work by paying for approximately two-thirds of a farmer's insurance premiums. On its face, this seems like a sensible reform. But many—me included—predicted the shift to crop insurance was at best cosmetic and, at worst, would have a host of negative unintended consequences. Those outcomes were predicted to include ballooning costs for taxpayers, a lack of transparency, and potential environmental consequences. Unfortunately, each of those criticisms has been borne out by Congress's so-called "reforms."

During the most recent debates over passage of a Farm Bill, Sen. Thad Cochran (R-MS) urged support for crop insurance, which he referred to as a set of "important risk management tools for farmers and ranchers nationwide" that "can help reduce costs."[26] Sen. Debbie Stabenow (D-MI), who chaired the Senate Agriculture Committee, of which Sen. Cochran is also a member, lauded the Farm Bill as "an opportunity to cut spending."[27] That's not how it's worked out. Rather, costs have skyrocketed under the new Farm Bill thanks to crop insurance subsidies. In 2011, before crop insurance supplanted direct subsidies, I noted in a *Baltimore Sun* op-ed that farm subsidies cost taxpayers approximately $15 billion per year.[28] With crop insurance subsidies now having gained favor over direct subsidies, the latest EWG estimates show farm-subsidy payments could reach $30 billion annually by 2018.[29] All of this was predictable. As I wrote in 2014, "the bill taxpayers may foot for crop insurance subsidies . . . may outweigh what taxpayers would have contributed in direct subsidies."[30] So much for reducing costs.

In addition to their staggering cost, farm subsidies have also helped promote consolidation and upsizing of farms in American agriculture. "Cropland [has] shifted to larger farms in most States and for most crops," a report by USDA official James McDonald noted in 2013. "The increases were persistent over time, and they were substantial."[31] An earlier report by McDonald reached similar conclusions. "Agricultural production continues to shift to larger farms in the U.S.," he wrote in a 2011 USDA report. The latter report noted that this shift has come "at the expense of small commercial farms."[32] A variety of factors is causing this shift. But subsidies certainly play a key role. As Ferd Hoefner of the National Sustainable Agriculture Coalition wrote in 2014, subsidies have served "as a stimulant to farm consolidation and the growth of mega farms."[33]

Although Americans may have a good sense of the unbelievable financial cost of farm subsidies, they may know less about just who's receiving those subsidies. It used to be that individual recipients of farm subsidies could catch heat from a watchful public—mostly thanks to EWG's excellent database. The most recent Farm Bill, though, eliminated virtually any transparency in farm-subsidy programs. The Center for Public Integrity, a watchdog group, reported in 2010 that in the wake of the 2008 Farm Bill, the USDA "is no longer centralizing the data that made it easier to pinpoint individuals who receive farm payments through their affiliation in farming corporations, co-ops and other types of business partnerships."[34] The 2014 Farm Bill neutered transparency even further, "deliberately keeping recipients of [farm] subsidies secret," reported the Sunlight Foundation, another watchdog, in 2014.[35] "Indeed, the final version of the law even dropped a bipartisan provision that would have at least required members of Congress and Cabinet officials to disclose such benefits." Jon Bon Jovi and Michele Bachmann might rest a little easier, but the farm-subsidy nightmares plaguing American taxpayers are only sure to grow.

If farm subsidies are a growing nightmare for America's taxpayers, their environmental costs are also staggering. Because crop insurance rewards farmers for maximizing their yields, regardless of consumer demand, it's a recipe for environmental degradation. A 2001 paper by University of California-Berkeley economist Jeffrey LaFrance (now at Montana State) and two colleagues concluded that "crop insurance policies may adversely affect the environment, in that any increase in overall acreage results in further contributions to sedimentation and siltation, oxygen depletion, [and] toxic and pathogenic pollution."[36] The expansion in crop acreage also tends to occur in marginal lands, which the report noted "may also require greater fertilizer, pesticide, and insecticide applications." Prof. LaFrance and his colleagues were hardly alone in reaching these conclusions. A 2006 USDA research report noted that "[a]lmost all studies on crop insurance subsidies have noted the potential for environmental damage due to expanded crop production."[37] What's more, that expansion typically means a farmer might grow a crop in a monoculture, a vast agricultural expanse featuring only one crop. It's no coincidence highly subsidized crops like corn and soy are most often grown in vast monocultures. And it's not just the subsidies that differentiate these monocultures from sustainable agriculture. A 1999 article on the role of biodiversity in agriculture, published in the journal *Agriculture, Ecosystems & Environment,* warns that the monocultures typical in "modern agricultural systems have become productive but only by being highly dependent on external inputs."[38]

Alongside this discussion of large farms and monocultures, it's important to note here that there's nothing about large farms that is inherently unsustainable, at least not any more so than there is anything about small farms that is inherently sustainable. As it applies to farming, the term "sustainability" refers to a set of practices and goals, not to the size of the property on which those practices take place (or don't) and where such goals are (or are not) aspired to. As the Environmental Defense Fund's Suzy Friedman wrote, "'big' does not equate to 'bad,' and 'small' doesn't necessarily mean 'good' when it comes to sustainable farming."[39] Subsidies are environmentally unsound at least in part because they promote unsustainable practices on increasingly larger farms. They'd be environmentally unsound if they promoted these same practices on small farms, too.

Encouraging the growth of monocultures is just one specific farming practice that farm subsidies promote and that should alarm sustainability advocates. They also incentivize farmers, wrote a trio of food and environmental law faculty, "to grow large quantities of commodity crops regardless of whether a market exists for these crops."[40] And the food crops the USDA directs taxpayer subsidies toward is telling. Corn subsidies lead the way, at nearly $85 billion from 1995 to 2012, according to EWG data, followed by wheat, soybeans, rice, and sorghum.[41] It's no coincidence one rarely sees these crops raised in any significant way by sustainable farmers.

Furthermore, corn and soy subsidies also serve as an indirect subsidy for the animal agriculture industry. As films like *King Corn* and countless critics have noted, most subsidized corn never makes it into the mouth of a human eater. At least not directly. Instead, roughly half of that corn—according to a 2005 Tufts University study—is used as feed.[42] We eat the animals and animal products produced using subsidized feed. The nonprofit National Family Farm Coalition said corn subsidies helped save "factory farms in the hog, poultry, egg, dairy and cattle sectors" more than $7 billion a year.[43] That's why corn subsidies—along with other subsidized crops like sorghum, much of which is also turned into animal feed—act as a discreet subsidy to livestock farmers.

What's more, subsidies don't just affect what farmers grow; they also help determine what farmers *don't* grow. The incentives created by corn "subsidies keep farmers from growing vegetables and fruit and from growing diversified crops, a very important part of sustainable agriculture," argued the Sustainable Table.[44] In 2012, Joel Salatin, the "beyond organic" farmer celebrated by Michael Pollan in his book *The Omnivore's Dilemma*, told me the push away from direct subsidies and toward subsidized crop insurance was a hollow promise "because it masks the true cost of tillage, annuals, and cropping. . . . As a result, it artificially stimulates the profits for those crops to the prejudice of competitors and other products. It continues to push American agriculture toward a simplistic, non-diversified handful of genetics and products, rather than the cornucopia nature enjoys."[45] As he often is on the topic of food policy, Salatin was right.

Subsidies also act as a boon to companies that grow genetically modified (GMO) crops. According to USDA data, nine out of ten corn plants grown in America is genetically modified. Nearly all of the country's soybeans, also subsidized and used in animal feed, are also produced through genetic engineering.[46] Subsidizing GMO crops that supporters claim are technologically superior to natural versions of the same crops is downright bizarre. If they're superior, let them—like most non-GMO crops—stand on their own without taxpayer subsidies.

Finally, there's the very real cost of farm subsidies to human health. The cost of corn subsidies in particular has been reflected in the American diet—and may also be reflected in our growing waistlines. A 2013 study by the nonprofit Public Interest Research Group found that nearly $20 billion in farm subsidies have been directed to the production of high fructose corn syrup and other corn-based sugars, which are used to sweeten packaged foods like cookies, crackers, cereal, and soda, over the past two decades.[47] "The government is subsidizing the obesity epidemic," said Pollan, in the Katie Couric-produced documentary *Fed Up*.

Even in the face of current and proposed reforms to farm-subsidy programs, the situation is still dire. Critics, Salatin included,[48] note that USDA funding still tilts massively in the direction of large agricultural producers.[49] The National Sustainable Agriculture Coalition, for example, noted in 2015 that modifications to farm subsidies would still mean that "mega-farms . . . continue to collect millions in federal subsidy payments."[50] Farm subsidies were created in the 1930s as a temporary scheme to help lift the nation out of the Great Depression. Along the way, they transformed into a permanent scheme to help farmers manage risk. In recent years, their costs have ballooned. Their negative unintended consequences for consumers, sustainable farmers, and the environment are staggering.

Record taxpayer subsidies to help farmers manage risk at a time of record profits recalls the great *Seinfeld* episode in which a second-rate hack comedian, Kenny Bania, thanks star Jerry Seinfeld for mistakenly providing him with a folder of information about risk management—Seinfeld buddy George Costanza ended up with the information intended for Bania, a lame bit about the drink Ovaltine—for a comedy routine. "That risk management stuff you wrote for me?" Bania says, excitedly. "It's killer!" Jerry responds, clueless to what Bania is talking about. "Aw," Bania says, "it's gold, Jerry! Gold!" The joke, of course, is that only an idiot like Bania would see risk-management material as comedy gold. But farm subsidies *are* risk-management gold—a gilded parachute for many farmers and other agricultural producers. In fact, farm subsidies are perhaps the most flagrant example of a government program that is openly intended to benefit large agricultural producers and that, consequently, serves to hurt smaller competitors.

Is there an alternative to farm subsidies? Indeed, there is. And it's a dramatic one. Congress should eliminate them all. Immediately. "Agricultural subsidies cost taxpayers more than $15 billion each year, and until those subsidies are eliminated, farming in America will never be sustainable," I wrote in my 2011 op-ed in the *Baltimore Sun*, during a contentious debate in Congress over their renewal. "Killing off agricultural subsidies can help ensure a sustainable future for farming in America."[51] Many supporters of sustainable agriculture already oppose farm subsidies. If you didn't count yourself among them before this chapter began—maybe you believed, like the Arkansas farmer I quoted earlier in this chapter, that farm subsidies are a necessary contribution to American farmers that helps keep food cheap and healthy—I hope you see now that they're a bad deal for the environment, sustainable farmers, and American consumers and taxpayers alike.

Other USDA Supply and Demand Games

In addition to farm subsidies, there are several other ways the USDA stacks the deck against small, sustainable agricultural producers. One such example exists in a decades-old set of USDA programs known as "marketing orders," which exist for a variety of foods, including everything from dairy products to raisins. One key purpose of these marketing orders is to restrict the supply of a designated agricultural product in order to make that product more expensive. Supporters claim this rewards producers and marketers by guaranteeing income, promoting the agricultural products to potential consumers, and fostering order in the marketplace.

USDA raisin marketing orders, for example, have been in place since the 1940s. Since that time, all raisin growers and handlers in California have been required by the USDA to take part in the program.[52] The USDA's raisin marketing orders are overseen by the agency's Raisin Administrative Committee (RAC). Each year, the committee and its staff of more than a dozen employees determine how much of the raisin crop they will order to be seized by the agency, kept off the open market to limit the raisin supply and raise prices. That amount varies from year to year. But it can be staggeringly high. In 2003, for example, the RAC determined that the percentage of raisins it would seize was 47 percent—or nearly half the total crop.[53] Sometimes the RAC pays for a percentage of the raisins it takes. In 2003, the RAC paid nothing for the raisins it seized. Once it obtains the raisins, the federal government can—and does—do virtually anything it wants with them. It can sell them abroad. It can pass them along as cattle feed. Surplus raisins often make their way into the USDA's National School Lunch Program. Or the raisins can simply be thrown out or left to rot. If you think that sounds wacky and needlessly convoluted, you're not alone. In 2006 the USDA itself referred to its own raisin marketing order program as "somewhat complex."[54]

In return for handing over their raisins, those who produce and market raisins enjoy the fruits of the RAC's marketing wizardry. Most famously, RAC marketing dollars created the "Heard it Through the Grapevine" series of advertisements in the 1980s, which featured a claymation band, the "California Raisins," in a send-up of the classic Motown song by the Temptations.[55]

You may love claymation raisins, but not everyone involved in the raisin business is happy with the RAC. One chief concern is that participation in the RAC is mandatory. If you are a California raisin producer or handler, you've had no choice other than to be governed by RAC rules.

After the RAC's 2003 marketing order mandated the seizure of nearly half of the raisin crop, one raisin handler—the USDA term for a middleman—decided he'd had enough. That year, the RAC ordered Marvin Horne, a sixty-something handler from California, to turn over 47 percent of his raisins (or their cash equivalent). This amounted to either giving the RAC more than 1 million pounds of raisins or writing them a check for more than $600,000. Horne soon filed suit against the USDA. To Horne, the USDA's actions were simply unconstitutional. "They took our raisins and didn't pay us for them," he said.[56] The Fifth Amendment's Takings Clause requires the government to compensate a property owner when it seizes his property. Clearly, as Horne described, the USDA and the RAC had not done this.

One good way to judge a law that's been taken up by the Supreme Court is to see which companies, businesses, advocacy groups, and others support or oppose the law. I wrote a brief opposing the RAC and supporting Marvin Horne, for example. Together, my arguments (and those of others who supported Horne) included that the RAC promotes uncertainty for all but the largest producers and handlers, those who can better tailor their production to fit into the government's scheme. This uncertainty no doubt prevents smaller entrants from getting into the market, which stifles competition. It takes agricultural production decision making out of the hands of the people who know best—individual farmers and handlers—and puts it in the hands of government commissioners and their staff. It puts taxpayers on the hook to fund the RAC, and forces consumers to pay higher prices for raisins as a result. It creates food waste by needlessly disposing of raisins. And it's unconstitutional.

One of the few parties to write a brief in support of the USDA in the case was raisin giant Sun-Maid, a cooperative of more than 600 raisin growers that bills itself as "the largest single marketer of raisins in the world." They're not kidding. California raisins make up a staggering 99 percent of all raisins on the American market.[57] Sun-Maid growers produce more than 60 percent of those raisins, and more than one of every eight raisins worldwide.[58] It would be unfair to paint Sun-Maid as some enemy of sustainability. Many of its members are sustainable farmers and producers who, for example, use nothing more than natural sunlight to dry their grapes.[59] So why would Sun-Maid support the USDA and the RAC? The company's brief to the Supreme Court argued, as the USDA did in defending the RAC, that the program "benefits the entire raisin industry" by stabilizing prices and supply. And they claimed that Horne was acting as a free rider—taking advantage of the higher prices guaranteed by the RAC's actions but not contributing to the pool of seized raisins.[60]

That may have been true. But Sun-Maid's defense of the RAC turned out to be half-hearted at best. In 2014, as the *Horne* case was pending, Sun-Maid revealed in its Supreme Court brief that it had written to the USDA to "express its concerns" about the RAC and explained to the agency "why volume restrictions are no longer necessary for the raisin industry."[61] Whether this turnabout was the result of an earnest belief that the sixty-five-year old RAC had outlived whatever use it may have had or whether the company simply saw the writing on the wall is unknown. What was clear was that the RAC no longer benefited Sun-Maid's growers as it had in years past. During these years, though, Sun-Maid's hundreds of growers could afford to bear the cost of complying with the program. Marvin Horne, though, along with other smaller competitors, simply could not. And for every smaller competitor such as Horne who faced hardship because of the program, Sun-Maid only grew stronger. Sun-Maid's support for the RAC may come down to little more than protecting its own market share.

That's what happens in many cases where rules benefit big producers. Rules that squeeze—or squeeze out—smaller competitors benefit larger producers not necessarily by helping them financially but by hurting smaller producers who are less able to cope under the rules. Even if those larger producers are hurt by the rules, too, their massive size and market share means they're better able to withstand that injury. And their ability to do so only makes them stronger when smaller competitors falter under the rules.

The RAC is a classic example of how sometimes large food companies, working with government, stifle competition and harm consumers. "In short, the economic arrangements for raisins are an example of what so often happens when economic policy is set by a combination of government and existing firms: the focus tends to be on profits for those existing firms, backed up either by government regulations that function like implicit subsidies or by explicit subsidies," wrote economist Timothy Taylor.[62] The RAC, he wrote, "lacks any meaningful representation from consumers, or other firms in related industries, or the public more broadly, or those who might wish to enter the market for raisins."

In June 2015, the Supreme Court ruled in favor of Marvin Horne, declaring the RAC to be unconstitutional.[63] Although that's great news, the win isn't a total victory for those who'd like to see decisions about growing crops left to farmers—and an end to USDA programs that promote large producers to the detriment of smaller ones. Victory is incomplete because the Supreme Court made clear that the USDA could have met its goals simply by establishing production quotas, for example. Indeed, quotas are key to many other marketing orders, which include orders governing almonds, apricots, avocados, cherries, Florida and Texas citrus, cranberries, dates, grapes, hazelnuts, kiwis, olives, many onions and pears, pistachios, California plums and prunes, many potatoes, spearmint oil, tomatoes, and walnuts.

Consider the USDA's spearmint marketing order, which is intended to "maintain orderly marketing conditions in the Far West spearmint oil market."[64] Anyone who's ever grown spearmint knows that while it's great in a mojito or a julep, it's also a vigorous weed. Spearmint's quickly spreading roots will do everything they can to take over an entire garden. No gardener has ever complained about not being able to grow *enough* spearmint. Doing so would be akin to complaining about a dearth of dandelions in a flowerbed. And yet, to the powers that be at the RAC-like Far West Spearmint Oil Administrative Committee, doing away with its USDA program would be tantamount to a spearmint apocalypse. "If our industry didn't have the marketing order we would have one person raising spearmint," said spearmint committee chair Kim Mills, in an effort to distinguish her industry's quotas and protectionism from that evident in the *Horne* case, shortly before the Supreme Court announced its decision in the case.[65] "The market would be a monopoly and the small family farmers would no longer be participating and no one knows what the price of spearmint oil would be." But that's just wrong. Without the Far West spearmint oil marketing order, there would likely be *more* spearmint producers, and spearmint would likely cost taxpaying consumers *less* money. That's no good for the current crop of spearmint producers who, the same piece noted, are currently "protected and secure" under the current spearmint marketing order.

Marketing orders aren't the only way the USDA props up large agricultural producers. USDA "checkoff" programs, which exist for beef, pork, poultry, and other foods, play a similar role. How do these programs work? "Today, when you buy a Big Mac or a T-bone, a portion of the cost is a tax on beef, the proceeds from which the government hands over to a private trade group called the National Cattlemen's Beef Association (NCBA)," read a 2014 *Washington Monthly* piece skewering the beef checkoff program.[66] "The NCBA in turn uses this public money to buy ads encouraging you to eat more beef." You've no doubt seen these ads that were paid for with your tax dollars. "Beef. It's what's for dinner." Pork producers long had their own ads: "Pork. The other white meat." Meanwhile, large dairy producers are so entangled with the USDA that they capitalize on both marketing orders *and* checkoff programs. USDA dairy marketing orders set minimum dairy prices, while the checkoff program takes money from dairy farmers to promote milk and other dairy products. Taxpayers have the dairy checkoff program to thank, for example, for the ubiquitous "milk mustache" advertising campaign. If there are any benefits to be had from either program, they aren't likely to be enjoyed by you or your local farmer, creamery, or dairy.

In addition to its marketing orders and checkoff programs—and, don't forget, farm subsidies—the USDA finds still more ways to shift millions of taxpayer dollars to large food producers. In 2011, for example, the USDA purchased $40 million of excess poultry in an effort to aid large poultry producers.[67] Two years earlier, the agency bought up a similar amount of pork "to boost America's hog farmers."[68] And millions of dollars in dairy checkoff funds were recently used by Domino's to develop pizzas that contain more cheese and to urge Americans to eat more of those pizzas.[69] In fact, the USDA regularly spends millions of dollars each year to prop up animal agriculture producers. In 2009, according to the Physicians Committee for Responsible Medicine, a pro-vegan group, the USDA spent more than $1.7 billion to buy surplus dairy, beef, eggs, pork, and poultry.[70] Paul Shapiro, vice president for farm animal welfare with the Humane Society of the United States, told me those industries often try to keep government at arm's length, but when they "suffer from lack of demand, their clamor for government aid is stark."[71] Using taxpayer money to redirect billions of dollars to large food producers no doubt helps those businesses. But it's a raw deal for the competing smaller, sustainable producers, as well as for

American taxpayers and consumers. "Relying so heavily on federal subsidies, handouts, and bailouts isn't a strategy for sustainability," Shapiro told me.

Government buy-ups like these from large producers don't just harm sustainable food producers by senselessly propping up large, wealthy competitors. "The checkoff partnerships undermine USDA's standing as a credible voice in promoting dietary guidance for Americans, and they must be a terrible embarrassment for the many people at USDA who seek to promote healthful eating," noted Tufts University nutrition professor Parke Wilde.[72] These checkoff programs also reinforce the agricultural status quo put in place by the USDA and Congress. For example, a recent outbreak of avian influenza at large poultry farms and egg-laying facilities in at least fifteen states, including Iowa, Wisconsin, and Minnesota, resulted in the death of nearly 50 million chickens and other birds.[73] Sunrise Farms in Iowa, for example, lost 3.8 million hens. The government reimbursed many farms for their losses.[74] Critics, including many food-safety, animal-welfare, and sustainability advocates, argued the massive size of the facilities and the cramped living quarters the poultry live in—typical CAFOs, where birds are stacked high and wide in cages—was responsible for the scope of the outbreak. Don Carr, a food and agriculture writer for Grist and other publications, told me that the USDA's decision to pay farmers for their losses has a direct, negative impact on efforts to promote a more sustainable food system.[75] In this way, the USDA is propping up large farms. That's the very definition of an unsustainable system.

Special Treatment for GMO Farmers

Although USDA programs such as farm subsidies, marketing orders, checkoff programs, and other ad hoc payments to large food producers are some of the better-known ways that the agency promotes large producers of some agricultural products to the detriment of smaller ones, they're by no means the only examples of such practices. A patchwork of other laws that govern the agency's actions are also noteworthy examples of such practices. Outside of the regular outcry against farm subsidies by sustainable food producers and their supporters, perhaps no law in recent memory was as widely derided for so baldly protecting one class of agricultural interests as was a provision inserted into a 2012 appropriations bill in Congress.[76] The law, dubbed the "Farmer Assurance Provision" by sponsors, so openly safeguarded the interests of farmers who grow genetically modified crops (commonly referred to as "GMOs") that critics nicknamed it the "Monsanto Protection Act." The law requires that, in the event a federal court was to overturn USDA approval of a particular GMO crop, the USDA effectively ignore the court ruling so as to guarantee "that growers or other users are able to move, plant, cultivate, introduce into commerce and carry out other authorized activities" for an indefinite period.[77]

GMOs are a hot-button issue. Supporters and detractors—and I know many people on either side of the debate—are equally fervent in their beliefs about GMOs. Before continuing on to discuss the Monsanto Protection Act, it's compulsory that I situate myself within this heated debate. I tend to characterize my position on GMOs as somewhere between disinterested and neutral. I neither support nor oppose them. That's no cop out. It doesn't mean I hold *no* views on GMOs. Hardly. In fact, I have strong opinions in two key areas pertaining to GMO agriculture. First, I believe farmers should be free to raise whatever types of crops they wish, whether those crops are of the conventional, organic, or GMO variety. Second, I believe that if a farmer who is not raising GMO crops finds evidence that genetically modified crops have cross-pollenated with his crops, that farmer should have recourse in the courts. I believe this because the presence of genetically modified crops in an organic farmer's fields could damage or destroy the value of his crops, thanks to USDA regulations that ban the presence of all but minute traces of GMO materials in organic crops.

Owing to its application to farmers (rather than to seed companies such as Monsanto), the name "Farmer Assurance Provision" is probably a more accurate term than is the "Monsanto Protection Act," although I've also used the latter, better-known moniker to refer to the measure. Although Monsanto supported the Farmer Assurance Provision, the language in the law protected farmers who raised GMO crops, rather than those who sold GMO seeds to the farmers.[78] It's for that reason that GMO soybean growers, for example, also supported the measure.[79]

Conveniently, supporters of the law were pigeonholed as GMO advocates, while detractors were pegged as anti-GMO activists. To some extent, this was true. But my neutrality over GMOs didn't stop me from inveighing strongly against what I saw as a law intended to protect one type of farmers (those who raise GMO crops) to the potential detriment of those who grow conventional or organic crops. Not only that, but the law did so in a troubling and manifestly unconstitutional manner. As I noted earlier, the terms of the law directed the USDA secretary to ignore any court ruling that invalidates USDA approval of a particular GMO crop.[80] In other words, America's legislative branch, Congress, passed a law that ordered an executive agency to ignore any ruling by the judicial branch (which includes the U.S. Supreme Court). In our American system of checks and balances, that sort of law has been unconstitutional at least since an 1803 Supreme Court case, *Marbury v. Madison*, one of this country's most important court rulings.[81] Worse still, the law appeared to controvert a 2010 Supreme Court decision pertaining to GMOs, which held that a plaintiff, such as a farmer, could sue if they were harmed by a USDA action that "arguably [ran] afoul of" agency rules.[82] Even USDA Secretary Tom Vilsack—the very person empowered by the law—appeared to see it as an unconstitutional power grab.

Vilsack expressed concern that the law "appears to preempt judicial review of a[n] action, which may make the provision unenforceable."[83]

The good news is that the Monsanto Protection Act was allowed to expire the same year it became law. The bad news is that Congress established a precedent—further precedent, if you consider, for example, the extent to which farm subsidies promote GMO agriculture in this country—for protecting GMO farmers at the expense of others in general, and organic farmers specifically.

Identity Crisis

The Monsanto Protection Act was as awful as it was unconstitutional. But it was limited in scope and came with a small silver lining, in that it expired after six months. Another area of lousy food rules, though, is so pervasive that it has affected generations of American eaters. And, as you'll see, it's particularly hard on many of the country's sustainable food producers. Those bad rules pertain to a food's "standard of identity," which establishes specific rules for what foods may be labeled under a given name.[84]

For a food to be labeled as a "hot dog," for example, the food's ingredients must comply with specific USDA rules dictating exactly what a hot dog must, may, and must not contain. The standard of identity for hot dogs requires that any food labeled as a "hot dog"—technically, the USDA standard oddly combines the two words into one: "hotdog"—must contain "raw skeletal muscle meat." It may (but need not) contain "poultry skin" and pig lips. It may not contain more than 30 percent fat. If a company fails to meet the exact standard of identity for a specific food—if, for example, its hot dogs meet all other standards but contain 31 percent fat—then in most cases the USDA can force that food off the market.[85]

Various federal and state agencies also have food standards of identity in place. The definitions they use to establish what is or isn't a hot dog—or countless other foods—can be confusing or even surprising. That's because "[n]ames for foods are not based on common vernacular or a definition in a dictionary," the National Milk Producers Federation explained. "Names for foods are determined by the FDA" or the USDA, or any number of state agencies.[86]

Supporters claim standards of identity establish uniformity, boost consumer confidence, and prevent fraud. Indeed, the impetus for creating these standards was the prevalence, in the early part of the twentieth century, of fraudulent food labeling claims. Since then, hundreds of food standards of identity have been established. The USDA, for example, has established countless standards of identity for a virtual grocery list of foods. Many read like recipes from bygone days. For example, USDA rules say a product may be labeled as "au gratin potatoes and bacon" only if it contains no less than 8 percent fully cooked bacon. Similarly, the USDA's standard of identity for meat patties (such as frozen ground burgers) prohibits the addition of paprika. The rules require any product labeled as "egg foo young with poultry" to contain at least 3 percent "poultry meat," though a product labeled as "egg roll with poultry" need contain only at least 2 percent poultry (with no mention of "meat").[87] The FDA has its own lengthy list of standards of identity. The one for white chocolate defines it as "the solid or semiplastic food prepared by mixing and grinding cocoa butter with one or more of the optional dairy ingredients . . . and one or more optional nutritive carbohydrate sweeteners." The standard also requires that white chocolate consist of no less than 20 percent cocoa butter, 14 percent milk solids, and 3.5 percent milkfat, and no more than 55 percent sugar.[88]

One of the main criticisms of standards of identity is that they are frozen in time. Detractors contend, for example, that they fail to take into account the fact that popular foods such as soy milk and soy burgers could be barred from using the terms "milk" or "burger" because they fail to meet rigid standards of identity. But it's not just new foods that are stifled by standards of identity. These rules are actually enemies of two diametrically opposite attitudes that often play out in the food sphere and that supporters of a more sustainable food system often support: tradition and innovation. Food innovation often happens in some of the least likely of places. Take boring mayonnaise, the off-white, congealed sandwich spread that often accompanies an American's lunch of a tuna fish (never just "tuna") sandwich. Unilever's Hellmann's brand is the nation's best-selling mayonnaise. A leading competitor, Kraft's Miracle Whip brand, was innovative when it first appeared on the market in the 1930s. Miracle Whip isn't mayonnaise but is instead a "salad dressing" —even if few people dress a salad in Miracle Whip. (My mom's Waldorf salad dressing is one exception.) The reason for the distinction is that although the FDA's respective standards of identity for "mayonnaise" and "salad dressing" contain similar language—including reference to vegetable oils, eggs, and salt—Miracle Whip contains less of some mandatory ingredients by weight than the FDA's mayonnaise standard requires. Other innovators have since followed Miracle Whip. Vegenaise, an imitation, vegan-friendly, egg-free mayonnaise that's made with soy, is touted neither as mayonnaise nor salad dressing but as "better than mayo."

And then there's Just Mayo, the most recent entrant on the market. Like Vegenaise, Just Mayo dispenses with eggs, opting instead to get its protein from peas. The company that produces Just Mayo, Hampton Creek, has quickly gone from a tiny San Francisco start-up to a staple at grocers from Whole Foods to Walmart, thanks in part to financial backing from heavyweights like billionaire Bill Gates. It's also become a darling of sustainability advocates, who claim Just Mayo is far more sustainable than mayonnaise. That's largely because sustainability is at the core of Hampton Creek's mission. "Our approach is to use plants that are much more sustainable—less greenhouse gas emissions, less water, no animal involved and a whole lot more affordable—to create a better food system," company founder Josh Tetrick said in 2013, right after Just Mayo launched.[89] Two years later, Hampton Creek's mission is still clear. "We care deeply about many of the challenges facing society today, sustainability being one of the biggest ones," Tetrick told me.[90] "And that is why we are so passionate about making products that are markedly more sustainable than the status quo."

What makes Just Mayo different? For one, Tetrick told me the company searched until they "found a varietal of the Canadian Yellow Pea that can be used in mayo just like a chicken egg and actually saves a whole bathtub worth of water with every jar." Saving egg-laying hens from living out their days in cages is also something that matters to Tetrick. But Hampton Creek's decision to use the term "mayo" in its product name—so suggestive of mayonnaise, as it is—caused Unilever, the Hellmann's manufacturer, to sue Hampton Creek in 2014. Unilever's suit claimed that Hampton Creek's use of the word "mayo" in the Just Mayo product name violated the FDA's standard of identity for mayonnaise.[91] Tetrick and others pinned blame for the lawsuit squarely on FDA regulations. "We're living in 2015 with laws written for food . . . over 60 years ago—and that's not okay," Tetrick told me. "We need to update our regulations to fit a modern world with modern problems . . . and some of the solutions that are being used to fix them. Especially in food."

The executive director of the Plant Based Foods Association, Michele Simon, an attorney who's followed Just Mayo's case closely, said it was the result of innovation simply outpacing dated regulations. "I admire Hampton Creek's mission to make healthier, more sustainable, and cruelty-free foods that are affordable and appeal to the mainstream consumer, all of which should be encouraged and not threatened with legal action," Simon told me.[92]

Still, Unilever is hardly a boogeyman to supporters of sustainability. In fact, sustainability advocates have long recognized Unilever as a leader—particularly for a corporation of its size. In 2014, the twentieth-annual survey of corporate sustainability efforts by consultancy GlobeScan ranked Unilever tops in the world for sustainability. It's a familiar spot for the company. "For the fourth year in a row, and by the largest margin yet, Unilever is regarded as the number-one corporate sustainability leader, with 33 percent of expert respondents identifying the company (up 8 points from 2013) as a 'leader in integrating sustainability into its business strategy,'" the report concluded.[93] One of those who sings Unilever's praises, in fact, is Hampton Creek CEO Josh Tetrick. "If you look at what Paul Polman, their C.E.O., says about sustainability requiring radical transformation and entirely new business models," Tetrick told the *New York Times* in the wake of the lawsuit, "I do think Unilever is on the front lines of getting it."[94]

Unilever no doubt "gets" bad press, too. Shortly after Simon pointed out that several Hellmann's mayonnaise products themselves didn't appear to fit the FDA's standard of identity for mayonnaise—a point I and others later expanded on—Unilever backed down. In dropping its lawsuit, Unilever had nice things to say about Hampton Creek in the process. "We share a vision with Hampton Creek of a more sustainable world," Unilever announced. But Unilever's statement also left the door open for the FDA to take its own punitive action, suggesting that Hampton Creek may need to work with the "appropriate regulatory authorities" on its label.[95] Sure enough, the FDA soon sent a letter to Hampton Creek, warning the company that its label was misleading.[96] Hampton Creek vowed to fight to clear—and keep—its Just Mayo name. Ultimately, in December 2015, the FDA forced the company to make changes to its label—including adding reference to the Miracle Whip-like salad dressing—but let it keep its product name intact.[97]

Governments and consumers can and should fight fraudulent labels. As I explain later in this chapter, it's courts and consumers—rather than lawmakers and regulators—that are our most effective defense against fraud. Standards of identity aren't the answer. We won't be able to innovate our way to the "more sustainable world" Unilever, Hampton Creek, and many others want until food standards of identity are relegated to the scrap heap. For more proof of that fact, we need to travel across the country, from Hampton Creek's base in San Francisco to the even hipper confines of the Williamsburg neighborhood in Brooklyn, New York, home to another innovative food that stood accused of running afoul of yet another standard of identity.

Early in 2012, Julie Van Ullen and her husband Greg launched OMilk, a high-end dairy alternative that's made from nuts, including organic almonds and cashews. They first sold their nut milks at the Brooklyn Flea Market. Although drinks like almond milk have been on the U.S. market for years, two key factors distinguish OMilk from many of its competitors. First, unlike many other nut milks, OMilk doesn't contain any stabilizers, powders, or preservatives. Its almond milk, for example, contains just four ingredients: filtered water, raw organic almonds, raw organic agave nectar, and sea salt. By comparison, stabilizers and preservatives in many competitors' products means a typical almond milk can contain at least ten ingredients. Second, OMilk is cold-pasteurized using a high-pressure method that—though more costly than heat pasteurization—keeps intact more of the milk's natural nut flavor. For more than two-and-a-half years, the Van Ullens marketed OMilk to a constantly growing number of customers. Ultimately, as demand outstripped supply—and Whole Foods outlets in New York City came calling—they were forced to give up their quaint practice of delivering OMilk to customers' homes.

OMilk had secured all the proper permits and licenses from New York State's agriculture department and had passed department inspections on several occasions over a period of two years. That all changed in August 2014, when an agricultural inspector informed the Van Ullens that OMilk's nut milks were no longer nut milks but were instead classified by New York State regulators as something called "melloream." What the heck is melloream? New York State's standard of identity for melloream defines it as any food "which contains vegetable fats or oils and proteins derived from animal or vegetable sources, and whose appearance, odor and taste is similar to cream, half and half, milk or a mixture of milk and cream, to the point of rendering these products difficult to differentiate from each other."[98] According to a 1970 *New York Times* article, melloream was introduced in the 1960s as a cheaper alternative to cream, particularly to add to hot coffee.[99] The melloream law, on the books since the 1960s, was clearly intended to protect the state's powerful dairy producers from lower cost imitators. A 1968 news article reports the Eastern Milk Producers Association, a dairy lobby, had urged state regulators "to protect the dairy industry" by cracking down on melloream sellers.[100]

What did their new status as melloream sellers mean for OMilk? It meant a lot of things—none of them good. That's because New York State law also contains draconian rules for melloream producers. First, the law states the word "milk" cannot be used on a melloream label, so the clear, honest descriptive term OMilk had used to describe its almond milk—"almond milk"—was no longer legally viable. The term "cashew milk" was out for its cashew milk, too. The law would also require that large lettering on OMilk containers identify the milks by one of a handful of others names, including "melloream" or "a vegetable oil product." Worse still, New York State law makes clear that a melloream producer is required to be "licensed as a milk dealer" and regulated not by the state's agriculture department, but by its milk and dairy department, a department whose scrutiny comes with a host of heightened rules—including mandatory *heat* pasteurization.[101] I spoke with Greg Van Ullen about the impact of a possible melloream designation for his nut milk. "[B]eing considered a melloream would have meant we needed to follow dairy regulations which would have made our kitchen unusable, forced us to pasteurize our product (eliminating much of our market advantage), and added tons of additional regulations for us to needlessly follow," he told me.[102] "It either would have forced us out of state or to close."

OMilk had distinguished itself from dairy milk and from other nut milk competitors—literally and figuratively—and built up a loyal customer base thanks to the fact its nut milks contain just a handful of natural and organic ingredients and because its costly cold pasteurization gave OMilk's product line a fresher and nuttier taste. Now New York State was telling the company that cold pasteurization was no longer legal, and that accurate descriptive terms like "almond milk" and "cashew milk" would have to be swapped out for terms like "a vegetable oil product" or "melloream"—terms that gave the company little chance of appealing to consumers who wanted to purchase an all-natural nut milk like OMilk's. (The melloream aisle at Whole Foods isn't just small, it's nonexistent.)

After the state agriculture department informed the Van Ullens that OMilk's departmental license was no longer valid, and that they would have to reapply for a license as a melloream producer, the company sought out the Food Law Firm, a small law firm located in New York State that specializes in helping small food entrepreneurs around the country navigate the complicated food-regulatory process. Jason Foscolo founded the Food Law Firm in 2011. Clients seek out the firm's advice for a host of reasons, including commercial agreements, licensing and inspection, compliance with food regulations, and, Foscolo told me, "often to respond to potentially adverse action from food industry regulators."[103] Many of the Food Law Firm's clients are start-up ventures. Foscolo loves helping small food entrepreneurs like OMilk grow their businesses. "The company's mission is really simple—just produce a great product that their customers can believe in," he told me of OMilk. "There are lots of things that make the company special, but my favorite has to be their origin story. Food enthusiasts idealize the humble origins of a food start-up, and OMilk embodies that. They started small, just one or two founders in a very modest facility. They focused intensively on just a few product lines and built a successful, growing business out of it."

Foscolo knows as much about how food laws affect small food entrepreneurs as does any practicing attorney. Like me, he's a graduate of the Agricultural and Food Law Program at the University of Arkansas Law School. Like me, he'd never heard the term "melloream" even once. "That one left us scratching our heads when we first saw it," Foscolo said. Even today, after being forced to become somewhat of an expert on melloream, Foscolo is left with some lingering questions. "I still don't know how to actually pronounce the word," he admitted. "Is it 'mellow-reem,' or is it 'melor-ee-ahm?' No clue."

Despite that confusion—which I share—the Food Law Firm was able to point out several key facts about the case to the state, including, namely, that OMilk's nut milks do not fit the definition contained within the state's standard of identity for melloream. First—and their argument really could have ended here—they tackled the definition's requirement that melloream must consist of "vegetable fats or oils and proteins derived from animal or vegetable sources." They kindly pointed out that that nuts are not vegetables, and that none of OMilk's vegan ingredients are derived from animals. Second, they noted that the "odor and taste" of almond milk and cashew milk is very different from that of dairy milk, making the drinks simple "to differentiate from each other." They also noted that at least one U.S. court has already ruled that reasonable consumers don't mistake milk made from nuts or soy from dairy milk.

Given these arguments, the state was forced to back down. But New York's decision to target OMilk nevertheless raises the specter of future standard of identity–related actions against a host of other food producers. That's because although it's clear that nut milks don't fit the definition of melloream because nuts aren't vegetables, makers of soy milk—made from soybeans—might not be so lucky.[104] What's more, OMilk's attorneys at the Food Law Firm say that the state regulates non-dairy ice cream made from nuts—including almond milk ice cream—under its milk laws. In other words, the overwhelming victory for OMilk hasn't resulted in any new thinking about standards of identity among New York State regulators. It's a win for a couple of innovators—the Van Ullens—but not *for innovation*. Not yet, at least.

As I mentioned earlier, standards of identity aren't just bad for innovative food producers. It may surprise you to learn that the negative impact of standards of identity on innovative foods like Just Mayo and OMilk is similar to their effect on many traditional foods. Don't standards of identity simply reflect time-tested definitions of food? In a word: no. Recall that the National Milk Producers Federation noted that the standard of identity of a food isn't based on the "common vernacular or a definition in a dictionary." In other words, the standard of identity for a food needn't even resemble what every American thinks of when they think of that food. That can be true even if the vernacular has embraced the use of the term—as in the case of "almond milk," which also happens to comport with the dictionary definition of "milk"—or even, astonishingly, as you're about to learn, in cases where a food's definition has been unchanged for centuries.[105]

Although many standards of identity for various types of dairy foods exist at the federal level, it's also true that many states have their own standards for dairy products that are obtained and sold only in each respective state. New York State's melloream rules are one example. To learn just how standards of identity can wreak senseless havoc on a traditional, sustainable food producer, it's informative to look at the story of a small creamery's unwanted fight against Florida's backward standard of identity for skim milk. Ocheesee Creamery is a small, family-run creamery in Florida's Panhandle. The creamery's owners, Mary Lou Wesselhoeft and her husband Paul, started Ocheesee in 2007. A 2013 *Tallahassee Democrat* profile of Ocheesee noted that the creamery caters to "health-conscious milk drinkers—people who demand an all-natural product with nothing added—no preservatives, no nutrients that don't come straight from the cow." Ocheesee uses traditional pasteurization techniques, which heat the milk to lower temperatures for a longer period of time to preserve flavor while still ensuring safety, and sells the milk in returnable and reusable glass bottles.[106]

Today, Ocheesee has three employees. The creamery sells its milk from the farm, at various farmers markets, and at markets like New Leaf Market co-op, an organic grocer in Tallahassee that profiled Ocheesee in a 2012 newsletter. New Leaf lauded Ocheesee's "commitment to natural, humane and environmentally sound methods of farming." Those methods include "grass-feeding their dairy cows and supplementing the grass diet with high-quality feed, vitamins, minerals, sea salt licks, and fermented hay (made right there on the farm)."[107] The Wesselhoefts raise a herd of about 200 grass-fed Jersey cows—rather than the more common Holstein breed—because the smaller Jersey cows require less tending to and are better adapted to thrive in Florida's hot climate. The farm also collects and composts all of its manure, which it reuses as fertilizer. In short, Ocheesee is a model of sustainability.

The creamery's problems began in fall 2012, when a Florida state agriculture department inspector suddenly ordered Ocheesee to stop selling its skim milk. The inspector hadn't found any food-safety problems at the creamery. Instead, he determined that the issue with Ocheesee's additive-free skim milk was not what it contained but what it *didn't* contain—mandatory additives. Ocheesee's skim milk was just *too natural.*

It turns out that Florida's standard of identity for skim milk requires that creameries and dairies add vitamin A to their skim milk. (Notably, the FDA standard of identity also requires the addition of vitamin A, but because Ocheesee sells its milk only in Florida, the FDA rules don't apply.) The inspector wrote on his stop-sale order, which effectively rendered Ocheesee's skim milk as contraband, the sole reason for his determination: "FAILURE TO ADD VITAMIN A." Ocheesee, which earned its many devoted customers in large part because of its dedication to all-natural milk and opposition to introducing any additives in its milk, was caught off guard. The Wesselhoefts had been selling their pasteurized skim milk as "pasteurized skim milk" for several years without any complaints from state inspectors or customers. Surely, the couple thought, this was some sort of mistake, and some compromise could be reached. Ocheesee offered to label its skim milk as "Pasteurized Skim Milk, No Vitamin A Added." The state balked, telling the company it must add vitamin A to its milk.

Ocheesee *could* add vitamin A to its skim milk. There was no physical or economic barrier preventing them from doing so. But the creamery built its reputation and its customer base on selling only all-natural milk that adhered to time-honored traditions. Many Ocheesee customers have since confirmed they wouldn't buy the creamery's products if they contained additives. "They didn't add vitamin A back in the 1800s," Wesselhoeft told the Tallahassee newspaper. She's right. One reason for that, as author Kendra Smith-Howard described in her book *Pure & Modern Milk*, is that skim milk was traditionally used as "hog slop"—pig feed—or went to waste. It was only during the last century that people began to consume skim milk.[108] Many people in this country also once suffered from vitamin A deficiencies. Mandating the addition of vitamin A to skim milk was at least *theoretically* defensible in the early 1900s. But there are also reasonable questions about the efficacy and advisability of adding vitamin A to skim milk. In fact, doing so may be a very bad idea, for a variety of reasons.

Because vitamin A is fat-soluble, the benefits of ingesting vitamin A in fat-free milk are questionable at best. Without fat in milk to which to bind, the vitamin may just pass through a skim milk drinker's body without conveying any benefits. Vitamin A also degrades quickly when it is exposed to light—as it is in many milk containers, including many plastic containers and Ocheesee's reusable glass bottles. What's more, although vitamin A is an important nutrient, most evidence shows Americans already get enough vitamin A in their diets. If there's anything we know about consuming vitamin A, it's that there's a very real danger—particularly to children—from consuming *too much* of it. In fact, a Florida nutritionist cautioned state residents in 2013 against ingesting "too much vitamin A, because your body can store it and cause damage to the liver."[109]

Despite all this evidence, Ocheesee appeared to be out of options. But the state soon offered one. The creamery could continue to market its skim milk, but it would have to adopt a new standard of identity for the milk. No longer would Ocheesee skim milk be called "skim milk." Instead, the state told Ocheesee it could sell its skim milk without adding vitamin A only if it labeled the skim milk as "Non-Grade 'A' Milk Product, Natural Milk Vitamins Removed." There could be no mention of "skim milk" on the label.

As descriptive phrases go, the expression "Non-Grade 'A' Milk Product, Natural Milk Vitamins Removed" doesn't exactly roll off the tongue. It also suffers from a variety of fatal defects. For one, it paints entirely natural skim milk as a milk *product* that no reasonable consumer would believe consisted solely of one ingredient: skim milk. The state's standard is misleading, too, in that it doesn't even allude to the very reason people buy skim milk in the first place—the fact that it contains no fat. It's also deceptive because it infers that *all* of the milk's natural vitamins have been removed, when in fact many natural milk vitamins remain in the skim milk. (This is the case because vitamin A binds naturally to fat, and removing cream from milk also necessarily removes a fat-soluble vitamin with the fat.) Perhaps most importantly, Florida's standard of identity for skim milk takes a food that's been defined and understood by the public to mean one thing and one thing only for centuries—skim milk has been defined as "milk with the cream removed" for well over 200 years—and redefines it in a way that makes the traditional and natural seem processed and unnatural.

Ocheesee proudly sold the very definition of skim milk, not some eight-word imitation "milk product." It was no surprise, then, that the prospect of using Florida's bizarre and misleading standard of identity to refer to their all-natural skim milk was unacceptable to the Wesselhoefts. In late 2014, after nearly two years of selling no skim milk—which cost Ocheesee thousands of dollars each week—the creamery sued the state of Florida in federal court, arguing that the state's decision to bar the creamery from honestly labeling its skim milk as "skim milk" violated the First Amendment. "Businesses have the right to tell the truth, and the government does not have the power to change the dictionary," Ocheesee's lead attorney, Justin Pearson, who heads the Florida offices of the Arlington, Virginia-based Institute for Justice, told me.[110]

I've been honored to serve as an expert witness in support of Ocheesee and its customers. In that capacity, I spent several hours testifying in a deposition administered by the state of Florida's lawyers. I also drafted a report describing how Florida's mandated standard of identity does not serve the interests of consumers in the state and tends to mislead consumers. In my report, I concluded that Ocheesee's skim milk, which contains only skim milk, is skim milk. I also concluded that labeling skim milk that contains only skim milk as "skim milk" does not mislead consumers.

In the course of working on behalf of the creamery, I've seen firsthand just how tortured arguments in favor of standards of identity can be. For example, Florida and its own expert witness admitted that Ocheesee's skim milk contains only one ingredient—skim milk. Yet the state went out of its way for more than a year to deny that Ocheesee's single-ingredient skim milk is "all natural." State agents ultimately admitted that Ocheesee's milk is, in fact, all natural. Still, at trial, lawyers for Florida's agriculture department argued that Ocheesee's all-natural skim milk should be labeled as "imitation skim milk." Finally, the same state expert witness who opined on the necessity of adding vitamin A to skim milk, ironically, is also the person quoted in the aforementioned 2013 newspaper article cautioning Floridians against ingesting *too much* vitamin A because doing so can cause liver damage.

In March 2016, a federal judge ruled that because Ocheesee doesn't add vitamin A to its skim milk, Florida may prohibit the creamery from labeling its skim milk as "skim milk."[111] The Wesselhoefts are fighting on. "Mary Lou refuses to mislead her customers, so she will continue to dump this perfectly safe, legal, pure skim milk until the courts vindicate her right to tell the truth," Institute for Justice attorney Justin Pearson told me in the wake of the U.S. District Court decision.[112] "We look forward to continuing this fight at the Court of Appeals."

When the federal government and state governments can use Orwellian logic to redefine the meaning of traditional foods such as skim milk—when they can mandate that "up" means "down"—and use standards of identity to disparage a 100-percent natural food such as skim milk as "Non-Grade 'A' Milk Product, Natural Milk Vitamins Removed," then standards of identity have failed to prevent food labels from misleading us. Instead, they serve to *promote* deception. Who benefits from this deception? Certainly not sustainable producers, their customers, or the buying public. Instead, it's large producers who benefit from these rules. It's perhaps no surprise, then, that the National Milk Producers Federation has urged the FDA to use its standards of identity to bar foods such as almond milk, soy milk, and other plant-based drinks from using the term "milk" to describe their non-dairy milk.[113] Consumers benefit from literal meanings—when food makers call almond milk "almond milk" and skim milk "skim milk." Instead, standards of identity often make the foods consumers buy subject to politicized meanings determined by politicians, food industry lobbyists, and regulators.

The standards of identity are the problem. It's not that *some* standards of identity are outdated. The *very idea* of standards of identity is, itself, outdated. Food labels should be open to any and all statements about a food that aren't demonstrably false. Such rules would certainly protect Just Mayo and producers of almond milks made from almonds and skim milks made from, well, skim milk. What they wouldn't protect would be the producer who wanted to market an almond milk that wasn't made from almonds, or use of just the term "milk" to describe, say, colored water. Federal and state agencies would be right to step in and prevent the use of the term "almond milk" and "milk" in those examples, just as consumers who bought the product thinking it contained almonds or who bought the colored water thinking it was milk would be justified in suing the company that sold the product. The Supreme Court also recently ruled—in a case that pitted pomegranate juice maker POM against fellow beverage maker Coca-Cola—that companies such as POM can sue competitors such as Coke when, as was the case, POM argued that the latter's Minute Maid pomegranate blueberry juice, which contained barely even trace amounts of pomegranate or blueberry, was deceptive.[114]

Attorney Michele Simon, who supported Just Mayo in its fight against Hellman's, agrees with me in part, but thinks we still need standards of identity to prevent deceptive food marketing—or marketing that falls just below the threshold of fraud. As an example, Simon cited the so-called "jelly bean rule,"[115] by which the FDA effectively bars the addition of vitamins to candies and other similar treats because, Simon said, doing so "would deceive the consumer into thinking the product is healthy when it isn't." I don't agree with Simon that a vitamin-enriched Snickers bar, for example, would fool anyone into confusing it for an apple. What's more, foods very similar to the Snickers bar are exempt from the jelly bean rule, meaning they're perfectly free today to add vitamins and other nutrients and to tout their healthfulness. A 68-gram chocolate-chip Clif bar, for example, touts the fact it contains "23 vitamins and minerals," is a good source of protein and fiber, and is "nutrition for sustained energy."[116] The Clif bar's nutritional profile indicates it contains 5 grams of fat, 150 milligrams of sodium, 44 grams of carbohydrates, 22 grams of sugar, and 10 grams of protein. Now take a 53-gram Snickers candy bar. It contains 12 grams of fat, 120 milligrams of sodium, 33 grams of carbohydrates, 27 grams of sugar, and 4 grams of protein.[117] These profiles are very similar. Yet the Snickers bar is just the sort of food that's prohibited from touting any added vitamins under the jelly bean rule. Setting aside the question of whether consumers are better off eating a Clif bar than eating a Snickers bar, is a person eating the Snickers bar somehow better off because it doesn't contain the added vitamins found in the Clif bar?

From Just Mayo to OMilk to Ocheesee Creamery and beyond, food standards of identity often restrict sustainable food producers of all sorts from sharing important, honest information about their foods with the buying public. These standards of identity favor large, incumbent food producers over smaller ones. But some food laws don't just govern food makers. They apply to everyone, including you. As you're about to see, these laws prohibit members of the public from sharing information about food with each other and with the general public—often under threat of arrest. As you'll learn, the sole purpose of these laws is to protect large animal agricultural operations from seeing their reputations damaged and their customers flee to smaller, often-more-sustainable agricultural producers.

The Battle Over Ag-Gag

In 2012, an animal-rights group called Compassion Over Killing (COK), a nonprofit that "exposes cruelty to farmed animals and promotes vegetarian eating," posted a video online that it had obtained from an allied activist working undercover at Central Valley Meat, a California slaughterhouse. I watched and wrote about the video shortly after it was posted. It's gruesome and disgusting. In the video, which runs about four minutes, slaughterhouse workers appear to use bolt guns to daze cattle before the cows were sent—alive, terrified, bleeding, and in pain—to be tethered in the air by one leg on the way to being slaughtered. One cow appears to be suffocated.[118] The practices depicted in the videos aren't just animal slaughter. They're animal cruelty.

Central Valley Meat is a USDA-inspected slaughterhouse that's supplied meat across the country, including to the USDA's own National School Lunch Program, and to big chains such as In-N-Out Burger, Costco, and McDonald's. USDA purchases from Central Valley Meat were enormous—on the order of tens of millions of pounds of meat. After the video surfaced, the USDA rightly punished Central Valley, though it closed the slaughterhouse for only a few days. Perhaps more importantly, the tape's existence and the resulting public outcry pressured In-N-Out Burger, Costco, and McDonald's to stop buying beef from Central Valley Meat.[119] I don't know who shot the COK video. But whoever did so is a courageous whistleblower, responsible for providing vital information to businesses, regulators, consumers, and the public.

In response to incidents like the one captured by COK, change is coming to farms and slaughterhouses in a growing number of states. But the change might not be the change you'd want or expect. Rather than pushing to incentivize or train employees better, for example, or inviting more openness and public scrutiny to help reassure the public that the nation's big farms and slaughterhouses can do what they're supposed to do—raise and slaughter animals for food without abusing them—the real "change" has often been much the opposite.

In a growing number of states, in fact, the act of capturing video such as that obtained by COK has been made illegal. These states—Montana, Idaho, Colorado, North Carolina, North Dakota, Iowa, Missouri, and Kansas—have decided that the problem with videos documenting livestock abuse is not the abuse but the *documenting of that abuse.* The language of the laws differs from state to state. Iowa's law prohibits "agricultural production facility fraud," targeting those who gain access to livestock facilities under false pretenses.[120] Kansas outlaws "enter[ing] an animal facility to take pictures" without consent from the facility's owner.[121] Some states force whistleblowers to turn over tapes to authorities immediately. In most cases, violators can face jail time and thousands of dollars in fines. But although the language used in these so-called "ag-gag" laws might differ, their intent is always the same: to hide abuse and the bad press that results when such abuse comes to light, and to stifle political speech that is protected by the Constitution's First Amendment.

Randy Parker of the Utah Farm Bureau, which supported its state's ag-gag law, said videotaping by groups like COK "is politically motivated for their anti-meat agenda."[122] Yes, it is. Parker is absolutely right. Chances are pretty good that a livestock whistleblower is a vegan, an animal-rights activist, or both. Groups such as People for the Ethical Treatment of Animals (PETA) and COK work with undercover investigators, invariably, to expose animal abuse, to raise money and awareness, and to turn people off the idea of eating meat and onto the idea of eating a plant-based diet. But Parker misses the point that the ag-gag laws he supports are politically motivated for his group's *pro-meat* agenda. The First Amendment protects pro-meat, anti-meat, and meat-ambivalent statements equally. With ag-gag laws, the only difference is that those who videotape livestock abuse are *exercising* their First Amendment rights, while ag-gag supporters are attempting to use the law to *stifle* others' free speech.

For supporters of a more sustainable food system, including even the most die-hard meat eater, it should take little thought to figure out whether to support ag-gag laws. Although they theoretically "protect" all farmers equally, many—if not most—sustainable farms typically invite consumers onto their properties. They greet you at the farmers market. They urge consumers to make on-farm purchases. They encourage questions and even welcome photography. They conduct farm tours. Their livestock often have names. These are just some of the reasons why some farm groups have opposed ag-gag laws. For example, the National Young Farmers Coalition wrote in 2013, on the topic of ag-gag laws, that "we know who they're looking out for, and it isn't the small farmer, the beginning farmer, or the sustainable farmer."[123]

Besides moral arguments, there's also a solid legal argument against ag-gag laws, on which courts are being asked to rule. In 2014, a coalition of animal-rights groups, the American Civil Liberties Union (ACLU), and others sued the state of Idaho over its ag-gag law. A federal judge rightly struck down the law in 2015.[124] Idaho soon appealed the ruling. And just as this book was going to press, I organized a group of nearly twenty food law and policy faculty around the country to work with Minnesota appellate attorney Mahesha Subbaraman on an *amicus curiae* brief in support of the free-speech rights of the animal-rights groups, ACLU, and others in the case.

Interestingly, the Idaho lawsuit followed the nation's first ag-gag arrests, in Utah. That state quickly dropped those charges. But it also followed up with trespassing charges. Trespassing laws are already on the books in all fifty states, and they represent another great argument against ag-gag laws. Farmers deserve to be protected—just like any other property owner—from the presence of unwanted persons on their property. Trespassing laws already do just that.

Undaunted by the growth of ag-gag laws, COK—like other groups—continues to launch undercover investigations. "This job requires 100% travel for extended periods of time and the ability to work long hours while performing heavy manual labor in filthy conditions," read one

COK job announcement posted at the Idealist website. It sounds like backbreaking—and heartbreaking, and important—work.

Ag-gag laws are perhaps the best counterweight to those who might argue with the premise of this book. If we simply need *more* food rules, then ag-gag laws are one logical outgrowth of that belief. That doesn't mean we need *no* laws, though. In chapter 5, I give credit where credit is due, highlighting some good food laws and examining what makes them effective. But first, we're going to explore more of the bad ones. In the next chapter, you'll learn about a host of federal, state, and local rules that promote incalculable tons of food waste.

CHAPTER 3

Wasting Your Money Wasting Food

IN JULY 2015, a series of new composting and recycling services debuted in Oakland, California. City officials touted the new program, part of their "Oakland Recycles" initiative, as "a huge step" forward in Oakland's goal to produce zero waste.[1] Although the new services were intended to make Oakland more sustainable, the details of the program show its early impact has been just the opposite. The leading criticism of the rules is that they effectively force restaurants to throw away tons of food that might otherwise be recycled as compost. Somehow, a new service intended to *reduce* waste has instead *promoted* the wasting of food.

That problem of food waste—which a recent paper by the Organisation for Economic Co-operation and Development (OECD) defines as "food that completes the food supply chain up to a final product, of good quality and fit for consumption, but still does not get consumed because it is discarded, whether or not after it is left to spoil"—is an enormous one not just in Oakland but around the country and the world.[2] I'll focus on other examples shortly, but let's stay in Oakland for a moment to see why and how the city's new municipal waste rules went astray.

One of the city's key missteps was creating perverse financial incentives. The *East Bay Express* reported that "restaurants that generate a lot of food waste can save a substantial amount of money by throwing the waste away rather than by composting it."[3] For some restaurateurs, the cost of composting has doubled under the new rules, making it more expensive to send food to compost than to the landfill. Gail Lillian, owner of an Oakland falafel shop, tells *Inside Bay Area* that she'll spend $3,000 more each year in composting fees under the city's new contract.[4] And an Oakland bar owner estimates she'd have to spend $8,000 more than she did in previous years for exactly the same composting services. The bar owner, Maria Alderete, said she'll throw away most of what she otherwise would have composted because of the sky-high costs. For years, Alderete and other restaurateurs in the city had used Recology, a San Francisco company, for their composting needs.[5] But Oakland's new contract and rules mean Alderete and others must use the city's costly, lone, new, approved compost and waste contractor.

Lillian, Alderete, and other outraged restaurateurs have protested the new fees, which are clearly out of whack. For example, one restaurateur with a handful of locations in the Bay Area said he pays nearly seven times as much for composting for his Oakland restaurant as he does for his San Francisco restaurant. "The sticker shock of the new compost fees could all but kill efforts to establish a citywide no-waste plan," wrote the *San Francisco Chronicle*'s Chris Johnson, "not to mention wreaking havoc with the restaurant community that has helped re-establish downtown Oakland as a place to go for Bay Area residents."[6] *East Bay Express* editor Robert Gammon called Oakland's new composting rules a "mind-numbingly dumb" waste solution.[7] In 2014, the *Chronicle*'s Johnson actually supported the contract with the waste disposal company, Waste Management, which has been managing much of Oakland's waste for more than 100 years.[8]

How did an Oakland program intended to reduce or eliminate waste end up creating mountains of food waste instead? The city signed a garbage contract that made it easier and cheaper for people who wanted to cut down on food waste to throw that food away instead. This was probably a case of shortsightedness rather than any willful attempt to create more food waste. It was merely an unintended consequence of the new Oakland services.

If rules promoting food waste were merely confined to Oakland, the problem might be a small one that lends itself to a quick fix. But the truth is that the problem of food waste is immense. It stretches across the country and, as you'll see, is a problem in many other countries. As you'll also see, rules that promote food waste aren't just confined to land. Some of the worst laws I'll discuss in this chapter promote food waste—sometimes on a massive scale—in oceans surrounding the United States and elsewhere. You'll learn that food waste piles up from good intentions just as easily as it does from lesser motivations. You'll also see time and time again in this chapter that rules that promote food waste usually arise from a combination of poor foresight and backward incentives—as in Oakland—and also from economic protectionism or outright ignorance. Even if the causes differ, the result is the same.

New research pointing out the incomprehensible extent of food waste is being published, it seems, almost monthly. Any way you look at the numbers, the sheer breadth of food waste is overwhelming. Generally, research indicates that nearly 40 percent of all food goes to waste.[9] The Food Waste Reduction Alliance, a coalition of large national grocers and restaurateurs that was formed in 2011, says a staggering 40 million tons of food waste end up in America's landfills every year.[10] A 2014 USDA report found that Americans wasted 133 billion pounds of food in 2010.[11] The leading foods wasted were dairy products and vegetables, at 25 billion pounds each. An earlier report by two USDA staffers found that the dollar value of retail and consumer food waste—food wasted by businesses and individuals in the United States—totaled more than

$165 billion each year.[12] Forty-one percent of that loss comes from meat, poultry, and fish. Ultimately, 10 percent of the money Americans spend on food goes to waste.

That's what's wasted. But the problem of food waste is not just about what's lost. It's also about the persistent negative impact of what's lost on the environment. Ninety-seven percent of food waste ends up in landfills. There, it breaks down into various components, the most harmful of which is methane, a powerful greenhouse gas. One group estimates that every ton of food waste generates about 3.8 tons of greenhouse gases.[13] Food waste is so pervasive, and methane so damaging—it's more than twenty times as potent a greenhouse gas as carbon dioxide—that a 2013 United Nations report identified food waste as the world's third-leading contributor of atmospheric greenhouse gases, pumping 3.3 gigatons (or 3.3 *billion tons*) into the atmosphere each year.[14] Food waste trails only two whole countries—China and the United States—in that category.

Food waste causes other, less obvious problems. That's because food waste doesn't just concern what we don't eat. Its impact also includes the resources we expend to produce food we don't eat. Consider that food that goes to waste still used all of the resources needed to produce the food—including any combination of water and fertilizer (to grow crops), pesticides (to keep them free of pests), farmland (often converted from wild lands and tilled, both of which release stored carbon), and oil (to power plows and harvesters). Those resources are all used up whether a food is eaten or is left to rot in a field or landfill. The United Nations report concluded that producing food that is then wasted each year uses enough water to empty Europe's Lake Geneva—which is forty-five miles long, fourteen miles wide, and more than 1,000 feet deep in places—three times.[15] The report also notes that food that is produced but uneaten "vainly occupies" nearly 30 percent of the world's agricultural land, or 3.5 billion acres of land. That's about 50 percent more land than you'll find in all of the United States.[16] And there are other costs, even if they don't lend themselves to such ready comparisons. "While it is difficult to estimate impacts on biodiversity at a global level, food wastage unduly compounds the negative externalities that monocropping and agriculture expansion into wild areas create on biodiversity loss, including mammals, birds, fish and amphibians," the UN report states.[17]

Given these figures, you'd think governments at all levels would be working to minimize the causes and effects of such waste. Instead, as in Oakland, many rules promote, rather than combat, food waste. You've already seen some of these rules. In chapter 1, you learned about food-safety rules that promote food waste, including the FDA's campaign against the use of spent grains as animal feed, which threatened to create millions of tons of food waste. The California law that required chefs and bartenders to don disposable gloves while preparing foods also promoted waste (in the form of gloves rather than food). In chapter 2, you learned about a Florida law that left Ocheesee Creamery with little choice but to throw out its all-natural skim milk. In this chapter, you'll learn about unconscionable rules that cause food waste on even greater scales.

School Lunch is a Big Waste

The USDA's National School Lunch Program is one of the best examples anywhere of a program that promotes food waste on a massive scale. But before we learn more about the program and how it promotes food waste, it's important to step back and address a few of the heated arguments one typically hears about the school lunch program—a program that has equally passionate supporters and detractors. That passion means the rhetoric around school lunches is often *so* heated that it can be difficult to separate facts from fiction. It means people tend to yell past one another instead of discussing real problems and looking for real solutions. I'm not particularly interested in personal attacks or bombastic rhetoric on this or any other issue. So instead, let's start with some key facts about school lunches that will allow for a discussion that's grounded in facts and norms.

First, many schoolkids in America depend on free- or reduced-price school lunches to eat lunch at school. Second, the USDA National School Lunch Program spends most of its school lunch budget not on food but, instead, on reimbursing schools for overhead costs. That means only about $1 of every $3 the USDA reimburses a school for serving a student a free lunch goes to buy food.[18] The rest goes to wages, equipment, food storage, and other costs. Third, the food served as part of USDA-funded school lunches has been and still is closely tied to excessive food production spurred by USDA subsidies. The USDA's 2010 budget, for example, requested more than $1.4 billion to buy "surplus commodities from the marketplace for distribution to Federal nutrition assistance programs such as the National School Lunch Program."[19] Fourth, this practice is nothing new. In 2003, for example, a *Mother Jones* writer criticized the program as one "designed to subsidize agribusiness."[20] Fifth, peer-reviewed research has shown that the USDA National School Lunch Program promotes food waste. More on that—lots more—shortly. Sixth, food waste is a long-standing problem within the USDA National School Lunch Program. It was a problem before First Lady Michelle Obama ever began lobbying for passage of the Healthy, Hunger-Free Kids Act (HHFKA) of 2010 in an attempt to improve the quality of food that kids eat as part of the program. Seventh, the First Lady's school lunch reforms may have improved the quality of food choices slightly, but they also increased food waste. I say "slightly" because school lunch menus have changed little, even after the HHFKA reforms. Eighth, the plan favored by many Republicans in Congress—to gut the First Lady's reforms and return the USDA National School Lunch Program to where it was five or six years ago—may worsen the quality of food choices slightly, but would probably decrease food waste. Lastly, recent fights over the USDA National School Lunch Program have made for some strange bedfellows. House Republicans, school lunchroom employees, liberal-leaning newspapers, and opponents of food waste have found themselves opposing congressional Democrats, the First Lady, and nutrition advocates on the issue of school lunches.

Those are the facts, bereft of the politicization that often accompanies school lunch–related attacks on the First Lady, House Republicans, and others. So just what is the USDA National School Lunch Program, and how does it contribute to the nation's food-waste problems? The purpose of the program, as Congress stated in establishing it in 1946, is "to safeguard the health and well-being of the Nation's children and to encourage the domestic consumption of nutritious agricultural commodities and other food." The origins of the program lay in federal government efforts in the 1930s "to encourage the domestic consumption of certain agricultural commodities (usually those in surplus supply)."[21] That's why chef Ann Cooper, a noted school-lunch reformer, calls the school lunch program "an agricultural commodity program."[22]

The 2010 reforms, championed by the First Lady in the form of the Healthy, Hunger-Free Kids Act, included several key changes to the USDA program. The new rules, which debuted in 2012, were intended to address "critical nutrition and hunger safety [issues] for millions of children."[23] The changes increased the cost of school lunches, though only by a few cents per meal. Among those key changes—including caps on salt, fat, and calories per meal—the rules increased the amount of fruits and vegetables given to schoolkids by mandating that a substantive piece of produce be part of every meal. Specifically, under the previous rules, lunches had to contain between one-half and three-quarters of a cup of fruits and vegetables combined. Under the new rules, lunches must offer students between three-quarters and one cup of vegetables *and* one-half to one cup of fruit. That's an increase of between three-quarters and one-and-one-quarter cups of produce in each meal. What's more, for a school to be reimbursed for providing a lunch under the new rules, every student who receives a school lunch *must* take at least one-half cup of fruits or vegetables (up from the previous requirement of one-eighth of a cup). So long as the student takes the minimum fruit or vegetable portion, the federal government will reimburse the school for providing the student with a meal. If the student does not take at least the half-cup of fruits or vegetables, the rules require the federal government not to reimburse the school for providing the meal.[24] Whether the student eats the fruit or vegetable or throws it away doesn't factor into the equation.

In addition to the First Lady's backing, these rules have many supporters, particularly among nutrition-policy activists. Margo Wootan, of the Center for Science in the Public Interest, for example, dubbed the new rules the "best ever."[25] Prof. Marion Nestle praised the rules as "a major step forward."[26]

The goals of the new rules are formidable and, oftentimes, appear contradictory.[27] Meals must both help fight obesity and ensure all students get sufficient calories. They must contain foods kids want to eat, but also must be healthy. Meals must be so generalized that they cater to the food preferences of all of America's millions of public-school students while also ensuring that they appeal to students who practice all sorts of diets—from vegans to pescatarians to Paleo dieters, students with nut allergies, student with seafood allergies, gluten-free eaters, and students who don't like green vegetables, beans, peanut butter, veggie burgers, meat, cheese, or any one of thousands of foods. In short, it's near impossible to please everyone.

That difficulty may be why, in many cases, foods served at schools *after* the HHFKA reforms look very much like the foods they replaced. In February 2014, I looked at the lunches offered in Montgomery County, an affluent Maryland suburb just outside Washington, D.C.

The lunches offered by the school system that month included a whole grain chicken patty sandwich with tater tots, whole grain cheese or pepperoni pizza, hot dog with tater tots, French toast sticks with sausage, mac 'n cheese with whole grain chicken bites, and whole grain chicken nuggets with blueberry bread.[28] Remember, these are the *new and healthier* lunches federal government regulators spent years dreaming up. These are some of the foods HHFKA defenders are fighting *for*.

Despite the fact today's chicken-nugget lunches look a lot like yesterday's chicken-nugget lunches, many students don't love the taste of the reformulated food. Since the reforms have taken hold, there's been a notable downward shift in the rates of students eating school lunches. Students are voting with their mouths. According to federal government data, the USDA School Lunch Program served 258 million fewer lunches in 2014 than it did at its high point, in 2010.[29] The number of students paying full price for school lunches today—now 8.8 million—is at its lowest point in recorded history. That's a drop of more than 50 percent in full-price lunch sales since 1970. Considering the growth of America's population in general during this time period—more than 100 million people—and of its school-age population specifically, this drop-off in school lunch participation is even more dramatic.[30] Kids receiving free- or reduced-priced lunches now make up nearly three of every four students served a meal.[31] That's an increase of 17 percent since just 2008. In short, schoolkids are fleeing the program. Kids whose families can afford for them to eat something other than USDA school lunches are doing just that. Increasingly, only kids who must eat school lunches do so.

The new rules have proven so controversial that they prompted student-led boycotts across the country.[32] Seventy percent of students at one Wisconsin high school boycotted their school's lunches. In Connecticut, a student-led petition forced the school district to give up on the new rules after "only a few days."[33] It's not just students and families that are outraged with the school lunch program. Whole school districts are fleeing the program, too. Data from 2014 showed that more than 1,400 school districts had opted out of the USDA School Lunch Program since 2010.[34]

Opposition to the new school lunch rules from many families, students, and school administrators was one thing. But it was the increase in food waste caused by the new rules—confirmed by independent reports and research around the country—that really made the media and the public take notice that the HHFKA was a deeply flawed set of reforms. The *Los Angeles Times*, for example, reported in 2014 that more than $18 million worth of food goes to waste in the city's public schools each year.[35] A few days later, the editors of the *Los Angeles Times* blasted the HHFKA's "rigid, overreaching regulations that defy common sense" and claimed they've "practically guarantee[d] that an enormous amount of fruits and vegetables will go to waste."[36] Similar stories appeared in cities and states around the country. For example, an investigation by consumer reporters at WEWS, Cleveland's ABC affiliate, found that "millions of dollars' worth of fresh fruits and vegetables are being thrown in the trash in school lunchrooms in Ohio and across the country."[37]

These news reports were backed up by research. A 2014 study by the School Nutrition Association (SNA), which represents school lunchroom administrators and employees and which has opposed the First Lady's school lunch reforms, found that food waste increased in more than four out of five schools nationwide after HHFKA implementation.[38] Other research touted by the SNA revealed that more than 45 percent of all food served to a cohort of five classes studied in one Maryland school over a one-week study period ended up as food waste.[39] The study found more than 96 percent of all salad and 94 percent of all unflavored milk served in the school ended up in the garbage.

Other studies somehow painted an even bleaker picture. "Our results suggest that across all these children the cost of providing the additional fruit and vegetable items will cost an additional $5.5 million each day, with roughly $4.9 million worth of these fruits and vegetables being discarded by students into the trash," concluded a study by Cornell University and Brigham Young University researchers.[40] Put in starker terms, the study concluded that 89 percent of the fruits and vegetables mandated under the HHFKA school lunch reforms—nearly $5 million worth of fruits and vegetables each day—ends up as food waste. Similarly, a 2014 study by the federal government's own nonpartisan General Accountability Office revealed that 96 percent of states—48 out of 50—reported they "faced challenges" from food waste under the new rules.[41]

Again, it's important to remember that the HHFKA did not create the problem of food waste in schools. It simply made an already bad problem worse. A 2013 study of food waste in Boston, Massachusetts, public schools, conducted by Harvard School of Public Health nutritionist Juliana Cohen and a team of colleagues, found that middle-school students in the city discarded more than $430,000 worth of food each year.[42] That represents more than one-quarter of the system's entire middle-school food budget. Disturbingly, the researchers estimated, through extrapolating the Boston data, that the amount of food waste generated by the USDA National School Lunch Program each year may mean that more than $1.23 *billion* worth of food is thrown out in the nation's public schools each year. Astonishingly, Cohen's study was based on data collected *before* the HHFKA rules took effect. And reports around the country, as you've seen, indicate the problem has only worsened.

The nutrition community was so sensitive to charges that USDA school lunch reforms had caused a dramatic uptick in food waste that they were relieved when Harvard's Cohen released another study in 2014 indicating that food waste had not risen since the passage of

HHFKA.[43] In fact, the new study suggested HHFKA was behind some positive trends. "With the healthier school meal standards, students are consuming significantly more fruits, vegetables, and whole grains," Cohen told me.[44]

But the study contains serious limitations. Food waste may not have risen in the four schools Cohen studied not because students are eating more of the fruits and vegetables they're taking but because they're simply taking roughly the same amount of fruits and vegetables in the first place. How is that possible under the new rules? It turns out the HHFKA rules contain an escape clause that doesn't mean students are actually given more fruits and vegetables. The catch, known as "offer versus serve," means that students need not take any more fruits and vegetables than they did under the previous rules.[45] Instead, they need only be *offered* the amount described under the HHFKA rules and need only *take* the amount offered under the previous rules. Schools can choose whether students are required to be served all that they're offered or a lesser amount. In schools where students aren't necessarily taking more fruits and vegetables, it's no surprise that waste would remain constant. In schools that don't follow the "offer versus serve" protocol, we can expect waste to be higher.

Have the changes under HHFKA caused an increase in food waste? Cohen's not sure. "The limited research conducted has found mixed results as to whether or not schools have experienced increases in food waste," she told me, "and it is currently unknown if this varies by region and/or school sociodemographic factors."[46] Based on data I've seen from around the country—including data I've discussed from the federal government's General Accountability Office, the Los Angeles Unified School District, and from the Cornell University and Brigham Young University researchers—I believe the HHFKA rules did increase food waste, likely because the rules force many kids who wanted to eat fruits and vegetables *and* kids who didn't want to eat them alike to take those fruits and vegetables, regardless of personal preferences. Even eating comparatively more of a larger portion size can still mean more waste. For example, under the old rules, let's say a student might choose two grapes, eat half of them, and throw away the other half. That would result in one grape's worth of food waste. Under the new rules, a student might have to choose eight grapes. If they eat five, that means they've eaten a higher percentage of fruit. But they've also tripled the amount of food wasted.

Some nutrition experts have even gone so far as to *defend* this sort of food waste as a necessary evil. They claim that merely being exposed to fruits and vegetables can lead kids to eat them eventually. University of California, Los Angeles Prof. William J. McCarthy, for example, told the *Los Angeles Times* that food waste caused by the USDA National School Lunch Program is "a small investment" in building healthy eating habits.[47] "Today's food waste is the forerunner to tomorrow's healthy eating and therefore is a worthwhile investment," said McCarthy.[48] But the data linking exposure to consumption seem far from conclusive, and are often focused on infants who are being weaned. What's more, McCarthy admits the "exposure" must involve not just throwing away the food, but actual eating. McCarthy explains how that approach can work in the real world. "We did a study this summer that showed that African American children, who initially disliked jicama, just two weeks and 10 exposures later, loved the jicama," he told me by email.[49] "Food service directors who make single attempts to introduce a new fruit or vegetable will only succeed in generating more food waste if they are not willing to prolong their experiment for 8–14 meals."

I like jicama. But not everyone does—regardless of how many times they're exposed to it. Everyone's palate differs. And the fruits and vegetables that students are exposed to in schools are often the same ones they've tried and disliked for years under both old and new school lunch rules. Now, though, they're often getting bigger servings of many of those same fruits and vegetables. And that's creating more food waste.

Those waste figures could balloon even higher, as other school lunch supporters urge expanding the USDA program. Author and USDA school lunch advocate Janet Poppendieck argued in her book *Free for All* that *all* students in public schools should be required to eat the same USDA-funded free school lunches.[50] Poppendieck said this is necessary to reduce what she calls the "stigma" kids of low-income families face because they are the only ones who have no choice but to eat USDA school lunches. Like Prof. McCarthy's suggestion that food waste is a necessary and acceptable consequence of school lunches, I believe Poppendieck's solution is no solution at all. It, too, would only increase food waste. And what of students with food allergies, students who keep kosher, students who are vegan, students who like to prepare their own food, and families who want to make lunch for their kids? I think Poppendieck, however well meaning, ignores their very real wants and needs. Like Poppendieck's proposed reforms, even if Prof. McCarthy's beliefs about produce consumption are ironclad, is it worth growing and wasting tons of fruits and vegetables to prove that point? We know the environmental problems that food waste causes. Isn't there a better way to get kids to eat good food without creating more than $1 billion of food waste every year? Thinking outside the box, is there any way school lunches could even help *reduce* food waste?

Everyone wants "healthy, nutritious meals for all students," wrote chef Ann Cooper, the noted school-lunch advocate who supports the changes implemented by the Obama administration.[51] "Where we disagree is how to get there." I agree with Cooper, who I appeared alongside on a Minnesota public radio segment focused on school lunch reform in 2012. But how to get there is the key. Cooper thinks a combination of the HHFKA and increased food education in schools is the answer to improving school food and reducing food waste in schools. But is more education really the only way—or even the *best* way—to get healthy nutritious lunches *and* help fight the food waste monster? I know it's not the only answer, or even the best answer. For a real solution, we need to look far beyond Washington, D.C. We must look instead to kitchens in every community in America. No, not *school lunchroom* kitchens. Instead, I'm talking about your kitchen. Your neighbor's kitchen. Local restaurant kitchens. The commercial kitchen at your local grocer and caterer. What do all of these kitchens have in common? They all prepare food that you and people just like you in your community eat every day. Each one prepares food. And each one—home kitchens, restaurant kitchens, and grocery kitchens alike—generates food waste.

A 2004 study by a University of Arizona researcher estimated that restaurants, grocers, and convenience stores generate more than 147 million pounds of food waste.[52] More recently, a U.S. Environmental Protection Agency official said in 2012 that 15 percent of food in landfills comes from restaurants.[53] And while fast-food restaurants make up the bulk of that total, nearly 40 percent of the waste comes from full-service restaurants and grocers. The problem of food waste is national in scope. But, at its heart, it's also a local problem. Food waste happens in restaurants, grocers, caterers, and home kitchens in every community. School lunches, similarly, are a national issue that plays out locally. School lunches are prepared and served locally. Food waste and school lunches are, then, local problems that, if tackled in every community—yours included—can have an overwhelmingly positive impact nationally both in terms of what foods kids eat and what foods we all waste.

The solution to these national issues starts in your kitchen. Every parent who can afford to make and pack a sandwich or other food leftovers for their schoolchild should do so. Every school day. Even better, every parent should teach their children to make their own lunches. Every school day. Every dollar a parent gives a child to buy a USDA school lunch contributes to our country's food waste problem. Every bit of food from their own kitchen a parent sends to school with their child—

from leftover meatloaf and green beans to a peanut butter sandwich and an apple and everything in between—helps end the cycle of food waste at home *and* at school. What, though, of students who receive free- and reduced-priced school lunches? As I noted earlier in this chapter, many schoolkids in America depend on low-cost and no-cost food to be able to eat lunch at school. Does urging kids who can afford to brown-bag it mean the kids in greatest need would be forgotten? Absolutely not. The answer may *start* in your kitchen, but the campaign to improve school food *and* reduce food waste works only if it also continues in countless kitchens across the country.

The reform I propose is relatively simple. First, families should take back control of what their kids are eating by preparing a simple brown-bag lunch for each child, every school day. This will reduce food waste at home and at schools. Second, communities should find solutions for kids whose families may not be able to afford to send them to school with a lunch every day. Restaurateurs, caterers, and grocers that throw away tons of tasty food that's good enough to bring home and serve to their own families the next day as leftovers can help end the senseless and needless food waste by donating that food to families in need. Kids with special dietary needs—such as vegans or students with food allergies—can bring foods from home that meet those needs. Alternately, families, schools, and restaurants, working in partnership at the local level, can ensure that a specific number of gluten-free meals, for example, are prepared each day.

Supporters of the USDA National School Lunch Program and the HHFKA might chafe at an alternative to the program. But they might not. The stigma that concerned Poppendieck would not exist. In many cases, kids eating restaurant food would likely eat better-quality food than those who eat leftovers and sandwiches from home. And Prof. Marion Nestle, who supported the HHFKA, called my proposal "a really interesting idea" when we appeared alongside one another on

California public radio in 2012.[54] We need to work together to solve the problems of school lunches and food waste. In schools, I see these as one problem with a shared solution. Having families pack brown-bag lunches, and having local restaurants, caterers, and grocers provide high-quality packaged lunches to students in need *is* a solution to the problems of what to serve kids and to the tons of food waste generated by those restaurants, caterers, and grocers. Everyone from Congress to nutrition advocates, food waste opponents, and families should recognize that there is no rational explanation why feeding kids requires the USDA to pay schools to hire staff to cook and prepare food. Not when a better, cheaper, waste-eliminating, common-sense alternative exists.

Any school lunch program should strive to reduce food waste or, at worst, not to contribute to food waste. A reformulated school lunch program could be—and should be—one that actually fights against food waste. Each state can and should require every local school system to develop a school lunch program that does just this. In addition to giving control over what goes into lunches back to families and reducing or eliminating much food waste, the move away from USDA school lunches would have many other benefits. The program could help improve childhood nutrition, reduce childhood obesity, let schools focus on what should be their core mission of educating students, control federal spending, reduce state and local overhead and costs, and even put a dent in USDA farm subsidies. Making changes to promote better food and reduce food waste won't be easy. Those changes won't happen overnight. But the need for real changes is one idea whose time has come.

Rules Waste Tasty, Ugly Fruit

If the USDA National School Lunch Program is directly responsible for promoting food waste on a massive scale, the impact of another set of rules is far more subtle in its impact. But the consequences of these rules, which help decide indirectly which foods make it to your local grocer and which are thrown away or left to rot in fields, are no less insidious. These rules pertain to USDA grading of fruits, vegetables, and other foods. You've probably seen "Grade A" eggs and "Choice" beef at your grocer. Before we learn how grading promotes food waste, let's look at the purpose of these standards and see what they really mean.

The earliest USDA produce grades date back nearly a century, when okra and blackberries were classified by the agency.[55] Today, graded produce includes apples, artichokes, blueberries, broccoli, cabbage, eggplant, garlic, kale, limes, mushrooms, onions, parsley, pears, potatoes, sweet potatoes, strawberries, tomatoes, and watermelons. These standards are surprisingly pervasive. In fact, the agency has at least 150 standards in place for fruits and vegetables alone.

Most produce and meat is graded. Typically, growers pay fees to the USDA to have their foods graded. Most USDA grades are voluntary, though some USDA marketing order programs mandate that all produce subject to the standards meet the grading requirements. Even if produce or meat is graded, rules typically do not require that a grade must be displayed on food for sale. Still, many grocers and other companies sell only graded produce and meat that displays the grading score prominently. For example, Rogers Orchards in Connecticut, a mail-order supplier of fruits, "ship[s] only our USDA Fancy grade apples and pears."[56] And some states, including North Carolina, have their own grading requirements.[57] This sort of devotion to USDA grading standards is common. "The three supermarket chains we contacted about the standards they adhered to cited the USDA guidelines as their own guidelines for purchasing," reported *Bon Appetit* magazine in an excellent 2014 piece on USDA grading standards.[58]

The USDA grading scheme, while pervasive, is far from uniform. Grades for some foods use designated terms like "fancy" or "choice," while others use number ("No. 2") or letter ("Grade A") grades to indicate the USDA rating. If that seems perplexing, that's because it is. A 1977 report by the federal government's Office of Technology Assessment, *Perspectives on Federal Retail Food Grading*, criticized this "confusing nomenclature," saying it fails to convey any meaningful information to consumers.[59] "Present Federal food grades impart little information to the consumer," the report concluded. Yet the grading system has changed little since the report was written in the 1970s. And problems persist. The USDA admits, for example, that all graded foods are edible —regardless of grade—and that higher grades merely reflect a greater amount of subjectively "desirable characteristics."[60] The agency even admits that a fruit or vegetable that doesn't achieve the highest grade will likely "taste exactly the same" as one that does.[61]

How does that apple grading play out in the marketplace? Grocery stores typically buy only apples that are graded as "fancy," which means an apple must have at least 40 percent red coverage, wrote Natural Resources Defense Council (NRDC) food scientist Dana Gunders.[62] Interestingly, fast-food restaurant chains are some of the biggest buyers of produce that might otherwise end up as food waste. As Gunders noted, many of the perfectly edible apples that won't cut it as "fancy" end up as snacks in McDonald's Happy Meals.

For further evidence of the subjectivity of the grading system, one need look no further than the USDA system for grading beef. The agency awards its highest grade for beef, "Prime," when a particular cut boasts "abundant marbling," or a high amount of fat within lean meat.[63] The singular value USDA puts on fat marbling means that grass-fed beef, which is typically leaner than beef from cattle that are fed grain, is less likely to earn a "Prime" grade.[64]

As the USDA explains, the agency grades foods based on "quality standards" it developed with the "interest and support" of the food industry.[65] The standards "are based on measurable attributes that describe the value and utility of the product."[66] The ability of large food businesses to determine what "measurable" characteristics determine "value" and "utility" means industry wields enormous power over the marketplace. An apple with a higher USDA grade, for example, has—in the USDA's opinion—greater "value" and "utility" than an apple with a lesser grade.

The USDA grading standards for bunched carrots are informative.[67] The standards, established in 1954 and not updated since, identify two grades of carrots: "U.S. No. 1" and "U.S. Commercial." A third category, "Unclassified," includes carrots that are not graded by the USDA. Some of the grading characteristics do pertain to objective standards of quality. U.S. No. 1 carrots must be free from rot and insect damage, for example. But many of the traits are qualitative and appear to be entirely subjective. U.S. No. 1 carrots, as defined by the rules, are those "of similar varietal characteristics the roots of which are firm, fairly clean, fairly well colored, fairly smooth, well-formed and . . . the diameter of each carrot shall be not less than three-fourths inch." U.S. Commercial-grade carrots, on the other hand, include irregularly shaped carrots, such as those whose roots are smaller or larger than the specified diameter. The unevenly shaped purple, yellow, and orange carrots I recently picked up at my local farmers market in Garrett Park, Maryland, were perfectly crunchy, sweet, and earthy. But neither a USDA grader nor your local grocer would know what to do with these ungraded carrots. Instead, virtually every grocer sells one- and five-pound bags of "U.S. No. 1" carrots that display the requisite "similar varietal characteristics"—they're uniformly orange, about the same length, and certainly (heaven forbid) not less than three-fourths of an inch in diameter.

If oddball shapes, sizes, and colors of carrots are sold at many farmers markets, those same nonconformist root vegetables might go to waste on a farm that supplies carrots to larger, commercial food sellers. That means most farms, most grocers, and most restaurants. Ninety-eight percent of produce is purchased at groceries and restaurants—which typically buy graded foods and which often market those foods as having earned a specific USDA grade—versus just 2 percent that's purchased at farmers markets. The small farmer can earn a premium by selling at the farmers market, but USDA grading largely cuts him off from selling his oddly shaped foods to the grocer. Which carrots fetch the higher price at the grocery? Simply put, the higher the grade, the higher the price a farmer can fetch. The difference in price paid to a grower can be significant. In an excellent segment on food waste on the popular HBO show *Last Week Tonight*, host John Oliver noted that a USDA grade of "No. 2" rather than "No. 1" can mean a farmer loses two-thirds of the value of his crop.[68] It's this economic component where grading agricultural products such as fruits, vegetables, and meat truly helps promote tons of food waste.

Little about the rules *prohibits* misshapen carrots, peaches, or apples from reaching consumers in the market. But the USDA rules make these edible foods that much tougher to sell and, consequently, that much easier to waste. If profit margins are thin, it's often easier to plow under or throw away the crop than to pay for labor to harvest a crop you might not be able to sell at a profit. The NRDC has noted that harvesting crews are trained to pick produce based on grading specifications, and not to pick produce that fails, in their estimation, to make the grade. The group estimates this happens with up to one-third of all fruits and vegetables.[69]

The attributes of graded foods may be *measurable*, but do those characteristics really establish objective quality? The USDA says the grading system is good for consumers and producers alike, but there's good reason to be skeptical. Recall that in chapter 1, for example, Lynda Simkins, of Natick Community Organic Farm in Massachusetts, described how NCOF doesn't sell graded maple syrup because, in her words, the USDA's maple syrup grading system is a joke. She noted that the USDA's voluntary maple syrup grading system is based on color, not flavor. And the color of maple syrup has nothing to do with its quality. "It's all just a marketing tool," Simkins told me by phone.[70] "It's not reflective of the quality of the product." So if NCOF doesn't grade the maple syrup it sells, how do customers know which syrup they want to buy? Simkins told me that NCOF bottles all of its syrup in clear glass bottles and lets customers choose whichever color syrup they want. Imagine that. (Notably, the USDA relaxed its standards in March 2015 to allow more syrups to earn top marks even if their color may have prevented them from doing so in the past.)[71]

Certainly, many consumers have come to expect produce, eggs, and other foods to look similar to others of their kind. Why do all of the tomatoes at your grocer look and taste the same? Why are the peaches you find at your farmers market sometimes misshapen, and boast different flavors? This is largely due to USDA grades for peaches, tomatoes, and carrots, but it's also thanks to a combination of grocers meeting consumer expectations. In short, we are all complicit in making families of fruits, vegetables, and other agricultural products look and taste uniformly.

Even if the USDA is just part of the problem when it comes to grading and food waste—a lamentable role it shares with America's finicky consumers and its bottom-dollar-focused food industry—agency rules for grading agricultural products like produce and meat play an enormous role in promoting food waste. The agency has been loath to acknowledge its role. "Consumers naturally tend to choose only the shiniest looking apple and freshest milk at the store," the agency notes at its website.[72] "So what happens to 'ugly,' misshapen, or slightly out of proportion fruits and vegetables that might have looked similar to the ones in your garden?" The USDA doesn't answer its own question. Still, even if the agency won't openly admit the role its grading rules play in food waste, it has spoken of their impact in the past. A 1997 report by four USDA employees, *Estimating and Addressing America's*

Food Losses, cited "minimum quality standards for fresh produce set by State and Federal marketing orders" as one of the leading causes of food waste emanating from the nation's farms.[73] The agency's authors noted that these "requirements" often force farmers not to harvest "small, misshapen, or otherwise blemished produce" at all.

But if the USDA seems unwilling to change, others are taking notice of the role that grading plays in promoting food waste. And they're starting to fight back. In fact, there's a growing movement that's not just questioning how grading feeds into food waste, it's working to find solutions to the problem. The NRDC, for example, has described sales that happen outside the traditional USDA grading system as "breaking the grade barrier."[74] One of those who's breaking that barrier is California organic farmer and author David Masumoto. "If we picked our friends the way we selectively picked and culled our produce, we'd be very lonely," Masumoto wrote in an excellent 2012 op-ed on produce grading. "No two peaches are nor should they be exactly alike. Natural variation is natural." Masumoto said the quest for perfect produce is "expensive, it's unproductive and it's unrealistic."[75]

Like Masumoto, a growing number of people and groups around the country—and around the world—are combating food waste. I came across the work of one such group, Fruta Feia, in summer 2014. I'd read a fantastic *New York Times* profile of Fruta Feia, a recently formed Lisbon-based food co-op, that was fighting food waste in Portugal.[76] In his profile, *Times* reporter Raphael Minder called Fruta Feia "a kind of countercultural movement." He noted it had become popular with budget-conscious Portuguese consumers and opponents of food waste, and also "provided a backhanded slap to overweening European Union rule makers." Europe, it turns out, has rules in place that are very similar to those the USDA uses to grade produce, meats, and other foods. In fact, some of Europe's rules, dictated by the European Union (EU), are just as bad as our own.

The rules, published a decade ago, set up what the EU calls a "general marketing standard" that establishes grading benchmarks for a host of produce, and "specific marketing standards" for a number of others.[77] For example, the rules for apples, which are governed by specific standards that take up *fourteen pages*, establish three classes of the fruit: "Extra," "Class I," and "Class II." The rules declare that Extra-class apples, the premium classification, must be "characteristic of the variety," of "superior quality," and free from cosmetic "defects," including in "shape, size and colouring." Class I permits "slight defects" in size or coloring that are generally no more than two centimeters in length, while Class II defects can be generally no larger than four centimeters. The rules also establish minimum sizes for apples in all classes.

When I first reached out to Fruta Feia, I heard back from staffer Maria Canelhas.[78] I met with Canelhas when I traveled to Lisbon in July 2014, about ten months after Fruta Feia's launch. By that time, the group—whose name literally translates as "ugly fruit"—had already helped prevent more than thirty-five *tons* of food waste.[79] When I contacted Canelhas ten months later, that number had ballooned to 130 tons.[80] Canelhas told me Fruta Feia is now preventing three tons of food from being wasted each week in Portugal.

I met Canelhas at an outdoor cafe in Lisbon around the corner from Fruta Feia's Intendente Square offices. Canelhas gave me a bunch of irregularly sized grapes and two undersized melons, examples of the type of produce that would be flagged for its size and shape by regulators and, consequently, which may previously have gone to waste. Notably, these small, irregularly shaped fruits were easily the freshest and best fruit I enjoyed during my trip through parts of Portugal and Spain. Then again, the EU rules—like the American ones for grading food—make no reference to taste. I asked Canelhas how exactly the EU rules promote food waste. The rules, she said, push consumers looking for good produce to use the EU's subjective grading system as an arbiter of quality. That has a ripple effect. "When noticing this trend, distributors and supermarkets started to buy from the farmers those classes only, leaving the others out," she said in a subsequent email, referring to those fruits and vegetables not meeting government standards.[81] "This explains the difficulty that farmers are facing trying to sell these fruits and vegetables, resulting in a huge amount of food waste. Nowadays, distributors and supermarkets aren't buying the less appreciated classes, so consumers don't have the choice to buy them, because this food isn't even arriving on the market." It's a vicious cycle. And it's one promoted by the EU rules. Notably, the *New York Times* report said Fruta Feia founder Isabel Soares believes these EU rules are "a striking example of misplaced regulatory intervention."[82]

"These rules lead people to think that category A or B is better quality than the rest of the categories," Canelhas told me.[83] "The higher you go on categories, the bigger and more perfect the food has to be. And the names of the categories also lead people to think it's a matter of quality when it's not. We're here to show people that even the [nonstandardized] fruit and misshaped vegetables can be of excellent quality," she said, echoing NCOF head Lynda Simkins's comments on the lack of any relationship between a maple syrup's grade and its quality.

Soares, Canelhas's colleague, launched Fruta Feia when she was living in Barcelona and working on renewable energy issues. There, Soares became interested in the problem of food waste, Canelhas told me, and spoke with an uncle of hers who farms. He told Soares he was often forced to throw away a large amount of edible produce because of a combination of EU rules and grocer and consumer preferences. Soares eventually decided to do something about the problem, and secured funds to launch Fruta Feia by entering and placing second in a Portuguese contest seeking groundbreaking ideas in social entrepreneurship.

Fruta Feia pays farmers who sell ugly fruit about half what they'd expect to receive from a grocer for produce that meets EU standards.

That's income a farmer wouldn't otherwise have. The group passes its savings along to members. People pay about seven dollars to join the co-op, then pay another five dollars each week for about eight pounds of produce that's available at a pickup point. The model is similar to an American CSA. It's just that consumers can expect to receive oddball shapes and sizes they'd never see in a grocery store. Those consumers come from all walks of life. "We have college students, foreigners living in Portugal, families with kids, and old couples," Canelhas told me.[84] "But they all have a few characteristics in common: they're people who are aware of this social and environmental problem and who feel like they can and want to do something about it. They're also unsettled by these EU rules and they want to help farmers sell their 'ugly fruit' because they know and understand that it's the same quality as the 'pretty food.' Also, they want to consume food that's produced locally and sold at a price that's fair both to farmers and to themselves as consumers.

"Fruta Feia's main goal is to fight food waste, although we also intend to raise awareness and to question the cause and impact of these rules to farmers, to the environment and to the consumer," said Canelhas.[85] "We intend to help changing the consumption patterns that are causing this food waste problem and help educating people that the 'ugly fruit' is the same quality as the pretty one." The group's outreach is working. As Fruta Feia's successes have grown, so too has the organization. In addition to Soares and Canelhas, Fruta Feia recently hired a third employee. The group also hosts eighty volunteers. Fruta Feia now has a trio of pickup points, Canelhas told me, and has widened its distribution network to include three-dozen partner farmers. Most are small- or medium-sized farmers, she said, but the group also works with a small number of large producers. Impressively, Fruta Feia was serving 800 consumers in summer 2015—nearly double those it served when I first heard about the group in summer 2014.[86]

The tons of food waste avoided and farmers and consumers served shows that the work Canelhas, Soares, and Fruta Feia are doing to prevent food waste is incredibly valuable and important. But there's much more to the story. In a country such as Portugal that's been hit hard in recent years by an economic downturn, where nearly one in four Portuguese may be unemployed, Fruta Feia's work is vital.[87] The group is not just preventing food waste and helping society reap all the benefits from doing so, it's helping struggling farmers make money and struggling consumers buy healthier food at a lower cost. Not surprisingly, Fruta Feia has won numerous awards for its work, including ones from the Yves Rocher Foundation, António Sérgio Foundation, Crédito Agrícola, and, notably, the Calouste Gulbenkian Foundation, which helped fund the group's launch.[88] The group's attention-grabbing motto, "beautiful people eat ugly fruit," has garnered plenty of press. British newspaper *The Guardian* recently ranked Fruta Feia in sixteenth place on its list of the fifty hottest international food trends.[89] It also just won new funding from an EU environmental body, which Canelhas told me will allow Fruta Feia to expand throughout Portugal over the next few years.[90]

So far, Canelhas said, Fruta Feia's work has focused on changing consumers' buying habits, rather than on changing EU rules. But those rules have inched in a better direction in recent years anyway. Unlike the United States, for example, the EU has actually scaled back its grading standards in recent years, Canelhas told me, from thirty-six to ten, for "specific marketing standards." Just like in the United States, though, the EU rules exist thanks to pressure from large agricultural producers and sellers. "The E.U. has set standards and follows an agricultural policy that is focused on what the big players in the food supply chain want, even if that means an incredible amount of waste," João Barroso, an environmental scientist, told the *New York Times*'s Raphael Minder.[91] Rules supported by large industries are difficult to change. Perhaps Fruta Feia's focus on changing palates, rather than laws, is sound.

Interestingly, the undersized produce favored by Fruta Feia and its customer base—the same fruits and vegetables deemed déclassé by EU and USDA regulations—may turn out not just to be particularly tasty. It may also have environmental benefits beyond the fact Fruta Feia has saved it from the landfill. That's because growing smaller produce may actually help water conservation efforts. David Masumoto—the California author and farmer—has been growing smaller peaches by using less water, dictated not by flavor but by California's ongoing drought. Masumoto told Civil Eats that he got his inspiration from campaigners for ugly fruits.[92] Others have, too. Across the country, in Boston, a new market that's being billed as "America's most local food market" opened in summer 2015, in the heart of the city.[93] The mission of the Boston Public Market is to sell only local produce, meats, seafood, and other goods—like cheese—that are made locally, using local ingredients. The market has asked vendors to keep prices low, so the foods sold there can be more affordable for everyone, including low-income consumers. That means ugly fruit. "For most farmers," the *Boston Globe* reported, "it means selling 'seconds,' or produce slightly bruised or oddly shaped, at a lower price." Although lower-priced items and seconds were hard to find on my first visit to the market, in October 2015, I'm optimistic such items might appear as the market grows.

Although most readers can picture what a misshapen carrot or a slightly bruised tomato looks like, it may be more difficult to figure out what the "seconds" of seafood sold at the Boston Public Market might mean. The idea of eating fish that's somehow imperfect seems less than appetizing and, perhaps, less than smart. As you're about to learn, though, fighting waste in our seas and oceans doesn't means eating rotten fish. Rather, it means embracing ideas such as trash fish, which, despite the name, means fresh and tasty seafood.

Throwback Rules

No discussion of rules that promote food waste would be complete without focusing on federal, state, and international rules that, together, promote the wanton devastation of countless fish and other marine life in the world's oceans and seas. Bycatch, the term used to describe much of this senseless waste, is the harvesting of nontarget fish and other marine animals. Bycatch is often what happens when fishermen literally cast a wide net, trawl the bottom of the ocean indiscriminately, or use other unsustainable fishing practices in the quest to catch a certain species—tuna or shrimp, for example—and end up also catching turtles, sharks, dolphins, salmon, and other species the fishermen did not intend to catch. The Safina Center at New York's Stony Brook University says most bycatch is "already dead when it hits the" boat. But bycatch also includes fish that are alive but are "the wrong size, poor quality, low market value, or [keeping them is] prohibited for conservation reasons."[94]

The data on bycatch are as stunning and depressing as any on food waste caused by school lunches policies, fruit and vegetable grading, or other food-waste sources. The Monterey Bay Aquarium reports that up to six pounds of other species die for every pound of shrimp hauled to shore.[95] A 2014 report on bycatch by the group Oceana, a nonprofit dedicated to protecting the world's oceans, noted that up to 40 percent of fish caught worldwide—or 63 *billion* pounds of fish, marine mammals, and other ocean dwellers—is bycatch.[96] The figures in the United States are slightly better, the group reported, with bycatch representing about one-fifth of the domestic catch.

Efforts to promote sustainable fishing, the Pew Charitable Trusts noted in 2015, focus on the dual goals of "reduc[ing] bycatch while allowing fishing to continue."[97] The leading law regulating U.S. fisheries is the Magnuson-Stevens Fishery Conservation and Management Act (MSA).[98] This law, adopted in 1976, established eight regional councils that support and protect fish stocks within their respective regions through various quotas, limits, and other policies. Much of the conversation about limiting waste and bycatch typically revolves around the need to strengthen or expand the MSA. There's indeed some truth to the need for strong laws. For example, in chapter 5—which focuses on good food laws—you'll learn about why the federal government's existing ban on the practice of shark finning is an important law that's worth supporting. But stronger new rules aren't always the answer. Stronger rules, as you've seen in this book, aren't even *often* the answer. Just as you've seen with the other examples in this chapter of laws that promote food waste, there are plenty of ways that existing rules for fisheries promote waste.

For example, Gib Brogan, of Oceana, told NPR shortly after the group issued its 2014 report on bycatch that "fishing regulations are partly to blame for wasted seafood . . . because fishermen who have permits to catch certain species must throw back other valuable species they accidentally catch—even if the fish are dead."[99] Brogan went on to explain that Alaska trawlers seeking fish that live on the ocean bottom, such as flounder and sole, also catch millions of pounds of halibut and cod. But the rules bar fishermen from taking the halibut and cod to shore and selling them—even if the fish are edible and dying or dead. Consequently, fishermen often discard living and dead bycatch at sea. This sort of indiscriminant waste has drawn criticism from many quarters. The United Nations Food and Agriculture Organization noted "fishery regulations may promote discards or do little to minimize or eliminate them."[100] In testimony before a U.S. Senate committee on the MSA in 2013, Brian Rothschild, president of the Center for Sustainable Fisheries, a group that promotes conservation and economic development, said that the nation's "fisheries management . . . system generates considerable waste."[101] In 2011, Rothschild described how rules approved by Congress cause 100,000 tons of fish to be wasted each year. That fish, Rothschild said, is valued at $300 million "at the dock" and four times that amount—$1.2 billion—on the open market.[102]

The practice of trawling, which I noted above, has itself drawn fire from many environmental advocates. Trawling involves dragging a weighted fishing net along the ocean floor, often to catch so-called groundfish. Although this practice may cause little or no lasting damage in some areas, it can also destroy marine habitat, promote bycatch, and damage fragile ecosystems such as coral reefs. Some restrictions on the practice rightly exist today. Others may be needed. But groups such as The Nature Conservancy are also finding creative alternatives to the practice of trawling. The group's novel Central Coast Groundfish Project in California is promoting sustainable fisheries management practices there.[103] As part of the project, the group has bought up trawling permits and, in turn, leased them to fishermen who agree to follow certain conservation practices (such as seining, instead of trawling) in exchange for using the permits. A 2011 *New York Times* report called this a "collaborative model for sustainable fishing."[104] An approach like this one that involves conservation groups playing a leading role in fisheries management may provide fishermen, consumers, fish stocks, and the marine environment with the greatest shared benefits.

Nonprofit environmental groups aren't the only ones taking the lead in this area. During the course of researching this book, I learned about the work of Sea to Table, a business that helps fight ocean food waste by partnering with small-scale, sustainable fishermen to open up new markets for their catch. I spoke with Sean Dimin, one of the founders, about Sea to Table's work. "Sea to Table works with independent fishermen and commercial docks around the country each day shipping their catch directly to restaurant chefs and more recently university dining halls and home delivery companies," Dimin told me.[105] "We work to build better choices within our food system and provide greater value back to the men and women responsible for the harvest."

Although Dimin praised wild fisheries in the United States as "some of the best managed in the world"—and noted that they continue to improve—he also pointed out that Sea to Table's work with individual fishermen around the country leads him and others to "often hear discontent and sometimes bewilderment at the laws and regulations that govern U.S. seafood policy." Dimin shared a disheartening YouTube link with me that shows what appears to be thousands of striped bass floating dead in waters off North Carolina.[106] Sadly, federal laws help promote this sort of waste. Under the Lacey Act, a federal law, it is illegal for anyone to transport or sell fish that were taken in violation of any federal rules.[107] That means a fisherman who catches a fish that turns out not to be legal—if, for example, a fish isn't the right size, if the fisherman doesn't have a permit to catch that species, or even if he has a permit to catch the species but the permit doesn't allow him to catch the species in the place where he caught it—must throw the fish back whether it's alive or dead. The Lacey Act is serious business. The U.S. Justice Department is presently prosecuting more than a dozen fishermen for taking striped bass in federal waters, which is currently illegal.[108] The men claim they took the bass legally in North Carolina state waters, which extend to three nautical miles from the Tar Heel State's seashore.

The line between what's legal and what's not, as in the North Carolina case, which concerns 90,000 pounds of striped bass, can be nebulous.[109] But that fuzzy line can be the difference between throwing away thousands of fish and keeping and selling them. It can be the difference between earning a profit or a huge fine. Dimin shared with me a story that helps illustrate this issue. Summer flounder, also known as fluke, is a species managed jointly in federal and state waters by three different federal agencies. States up and down the Eastern Seaboard, from Maine to the Carolinas, also manage fluke fishing within their respective state coastal waters. States set quotas, Dimin said, to comply with a federal maximum fishing target, "with each state allowed to set limits and seasons as long as the overall conservation goal is achieved."[110] Dimin said it's common for fishermen to "hold quota"—or, to be licensed to take a fish, such as fluke—in several states. But because states are allowed to set limits and establish open and closed fishing seasons, complications can arise. And those complications have resulted in enormous waste.

"One vessel we know out of Montauk, New York, traveled southwest to New Jersey to fish quota as the New York season was closed," Dimin told me. "At the end of a productive day a storm began to brew threatening the vessel's safety. The captain had to make a decision; either ride into the storm to offload his catch legally in [New Jersey] or dump the fish and hightail back to his home port in [New York]. Had he carried his fish back to [New York] during a closed season he would have been subject to heavy fines for possessing an illegal catch. This all happens on bordering states with bordering waterlines. Needless to say, the captain chose the safety of his vessel and crew, dumping the fish overboard and heading home to port."[111]

Forcing fishermen to throw away edible fish that may not be "legal" for reasons such as these—to force edible *catch* to become wasted *bycatch*—is a bizarre conservation strategy. It's similar in effect to the destruction of ivory seized from poachers, something the federal government and African governments have done in recent years. Although poaching ivory is rightly illegal, the destruction of seized ivory only serves to restrict the supply, which in turn drives up the price for ivory, which in turn makes ivory poaching more profitable, a vicious cycle that the late Brookings Institute senior fellow Mwangi S. Kimenyi discussed in 2015.[112] A better solution to the ivory problem would be to seize the ivory, flood the market with it, and use the proceeds to protect elephants, rhinoceroses, and other animals, which would serve to depress ivory prices and make poaching less profitable and more difficult.

Similarly, rules that would allow fishermen to sell fish they've caught—but don't have permission to sell—and that are dead or dying but edible is simply smart policy. There's no saving a dead fish. But allowing that fish to be sold means less fish of that and other species will die. That dead fish can't be saved, but its sale can help save its living cousins. The *New York Times* article on The Nature Conservancy's efforts showed how that group's conservation efforts embrace this approach.[113] For example, the report noted, one fisherman working with the group caught hundreds of a threatened rockfish species that's protected under federal fisheries rules. Instead of throwing the catch back, though, the fisherman used an iPad to document and report the catch to others in the area (so they could avoid making the same mistake he had), brought the catch back to shore, and sold it. The catch counted against his annual quota.

"The conservancy's model is designed to take advantage of radical new changes in government regulation that allow fishermen in the region both more control and more responsibility for their operating choices," reported the *New York Times*. "The new rules have led to better conservation practices across all fleets, government monitors say."

Just as with food waste caused by the USDA National School Lunch Program and by domestic produce grading and EU produce standards, changing the rules is a key step to reducing food waste. Governments can—and should—impose some limits on the quantity of fish that can be taken, on the length or time of seasons for harvesting various fish, and on some methods of fishing. But these rules should not compel waste. Still, it would be a mistake to simply blame bad rules for the problem of overfishing and ocean waste. Although rules and practices at sea must change, so too must sales, marketing, and consumer behavior.

In addition to Sea to Table, other advocates for sustainable seafood are making waves in this area by suggesting a variety of solutions. I first met Ben Sargent, the seafood-obsessed author of the cookbook *The Catch* and host of the television show *Hook, Line, and Dinner*, several years ago while writing a profile of his colorful, avant-garde, underground-lobster-roll salesman alter-ego, Dr. Klaw.[114] Sargent has seawater running through his veins. His grandfather, father, sister, brother, and brother-in-law have all been deeply involved in fishing and related environmental and regulatory issues. He's passionate about sustainable fishing and outraged by waste.

"The most disgusting thing we are doing is targeting fish and throwing bycatch into the ocean," Sargent told me by email.[115] "It's so repulsive I can't even believe it's still happening. That to me is about the worst thing out there." Sargent is so angered by overfishing that he's skeptical about the future of all fishing. "At this point," he told me, "sustainable fishing means no fishing at all." But that skepticism quickly changes to potty-mouthed glee when you ask Sargent about invasive species. "We can eat the shit out of those because they eat everything in their path and it's a real problem," he said. Sargent pointed out that many invasive species taste great. (That many wasted foods taste great is a popular refrain I've heard many times when it comes to strategies for preventing food waste.) Sargent noted that snakehead fish, an invasive species in the mid-Atlantic states, and one I've eaten and enjoyed thoroughly, tastes fantastic. Sargent told me we should "fish the crap out of" the snakehead. But, he said, we'll need to relax rules to make it easier to serve invasive species. "Bend the laws a little about serving fresh water fish or give people a license to be able to sell them to the local fish and chips joint," he told me, referring to many existing laws that restrict the sale of freshwater fish.[116] That's still more rules that need bending.

Others have committed to turning bycatch into dinner. Houston, Texas chef PJ Stoops took it upon himself to popularize eating all sorts of fish that previously had gone to waste. Stoops is a giant in the "trash fish world," a term Sea to Table's Travis Riggs used to describe to me a world I didn't even know existed.[117] Trash fish, a term for unpopular species of bycatch, is—like invasive species—slowly becoming an increasingly popular menu option. A 2012 article in *Bon Appetit* magazine said Stoops had helped make trash fish hip.[118] He did so first by creating a market for the bycatch with fishermen, urging them to sell him what they'd otherwise throw away. Then he put bycatch on his restaurant menus, and also sold it to fellow chefs and other consumers. "Stoops cite[s] sustainability as the biggest impact of bringing bycatch to the mainstream," the piece noted. Stoops helped create a market out of waste, and helped ease the burden faced by overfished species in the process.

Innovators like Stoops, Sea to Table, Sargent, and Fruta Feia are helping to reduce food waste by creating new markets for food that might otherwise be squandered. Government rules are too often the cause of this waste, and eliminating them is an important step in ensuring a more sustainable food future. From disincentives for restaurants to compost to ineffective school lunch programs to the marginalization of edible fruits and vegetables, these rules are vast in scope and number. They also stretch across borders. EU produce standards are but one example.

But remember, it's not just the waste itself that's the problem. It's also the problems that waste causes, including the fact that wasted food ends up belching methane in landfills. That's why sustainability—"sustentabilidade" in Portuguese, as Fruta Feia's Maria Canelhas explained—is a term that applies not just to preventing waste but also to eradicating its secondary impacts. The campaign to promote ugly fruit helps put to good use the resources that were used to grow the food. It helps reduce pesticide use, Canelhas noted, by selling fruits and vegetables that weren't economically valuable enough to spray. And smaller fruits, as David Masumoto noted, require less water.

Yes, the rules must change for sustainable food to supplant food waste. But so must we all. Changing consumer behavior—like Fruta Feia, David Masumoto, Sea to Table, and others are doing—is another important step for reducing food waste. But it takes will. With school lunches, we've got to show a willingness to save, prepare, and eat leftovers. With fruits and vegetables, we must be willing to eat so-called ugly fruit. With seafood, we must be willing to choose the so-called trash fish.

We need to change. But what about consumers who are ahead of the curve, who've *already changed*? What about those who are so certain of their food choices and so committed to obtaining their own food that, in some or even most cases, they don't even want to be *consumers*? By that I don't mean people who don't want to eat but, rather, people who want to grow, raise, produce, share, or obtain food for themselves and their families—firsthand. Surely no rules would interfere with a person's ability to grow their own fruits and vegetables—ugly or not—right? What about the farmer who sells some wheat but keeps some for his family? Certainly that's well within the law. What about the person who wants to forage for wild berries or mushrooms? What of charitable people who volunteer to share food with those in need, including the homeless and less fortunate? There's no way rules would outlaw these practices, right? In fact, a web of different rules prohibits these and other traditional and sustainable food practices. Such rules exist at all levels of government. As you're about to see, they may constitute the most outrageous and indefensible sort of food rules imaginable.

CHAPTER 4

I Say "Tomato," You Say "No"

In the introduction to this book, you learned about Ohio farmer Roscoe Filburn, who in 1941 challenged a USDA rule that barred him from keeping a quantity of wheat for his own family's use. The lore around the case has Filburn claiming he and his family were using the surplus wheat to make bread. That may not tell the whole story. "To consume the 239 excess bushels at issue in the July 1941 wheat harvest," wrote law professor Jim Chen, in a definitive *Emory Law Journal* article on the case's legacy, "the Filburns would have had to consume nearly forty-four one-pound loaves of bread each day for the following year."[1] As I noted in this book's introduction, Filburn and his family sold the amount of wheat the USDA said they could and kept the rest to make bread—yes—and also to feed to the family's livestock and to save some for seed. Farmers have been doing exactly this since the dawn of farming—selling (or trading) some of the food they produce, using another portion of the food to feed themselves and their family, saving some for next year's planting, and using the rest to feed their pigs, chickens, goats, and cattle. Still, the Supreme Court ruled against Filburn, saying the

USDA had the power to order him not to keep any of the wheat he grew to make bread, to feed livestock, or for any other reason.

This was an unfair and incorrect decision in 1941. It still rings that way today. And while Roscoe Filburn's case has remained an important one for courts and legal scholars interested in the constitutional questions underlying the case—including the boundaries of the Constitution's Commerce Clause—what this case says about sustainability and peoples' rights to feed themselves, their families, and others has largely been ignored. To me, the case says much—too much, perhaps—about the ways governments and courts view such rights. There's nothing more notionally sustainable about eating than when people choose to feed themselves—and their family, friends, and others—with food they grew, raised, hunted, fished, foraged, found, shared, or otherwise obtained all by themselves.

In *The Omnivore's Dilemma*, for example, author Michael Pollan wrote that "the perfect meal" is the one he obtains solely of his own accord.[2] His first rule for such a meal, Pollan wrote, is that every single menu item "must have been hunted, gathered, or grown by me." Pollan went on to point out that for most, eating this way regularly is as "unsustainable" as is eating fast-food regularly. He's right. Most of us have jobs or other responsibilities that prevent us from farming, hunting, gathering, and fishing to the extent that it can provide all the food we need. But in each case—be it the perfect meal or the fast-food meal Pollan posited as its opposite—there are those who *do* make this choice. Whether it's eating only what you've hunted, gathered, and grown or eating only what a fast-food chain has pieced together for you, a few facts hold true. Many people choose to eat this way sometimes. Some people choose to eat this way often. And a few people—very few—choose to eat this way always.

Pollan has *his* rules for a perfect meal. They require him to hunt, gather, and grow everything he puts on his dinner table. In his perfect meal, he hunts the pig, forages for the mushrooms, and grows the vegetables. Then he cooks the dinner. But federal, state, and local governments have *their* rules, too. What if government rules like those that barred Roscoe Filburn from using his own wheat to prepare dinner also prevented Pollan from obtaining his perfect meal? In fact, this happens all the time; if not to Pollan himself, then to millions of other Americans. Federal, state, and local governments can—and do—tell people all the time that they can't grow, can't raise, can't forage, and can't share food. As you're about to see, some rules even prevent people from using water from their own wells. If the federal government of the 1940s was "skeptical of amateur farmers"—as I noted in this book's introduction that *Time* magazine had reported at the time today's federal, state, and local governments are skeptical of gardeners, foragers, good Samaritans, and others who make, obtain, and provide food outside the commercial mainstream.

If sustainability starts at home, then so too do rules that determine just how sustainable you can be in your home life. Farmers can rely on their own crops and livestock for food, compost, clothing, and a host of other solutions. Gardens can be a great place for homeowners to help feed a family and use composted waste. Even other less obvious home-based pursuits can feed into sustainability efforts.

For example, brewing beer—whether from ingredients grown at home or obtained at a farm or store—can help reduce packaging and transport costs, help out local farmers keen to receive spent grains, and give homebrewers the ultimate control over what they're drinking. The explosion of homebrewing in America in recent decades is a great example of how federal rules can affect your home. Before 1978, it was illegal for Americans to brew beer at home. That year, President Jimmy Carter signed into law a bill that allowed Americans to make beer (and wine) at home, so long as they didn't sell it.[3] In addition to letting Americans brew beer at home for the first time since Prohibition, the law is credited with helping to set in motion the explosion of craft brewing in this country, as many of yesterday's homebrewers went on to become today's commercial craft brewers. Although the ban on homebrewing is one of the best known examples of a prohibition on producing one's own food at home, many arguably more sustainable food practices—ones far more mundane than brewing beer—are banned at home by a tangled web of local rules.

Growing food in home gardens is among the easiest, most popular, and most personal ways to promote and consume sustainable food. It's also a practice that's exploded in popularity in recent years. A 2009 report by the National Gardening Association found that nearly one-third of American households raises some combination of fruits and vegetables at home.[4] A 2014 report by the same group found that the number of edible gardens had grown since the earlier report by 17 percent.[5] A 2012 report by the *New York Times* noted that home food gardens are a byproduct of the "growing interest in sustainability."[6]

Despite the mushrooming popularity of raising food at home, gardeners around the country have faced a dizzying number of bewildering restrictions in recent years. "Jason Helvenston was at work on his second crop, spreading compost to fertilize the carrots, bok choy, kale and dozens of other vegetables he grows organically on his property in Orlando, Fla., when the trouble began," reads the lede of that same *New York Times* article, which focuses on municipal battles over home gardens.[7] A neighbor's landlord had complained that Helvenston's neat little garden made his house look "like a farm." Helvenston, a sustainability consultant, squared off against city officials intent on forcing him to rip up the garden in his front yard. The city backed down in 2013, and Helvenston was able to keep his garden. But others haven't been so lucky.

In some cases, local governments have gone so far as to rip food-bearing plants from the yards of residents. Denise Morrison of Tulsa, Oklahoma is one such victim. In 2012, Tulsa code enforcement officers walked into Morrison's front yard without her permission and uprooted her edible garden. Morrison, who was unemployed at the time, was using the foods she grew to sustain herself during a difficult period. Code officers, on the other hand, were enforcing a city ordinance that said plants cannot be higher than twelve inches "unless they're used for human consumption." Morrison's garden contained "lemon, stevia, garlic chives, grapes, strawberries, apple mint, spearmint, peppermint," fruit trees, and other foods that would have been used for her consumption had the code enforcers not cut some down and ripped others right out of the ground.[8] The city claimed Morrison's "yard did not contain any organic garden, but had large amounts of untended, dead and decaying vegetation; unhealthy trees; dead tree limbs; and rotting tires."[9] Morrison—who had taken photos of her edible garden and shared them with the city—fought back, filing a civil rights lawsuit against the city. Amazingly, two successive federal courts dismissed her lawsuit. They determined Tulsa officials had provided Morrison with adequate notice before taking action.[10]

Although Morrison's case may seem extreme, others have even faced jail time for nothing more than growing food in their own yard. In 2011, an Oak Park, Michigan, woman was threatened with more than three months in jail for keeping a beautiful, well-manicured, edible garden in her front yard.[11] City officials charged Julie Bass with a misdemeanor, arguing that Bass's basil, cabbage, carrots, cucumbers, tomatoes, and other edible produce were not "suitable live plant material." The city has its own definition of what "suitable" means. "If you look at the dictionary, suitable means common," city planner Kevin Rulkowski told local station WXYZ. Rulkowski is wrong not just about Bass's garden but about the meaning of the word "suitable." It means—among other terms that do not include the word "common"—"similar," "matching," "adapted to a use or purpose," or "proper," according to *Webster's Dictionary*.[12] In fact, "common" isn't even a synonym for "suitable." For these reasons, perhaps, the city eventually dropped the charges against Bass.[13]

Other examples of cities and towns cracking down on residents' vegetable gardens are less extreme, if no less ridiculous and maddening in nature. In 2012, for example, Newton, Massachusetts officials ordered a town resident to remove his hanging tomato garden from his front yard.[14] Officials said the hanging garden violated a city ordinance prohibiting the construction of "swing sets, swimming pools, or sheds" in a front yard. Newton resident Eli Katzoff was forced to move his plants to the grounds of Andover Newton Theological School, a nearby seminary. The seminary was happy to take in the tomatoes, but its leader was perplexed by the town's behavior. "Who can be against tomatoes?" wondered then-seminary president Nick Carter.[15]

Tomatoes—a fruit—are probably fine in Miami Shores, Florida. But vegetables are not. The city code was amended to prohibit growing vegetables in a front yard in 2013. Hermine Ricketts and her husband Tom Carroll had been raising vegetables in their front yard in the city for more than fifteen years. The couple had a host of vegetables growing there—including arugula, cabbage, kale, and onions—when the city changed the code. Days later, a city code enforcement officer showed up at their home and ordered them to rip up their garden or face fines of $50 per day. "I politely asked the Village to leave me in peace and let me do my gardening," Rickets told her local CBS affiliate, "but they refused to do that."[16] The couple, devastated, was forced to uproot the garden. "When our garden was in full production, we had no need to shop for produce," Rickets told the station. "At least 80 percent of our meals were harvested fresh from our garden. This law crushes our freedom to grow our own healthy food. No one should have to expend time and energy dealing with such nonsense." The couple fought back, suing the city in 2013.

Prohibitions on gardens such as those in Orlando, Tulsa, Newton,

Miami Shores, and elsewhere arise largely out of zoning regulations. Zoning, supporters contend, is intended to prevent conflicts and nuisances from arising. There's probably some truth to that argument. But sometimes, as in the case of the prohibitions on edible gardens detailed in this chapter, zoning itself *becomes* the nuisance and the source of conflict. In Orlando, for example, where Jason Helvenston raised his garden, the city admitted its zoning rules were too vague to charge Helvenston with violating the city code. But the specifics the city proposed as a fix to that code—including a rule that would confine annual crops to no more than 25 percent of a front yard—simply replaced untenable vagueness with indefensible arbitrariness. "We think 25 percent is more than sufficient to provide for kitchen gardening in the front-yard area," chief city planner Jason Burton said at a contentious hearing attended by what the *Orlando Sentinel* characterized as "[d]ozens of garden lovers."[17]

In the end, the real purpose of zoning is to protect property values. Because many owners and buyers prefer the look of a manicured lawn to that of an edible garden—just like USDA rules prefer the look of a perfectly symmetrical tomato to that of an "ugly" one—zoning rules tend to reflect those wishes. As the examples in this chapter suggest, change to those rules has been slow to come. But change is coming. In 2007, Sacramento, California, revised its zoning code to eliminate a ban on front-yard gardens.[18] In nearby Berkeley, the Ecology Center reported in 2010, city government laid plans to encourage residents to raise edible gardens.[19] That same year, Seattle lawmakers eased restrictions on a host of home-based agricultural practices.[20] But in cities such as Miami Shores, where Hermine Ricketts and her husband Tom Carroll have to deal with the "nonsense" underlying the city's ban, a court will decide the matter.

The alternative typically proffered by opponents of front-yard edible gardens—limiting your garden to your backyard only—ignores two very real issues. First, backyards can be imperfect—or even nonexistent. Those that do exist may be tiny, rocky, wooded, or otherwise unsuitable for gardening. Some people don't get enough sun in their backyards to grow fruits and vegetables, which require ample light to flourish. That was the problem faced by Helvenston and by Ricketts and Carroll. Second, lawns—the conventional choice for yard vegetation—typically use more water than do edible gardens. Estimates of water savings vary, but most sources agree that fruit and vegetable gardens use less water than would a lawn in a comparable space.[21] Those who want to live more sustainably often choose to grow some of their own food and find ways both to reduce their reliance on commercially bought food and lower their water use. Swapping out a lawn for an edible garden can help achieve both goals.

NIMB(OF)Y [Not in My Back (Or Front) Yard]

If zoning rules can pose serious challenges for those like Helvenston and Ricketts and others who want to raise edible gardens in their own yards, these challenges often pale when compared to those faced by people who want to raise yet another form of sustenance in their yards: livestock. Chickens—or, more specifically, egg-laying hens—have become the face of backyard livestock. Supporters of keeping backyard chickens note the birds are a prized addition to any yard, providing a regular source for fresh eggs and fertilizer and a natural means of controlling pests such as grubs.

Data show chicken ownership is growing. A 2013 USDA report, *Urban Chicken Ownership in Four U.S. Cities*, looked at the "growing phenomenon" of chicken ownership in Denver, Los Angeles, Miami, and New York City and their surrounding areas.[22] The report found that more than 4 percent of single-family homes in those cities with at least an acre of land raised chickens, and that another 4 percent of all households without chickens planned to begin raising them within the next five years. A 2010 report submitted to a Georgia town's planning commission, which was considering new rules to permit raising backyard chickens, declared that "the raising of backyard chickens yields several bona fide and scientifically demonstrable ways to open the eyes of the average citizen to the world of sustainable behaviors as it provides for a safe source of eating."[23] In 2014, the website BackyardChickens.com claimed to have more than 280,000 active users.[24] Chicken-ownership magazines such as *Backyard Poultry* and *Chickens* appear to be thriving.

Salt Lake City relaxed its rules for keeping backyard chickens in 2010, as part of its SLC Green initiative. The city appears pleased with the results. "Residential chickens benefit our community in a variety of ways while providing a sustainable, healthy and fun source of food," the city reported.[25]

Despite what the 2013 USDA report called a "growing acceptance of urban farming" in places like Salt Lake City, Seattle, and elsewhere, detractors lob a host of charges against chickens: they're unclean, smelly, and noisy.[26] Those charges don't stick. For example, cities and towns that permit the keeping of quiet egg-laying hens invariably—and rightly—prohibit raising noisy roosters, and have other rules in place to prohibit nuisances from disturbing neighbors.

Still, while the number of cities and towns that permit keeping chickens has expanded alongside growing demand, opponents still represent a formidable challenge to backyard chicken advocates. In Omaha, for example, backyard chickens have pitted neighbor against neighbor in a heated courtroom drama. "After a hearing Thursday in which one neighbor asked a judge to order the removal of the other neighbor's chickens from the woman's yard, attorneys for both neighbors refused to let their clients answer any questions," the *Omaha World-Herald* reported, somewhat incredulously. "About chickens."[27] Opposition isn't confined to metropolitan areas such as Omaha. Consider that in August 2015 alone, South Lyon, Michigan, a Detroit suburb, upheld its poultry ban, a Springfield Township, Pennsylvania family was fined for keeping chickens on their property, and the Waukegan, Illinois city council voted against an ordinance that would permit keeping chickens in the Chicago suburb.[28] These examples are just a sample of losses supporters of raising chickens sustained during that one summer month.

In 2012, a woman in Pekin, Illinois, a three-hour drive down I-55 from Waukegan, was forced to fight county officials who wouldn't permit her to raise livestock on her land because it was zoned as residential property.[29] The zoning rules stated that only homes of greater than twenty acres were permitted to raise so much as one chicken. As I described in a 2012 article, Kelli Otting's wish to raise chickens and goats at her one-acre home—located in a rural, unincorporated part of downstate Illinois—met strenuous opposition from the county land commission.[30] "I don't understand why a county would put restrictions so severe in place that homeowners couldn't use their property for a sustainable food supply," Otting said.[31]

Although egg-laying hens have become the face of the backyard livestock movement—bees get a good deal of buzz, too—people like Otting who wish to raise goats likely represent the next wave of possibilities for sustainability and local-food advocates seeking to raise more of their own food. The Nigerian Dwarf goat, a breed that grows no larger than two feet tall, is the most popular type of goat to raise at home.[32] A 2005 USDA report on emerging issues pertaining to goats noted the "potential" of Nigerian Dwarf goats as both dairy animals—they're "prolific milkers" and can produce four pounds of milk each day—and as pets. The agency was right. When that report was issued, according to subsequent USDA data, there were only about 1,000 Nigerian Dwarf goats born annually in the United States. As of 2012, that number had grown to nearly 7,000 births per year, and more than 37,000 purebred Nigerian Dwarf goats were calling the United States home.[33]

Some cities have responded to the growing demand for keeping goats by writing reasonably relaxed rules—permitting goats and often suggesting or even requiring that residents who want to raise goats choose dwarf varieties. San Diego's rules for keeping goats, adopted in 2012, list some of the benefits of keeping dwarf goats, the only type of goats the city allows to be raised.[34] In addition to San Diego, larger cities such as Berkeley, Cleveland, Fort Worth, Oakland, Pasadena, San Francisco, St. Louis, and St. Paul now allow residents to raise dwarf goats.[35] But—as with edible gardens and chickens—many cities and towns still prohibit raising goats. Some cities that have permitted backyard chickens, including Harlem, Georgia, still prohibit keeping goats.[36] Others take a less sanguine view of all livestock.

Visalia, California, zoning enforcement officials recently forced resident Gingi Freeman to send her Nigerian Dwarf goats, Idee and Eos, back to the breeder who had sold them to her. After a neighbor complained about Freeman's goats, the city moved swiftly to evict Idee and Eos. The city had threatened Freeman with a fine of up to $1,000 per day if she didn't comply with their order. The city's demand was based on a 1978 Visalia law that prohibits keeping livestock—including chickens, cows, and goats—in the city.[37]

Freeman had bought the goats to gain access to their milk, which she used to help feed her two young children. Freeman would feed her children with her own breast milk if she could, but she's unable to do so because of corrective surgery she had as a teenager. She could buy milk or formula, but the former is expensive—she chooses to eat only organic food—and the latter contains manmade ingredients she opposes. "If you have unlimited finances, or a good lactating friend who is an overproducer, sure," said Susan Walsh, a Visalia resident and advocate for goat legalization who reached out to me in spring 2015, after I asked her about why various alternatives won't work for Freeman and others.[38] "But with breast milk donations being hard to come by, and [with] raw organic goat milk costing [more than $30] per gallon in California, the steadiest and most affordable option is to raise your own food supply, where quality, cleanliness and sanitation [are] all in your own hands," Walsh told me. She explains why Freeman chose to raise and milk her own goats. "In the absence of breast milk, the only options for a mother [who is] unable to lactate [are] infant formula or goat milk," she said. "More than 90% of infant formulas sold in the United States use GMO based ingredients. . . . At the moment, the only goat milk available for purchase in Visalia, California is ultra pasteurized non-organic goat milk from big box stores like Walmart."

Goat milk seemed like the perfect solution for Freeman. It's nutritious and it doesn't contain additives and ingredients she doesn't want in her children's food. One irony is that if Freeman lived in a big city such as Seattle or San Diego, large cities that aren't known as agricultural hubs but which allow residents to raise goats in their yards, Idee and Eos wouldn't be an issue. But Freeman lives in the storied agricultural city of Visalia, which lies in California's fertile San Joaquin Valley. It's a region that's been called "the most productive agricultural region in the world."[39] Livestock are common in the area. Cattle, hay, and milk—livestock, livestock inputs, and livestock outputs, respectively—make up nearly one-quarter of the San Joaquin Valley area's enormous agricultural output. Visalia itself is home to a museum of agriculture.[40] The museum is shaped like a barn and even painted red to resemble one. The city has been touted as "the city that represents agriculture worldwide."[41] Yet a pair of tiny goats aren't welcome here?

Freeman found a host of allies in Visalia, and together they're fighting to legalize dwarf goats (and chickens) in the city. Supporters launched a website, ImProGoat.com, to make their case. And they've pushed for change before the city council. "We want to see . . . Freeman's goats returned, and for the City of Visalia to amend [its] outdated ordinances against small, useful and eco-friendly animals within city limits," Susan Walsh told me. "With thousands of supporters in Visalia, and thousands more nationwide, we have a fair chance of success provided citizens step up and speak out and demand change."[42]

On the issue of whether goats constitute a nuisance, pro-goat forces argue that female goats—the ones that produce milk, and the ones Freeman kept—don't smell. But they also point out that there's no need to ban goats, because existing laws can address any problems that might arise. "If a neighbor complains about an animal's odor—whether that animal is a dog, a cat, a rabbit or a miniature goat—the neighbor can appeal to the cit[y']s preexisting health and nuisance ordinances to have the issue resolved," Walsh told me.[43]

But that's not enough for the city or for Jerrold Jensen, a particularly outspoken opponent of backyard livestock in Visalia. Jensen highlighted—in a fist-shaking op-ed in the city newspaper—the growing tension in the city caused by what he calls "the illegal goat crisis."[44] Jensen appealed to fellow residents to uphold the city's "conservative family values" against the existential threat posed by goats, which he said would somehow remake Visalia to "look more like politically liberal San Francisco." But the pro-goat forces hardly sound like they're trying to overturn the values Jensen claims to uphold in Visalia. "[E]veryone has the inherent right to plant, reap and eat foods of their choosing on their private property," Walsh told me, echoing a traditional defense of property rights that should appeal to conservatives like Jensen.[45] And while Jensen's correct that San Francisco allows residents to raise goats, as do fellow liberal enclaves such as Berkeley and Seattle, voters in San Diego and Pasadena—which, remember, also permit raising goats—may be as staunch in their support of "conservative family values" as is Jensen. Put simply, issues of goats and gardening aren't about left or right. They're about right and wrong. Here and elsewhere in this book, you've seen evidence that a growing number of people who agree on very little when it comes to politics find common ground when it comes to people's rights around food.

After impassioned debate, the Visalia city council voted 3–2 against a measure that would have allowed residents to raise backyard chickens, and tabled any future discussion of allowing goats.[46] That's forced Freeman, Walsh, and their allies to gather signatures to push for a ballot measure that could allow city residents to raise livestock.[47]

So maybe you don't have a right to grow your own vegetables or to keep chickens or goats on your property. Those sustainable food practices can be banned. As you've seen, they often are. But what about the right to obtain milk from a cow you legally own? Surely *that's* always legal. According to a 2011 court ruling, it's not.[48] The ruling, issued by a Wisconsin state court, centered largely on the question of whether a farm in the state was operating as an unlicensed dairy. The farm, owned by Mark and Petra Zinniker, was providing unpasteurized (raw) milk to customers in the state. Wisconsin law prohibits all but "incidental" sale of raw milk anywhere in the state. But the farm wasn't selling raw milk. Rather, Zinniker Farm had implemented a herd share agreement with customers.[49]

Under a herd share agreement—or its close cousin, the cow share—a consumer buys an ownership stake in a farmer's cattle herd that grants the customer, as part owner of the cows, to obtain some of its milk. A 2009 *New York Times* piece on herd sharing noted the growing popularity of the practice.[50] According to the Farm-to-Consumer Legal Defense Fund (FTCLDF), a nonprofit group that advocates and litigates for the rights of small farmers and their customers, often in cases pertaining to raw milk, herd share agreements are legal in eight states.[51]

Despite the state ban, support for legalizing raw milk in Wisconsin is strong. The state legislature passed a law that would do so in 2010, but then-Governor Jim Doyle vetoed the bill.[52] With Wisconsin's governor siding against raw milk, Zinniker Farm was forced into a catch-22. It could apply for a license to operate as a dairy and to sell raw milk, but the state never would approve any application for a dairy that sells raw milk. And applying for a license would put the farm on the radar of state regulators, who don't look kindly on efforts to dance around the edges of state law.

Wisconsin's law is indeed vague. For example, the question of what constitutes "incidental" sales of raw milk under state law is very much at issue. Although the FTCLDF says sales are legal on the farm, the state has a very different take. "No," wrote the state agriculture department in response to a question it posted about whether a dairy farmer may sell raw milk legally in Wisconsin.[53] "The sale or distribution of raw or unpasteurized milk is illegal. The law exempts the 'incidental sale' of raw milk directly to a consumer at the dairy farm where the milk is produced, for consumption by that consumer (or the consumer's family or nonpaying guests). But those sales are also illegal if done as a regular business, or if they involve advertising of any kind."[54] Where is the line between incidental and regular sales? It's dangerously unclear for the state's farmers.

The Zinnikers' certified-organic farm, in business since 1943, is a model of sustainability. The owners claim it's the longest continuously operating biodynamic farm in the country. "Most of our land is used to grow pasture and hay, but a few acres are planted in corn, oats, barley, peas, and wheat to sustain the poultry and pigs," Zinniker Farm proudly proclaims.[55] "Our land enjoys a wide biodiversity of clovers, grasses, dandelions and specialty herbs, some of which the grazing animals eat directly and some that supply the organic plant material for our biodynamic preparations."

None of that mattered much to the Wisconsin state court, which ruled in August 2011 that herd share agreements were void in the state, and that the Zinnikers effectively had been operating a dairy without a required state permit.[56] That might have been the end of the case. If it had been, then the case might have had little to say about the subject of this chapter—rules that prohibit growing, raising, obtaining, and sharing sustainable food close to home. After all, Zinniker Farm is a farm business, and not just a home. But in light of the ruling by Wisconsin state judge Patrick J. Fiedler, the FTCLDF and the Zinnikers wanted more clarity. The FTCLDF had argued in its court filings that individuals like the Zinnikers and those involved in their herd share have a right to obtain milk from their own cow. Judge Fiedler hadn't addressed that issue in his August ruling. So the FTCLDF filed a motion asking the judge to issue a subsequent ruling on that question.[57]

Weeks later, Judge Fiedler issued an order to "clarify any confusion" that may have arisen in the wake of his original decision.[58] Although that earlier decision raised few eyebrows, his terse clarification—not even five pages long—caused outrage nationwide. Judge Fiedler explained, rather infamously, that a person does "not have a fundamental right to own and use a dairy cow." They "do not have a fundamental right to consume the milk from their own cow." They "do not have a fundamental right to produce and consume the foods of their own choice."[59] The FTCLDF had gotten clarity on the issue. And so had the people of Wisconsin and many others around the country who had learned about the case.

The Forager's Dilemma

Remember that "perfect meal" Michael Pollan prepared in *The Omnivore's Dilemma*? One of the key ingredients was foraged mushrooms. As he explains in the book, Pollan gathered his chanterelles in Eldorado National Forest, which is located about 150 miles northeast of San Francisco, along the border between California and Nevada. Eldorado offers a limited number of seasonal permits to gather mushrooms, at $20 each.[60] But most other parks in California—along with many others around the country—take a far more dubious view of foragers. In fact, the mere act of plucking a few berries from a perennial bush can result in a big fine.[61] Call it the forager's dilemma.

I'm neither a good nor a frequent forager. But I've been foraging badly, occasionally, for decades. My partner still teases me about the "strawberry" I picked, put in my mouth, bit into, and then spit out around the corner from our Washington, D.C., apartment in the mid-1990s. It resembled a strawberry, to be sure, but I knew strawberries weren't supposed to make my mouth tingle. Long before that incident, Roxanne had sworn off eating any food I picked up in a park or on the street. Maybe I'm more careful since, too. But I'll still take any opportunity to pick a handful of berries, fruits, herbs, chives, figs, mushrooms—or at least the hen of the woods variety my friend Anthony showed me how to identify, pick, clean, and sauté several years ago—and pretty much anything else I can eat on the spot or use in that night's dinner. I picked and ate as much as I could of the wild blueberries and rose hips I saw in Maine and the Canadian Maritime provinces during a recent summer trip with Roxanne and our friend Michael. I love visiting my barber in a busy part of Washington, D.C., during the summer because I know I can also pluck a few ripe figs from a mature tree growing in the alley around the corner from his shop (located adjacent to a nail salon and across from a 7-Eleven).

Such was the case in late June 2015, when, as Roxanne and I walked through a park near our suburban Maryland apartment, I happened upon a thicket of raspberries by the side of the road. We'd grown raspberries and blackberries in our Washington, D.C., victory garden years before, and had just bought some from our local farmers market, so identification wasn't an issue. Still, she was wary. But I dove right in, happily devouring a few of the ripest I saw—perfectly plump, sweet, and sour—before continuing our walk. I'd have forgotten all about my berry picking were it not for a Twitter search the next day. In my feed, I came across a tweet from a man who claimed to have been issued a $50 ticket for foraging berries in a park a mile or so from the site of my own foraging. Clearly, this had to be a mistake. Was my foraging somehow lawless? It turns out it was.

I reached out to the man who'd been fined, Greg Visscher, and asked to see a copy of his ticket. Sure enough, as the image Visscher sent me revealed, he'd received a $50 ticket for "destroying/interfering with plants to wit: berries. Without a permit on park property." Visscher told me he was picking raspberries in a public park—which he's been doing with his family for years—when an officer approached him.[62] Two more officers soon appeared. "They were friendly fellows but it was still pretty amazing to me that I was picking berries one minute and then surrounded by 3 cops the next," said Visscher. All this seemed like overkill for having picked a quart of berries.

Visscher told me he's been foraging since he was a boy in Michigan. "Foraging is just something people in the Midwest and Northwest just *do*," he said. "I never even thought of it as foraging—it was just a fun outing to go find some wild fruits to harvest because nobody else did and we knew the land would provide for us." He said his parents instilled in him a love of foraging and respect for nature. "My mother is from Iran—they don't have a concept of 'foraging' necessarily . . . it is just, go out into the mountains or wilderness and bring back what you can to make a meal with."[63]

Visscher listed the foods—mostly fruits, he said—that he and his family favor. They include blackberries, raspberries, wine berries, crab apples, wild peaches, and wild cherries. "But lately, I've also learned a lot of about edible plants like broad leaf plantain and 'poke salad,'" he told me. Visscher's family ate the fruits raw and also cooked with their harvest—from his mom's pies to her mom's jams and fruit breads. "It was always better this way—the fruit tasted remarkable," he said. With his wife, he's now carrying on the tradition. "My wife's family, who have lineage in Maryland and Washington, D.C., going back 200+ years, they will forage for poke salad and boil it and eat it just like boiled kale," Visscher told me. "Or they will get blackberries and make preserves and jam out of it."[64]

The fact that Visscher's wife's family has been foraging in the area for centuries makes his ticket all the more bizarre. The rationale behind the ticket is also inexplicable. "Essentially, they are lumping in the 'picking of berries' with destruction or removal of park property," Visscher said. "It is ludicrous." He said the police made reference to a need to obtain a nebulous "permit" for harvesting berries, a permit that appears not to exist. "There is no sign anywhere saying that berries cannot be harvested," said Visscher. "To my knowledge, there is nothing in the park that even highlights this."[65] Maryland law does say, though, that any such prohibition must be posted conspicuously at park offices. I visited the park where Visscher received his ticket and found no such posting, nor any park employee who could explain whether foraging in the park is permitted. Lt. Rick Pelicano, of the county park police, informed me that it was indeed a punishable offense to pick even one berry in a public park in Montgomery County, thanks to the aforementioned prohibition on "destroy[ing] or interfer[ing] in any way with any . . . plants" on public property.[66] Lt. Pelicano told me such fines are rare. In 2014, Pelicano told me, the park service issued only two fines like the one Visscher received.

Rare or not, as interest in foraging has grown, efforts to rein in the practice are also on the rise. In 2013, a *Chicago Tribune* columnist detailed the story of "an old man barely making it on Social Security" who was ticketed $75 for picking dandelion greens in a Chicago park.[67] The man punished for voluntarily weeding in the park, John Taris, had picked the greens to make a salad for himself and his wife. New York City cracked down on foraging in Central Park in 2011 amid concerns the park couldn't sustain the growing number of people making off with ginger, mushrooms, and even fish.[68] Unlike the cases of Visscher and Taris, this latter example appears reasonable. Ginger and mushrooms are fragile, and a relatively small park in the midst of more than ten million people is far less likely to be resilient in the face of foraging than is an expansive suburban or rural park space. Another example of unsustainable and damaging foraging has arisen in California's Salt Point State Park, which—along with Michael Pollan's Eldorado—is one of two public lands in the state that permits foraging. There, reports NPR, "mushroom hunters sometimes carve new trails into the forest, trample small plants, and illegally use rakes and shovels to turn over the forest floor in search of young, budding mushrooms, according to [park ranger Todd] Farcau. Some, he adds, leave trash piles by the road and toilet paper in the woods."[69]

Although there may be some gray areas, it's not terribly difficult to distinguish between sustainable foraging, in which an individual such as Taris, Visscher, or Pollan harvests berries, nuts, fruits, seaweed, greens, or some other renewable resource for their personal consumption, and foraging that involves real destruction of flora, fauna, or public property. These latter practices should be banned. But the former should be encouraged. Blackberry bushes are practically begging passersby to pick their berries. Mushrooms don't mind a bit if you to pick them so long as you don't drag a rake around and destroy their habitat in the process.

In his fascinating book *Crimes Against Nature*, Columbia University historian Prof. Karl Jacoby explores the ways that traditional practices such as foraging have been criminalized in our nation's parks.[70] He describes, for example, how foraging for ginseng, berries, herbs, and other wild plants—along with hunting—helped form the basis of the economy and food stores of many of those living in the Adirondack region of New York in the nineteenth century. The push to protect the land came not from those living sustainably in the region but from outsiders. The move to restrict hunting and foraging in the region, embodied in the creation in the 1890s of the Adirondack Park, wrote Prof. Jacoby, came about in large part of "a distrust of the inhabitants of the countryside, particularly the small-scale farmers who made up the bulk of the residents in places like the Adirondacks." Elitist outsiders saw these residents, wrote Jacoby, as "lacking the foresight and expertise necessary to be wise stewards of the natural world."[71]

I spoke about foraging laws, including Visscher's case, with Iso Rabins in San Francisco, a leading forager I've known for several years. You may recall Rabins from chapter 1, where he starred in helping lead the successful fight against a California law that required chefs and bartenders to wear disposable latex gloves. Rabins's activism carries over to his day job. He runs Forage SF, where he organizes foraging tours for abalone, mushrooms, seaweed, and other wild foods and sponsors dinners where these foraged foods are served. Rabins told me that it's "usually illegal to pick anything in a park unless specifically permitted. Often berries are permitted, but again, [it] varies."[72]

Rabins has been foraging for years. "I forage because I like it," he told me.[73] "I like the way it connects me with the place I live, and gets me out into the wilderness (or at least into the city parks), and that's why I try to introduce it to other people too. When you start to forage you begin to have a better relationship with the natural world around you, something I think we could all use a bit of." Rabins forages in plenty of idyllic spots. He told me he dives for abalone and spearfishes in Sonoma. He gathers morel mushrooms in the same Sierra Nevada mountains where Pollan foraged for chanterelles. Rabins gathers edible flowers nearer the Bay Area. And he grabs seaweed anywhere it drifts along the coast. Some of his foraging spots are far less scenic. Rabins told me he's also foraged under bridges, along roadsides, and behind convenience stores.

Despite his concern for and close relationship with the natural world, early on Rabins drew the ire of some environmentalists, who opposed any commercial foraging. But as Rabins's work and belief system have become better known, those concerns seem to have faded. In 2010, the *San Francisco Bay Guardian* called Rabins a "local hero" thanks to "his ability to communicate his vision of feeding communities without the agro-industrial machine—by recognizing the soil-generated bounty available to all of us if we know where to look."[74] A 2012 profile of Rabins by the Sierra Club touted his work as both "eco-friendly" and "gourmet."[75]

If many environmentalists and others today view Rabins as a gallant sustainable forager, many regulators view him as an outlaw. Rabins isn't immune to facing fines like those Visscher received. And if Rabins's name sounds familiar, that may be because he made news when his beloved Underground Market was shut down by local and state regulators in 2011.[76] The *New York Times* called him "charismatic" and "scruffy."[77] He's both. And Rabins is seemingly as resilient as the foods he obtains from the wild, as I learned when we first met that year.

A *San Francisco Weekly* profile of Rabins in 2009 said his dogged pursuit of the foods in our midst raised no less than the existential question of how foraging, "one of humans' most elemental and ancient activities—finding and eating food in the places we inhabit," had become so problematic.[78] Rabins told me the same is still true. "Currently foraging is pretty much illegal across the board," he said, noting that foraging tends to be banned unless expressly permitted. That doesn't prevent foraging, though. Rather, it simply drives it underground—sometimes, he said, with disastrous consequences. "What this does is encourage people to forage illegally, to hoard spots and when they find a spot to take as much as they can," he said. "These policies are of course in place because the parks service imagines if they legalized it all the plants would be gone. I personally think this is ridiculous, and that open, legal, well-educated foraging only adds to the stewardship and use of our parks."[79]

Sustainable foraging, of the sort practiced by Michael Pollan, Greg Visscher, Rabins, and even—from time to time—me, should be encouraged. "Foraging sustainably for me is knowing what I can take and where without adversely [a]ffecting the future of the resource," Rabins told me. "So in one spot that might mean filling up a bag with seaweed, and in another it might mean just taking a handful. Being familiar with the places you forage, as well as the techniques for collecting individual species[,] is the most important thing. With that said I think the fears of city parks being picked bare by hipster foragers are a bit overblown. People who forage are by nature more concerned/aware of the natural world than most, and have the most interest in preserving the resource."[80] It's interesting to note that Rabins, a self-described independent Democrat, and Visscher, a Republican, agree about the parameters of sustainable foraging. "We always take care of the plants we harvest from—we want the resource to return the next year and the year after that," Visscher told me. "We aren't interested in just pillaging the plant one time or taking everything in one sitting. It is a sustainable harvest. And of course, we realize it is on potentially 'public' grounds and that someone else might beat us to it! That's part of the fun!"[81]

Sensible limits do exist in some parks, such as those that issue permits and limit them by number or season, including Eldorado. Others have instituted lottery systems.[82] These restrictions make sense when demand outstrips supply. Visscher agrees. "I would support some intelligent limits on foraging for fruit or a quickly-replenished plant/mushroom or food source only where the data clearly shows that people are harvesting too much and the ecosystem and plant life is being destroyed," Visscher said. "I do not think it should be legal to chop down a tree for firewood—that tree might take 20, 30 years to grow. But a berry is going to come back, hopefully, year after year. As long as that berry bush or mushroom spot isn't being completely pillaged and stripped of everything, I see no reason why the public can't enjoy it."[83]

Although I've had the misfortune to see trees chopped down for firewood while on hiking and camping trips along the C&O Canal National Park in Maryland, much foraging in the state, where Visscher was ticketed, hasn't reached the level of pillaging and stripping, according to a 2009 National Park Service report on mushroom foraging.[84] Although the state imposed smart restrictions on ginseng harvesting after wild populations of the root plummeted, berries aren't threatened.[85] In fact, the report indicates that Visscher's berry foraging—and my own—would likely have been allowed in other area parks. The National Park

Service report focuses on discrepancies such as this. The C&O Canal Park, which stretches from Washington, D.C., for more than 180 miles into far-western Maryland, for example, has the most liberal policies of the three parks discussed in the report. "Edible fruits, nuts, berries, and mushrooms may be gathered by hand for personal use or consumption," the report states. "Commercial use is prohibited. Removal of fruits, nuts, berries, and mushrooms cannot disturb the remainder of the plant." Catoctin Mountain Park in Maryland, a fantastic hiking area that borders the presidential retreat at Camp David, is slightly more fickle. In 2006, the report indicated, the park allowed visitors to remove "small amounts" of berries or mushrooms. That nebulous limit changed to "less than one gallon" the next year, and changed again in 2008, when the rules changed to "less than one gallon" of berries but no more than one-half gallon of mushrooms. But Rock Creek Park—which stretches from the heart of Washington, D.C., to its northernmost center, right along the District's border with Maryland—bars visitors from taking any "fruits, nuts, berries, seeds, [and] mushrooms . . . for personal or business use or consumption."[86]

These parks are nearby one another. And yet the rules change from park to park, and even from year to year within the same park. Indeed, rules seem to vary almost haphazardly, something the report noted. "This confusion generates resentment and causes some local residents to avoid the parks altogether," it stated.[87] Visscher echoes the National Park Service. "I'm actually of the mindset that underutilized park land should be put to good use: namely sustainable food production!" he said. "These berry bushes bring people out to the park. I thought that was the whole point!" Visscher's right. Thankfully, around the time I was completing this book, a judge dismissed Visscher's ticket after the county was unable to support its claim that picking berries in a county park requires a permit.[88]

Although public parks can, should, and sometimes do promote

responsible foraging, another relatively untapped area for foraging on public lands is subject to a host of restrictions. This type of foraging is also far more likely to raise the so-called "ick factor": harvesting roadkill. Roadkill is a widespread problem.[89] Millions of animals are killed on America's roads every week. For some, foraging roadkill is seen as a way to eat sustainably. The *Ecologist*, a British environmental journal, reported in 2012 that a growing number of Brits were turning to roadkill as an alternative to eating animals that were raised for food.[90] "Aficionados claim that roadkill is a cheap and ecologically sustainable source of fresh meat, both nutritious and, if you can swallow it, delicious too," wrote *Ecologist* blogger Ben Martin. Even PETA, the animal rights group, urges people who want to eat meat to choose roadkill.[91]

Journalist Jane Eastoe's excellent book *Wild Food*, which centers on responsible foraging and preparation of foraged foods, devotes an entire chapter to roadkill.[92] Eastoe called the "highway supermarket . . . a real test of our commitment to eating wild food." Recognizing that a deer, boar, or squirrel found lifeless along a roadway could sicken the human who chooses to eat it, Eastoe suggested several visual and olfactory cues for weeding out dangerous carrion. She also provided helpful cooking tips for pheasant, pigeon, and rabbit. Eating roadkill has even caught the eye of scholars. In a 2004 article on roadkill as food, author Mike Michaels said eating roadkill "mediates contradictions and ironies in American identities concerned with hunting, technology, and relationships to nature."[93]

Those American ironies also include prohibitions on foraging roadkill. A 2012 Associated Press report indicated that at least fourteen states have some laws permitting the harvesting of roadkill.[94] Many of the three-dozen remaining states either don't have rules or have laws that ban the practice. Nevada, one such state, has threatened to lob poaching charges at anyone foraging for roadkill.[95] Texas also bans harvesting roadkill.[96] California is another such state, as writer Catherine

Price recounted in a 2011 article in *Slate* that focused on the events that transpired after she hit and killed a rabbit with her car. "This rabbit was wild, grass-fed, and presumably antibiotic- and artificial hormone-free," wrote Price.[97] "Except for the car that had hit it, no food miles had been accrued delivering it to us. So why not bring it home for dinner?" And so she did.

Movement to allow foraging for roadkill has grown in recent years. Montana lifted its ban on harvesting roadkill in 2013. The law requires residents to obtain a free permit to harvest any roadkill. Residents must take the whole animal—both to remove it as a potential obstacle for other drivers and to keep other animals that might eat it (and themselves fall prey to traffic) out of the roadway. The law has been a tremendous success. In the first year after the ban, Montanans harvested more than 700 dead deer, 100 elk, 30 moose, and 5 antelope from state roadsides. "It really exceeded my expectations," said Montana state Rep. Steve Lavin, who sponsored the bill, in comments to *The Daily Inter Lake*.[98] "People seemed to really take advantage of the bill, and it is cool to see that it helped a lot of people." A few states have followed suit. Michigan relaxed its roadkill laws, also in 2014.[99] Wisconsin did the same in 2015.[100] Colorado, Florida, Illinois, West Virginia, and Georgia also have laws permitting the harvesting of roadkill.[101]

But if roadkill laws are slowly moving in the right direction, another set of laws—those that govern sharing food with people in need—is moving in exactly the opposite direction. These laws may be the cruelest and worst rules you'll see anywhere in this book.

Shackling the Food Samaritans

Sometimes, food donated to those in need is food that would otherwise go to waste. But even if it wouldn't go to waste, there may be no better (or more sustainable, in the literal sense of the word) use for food than to share it with those in need. Beginning in the mid-2000s, though, many cities around the country began to crack down on good Samaritans—let's call them "food Samaritans"—who provide food to the homeless and less fortunate. In one of the first such cases, Nevada's American Civil Liberties Union (ACLU) chapter sued the city of Las Vegas over that city's ban on sharing food with the homeless.[102] That ban imposed steep penalties—including a $1,000 fine and up to six months in jail—for anyone caught giving away food in public to more than a handful of people without a permit. "When the ACLU of Nevada took issue with this interpretation of permit laws, the City took a more direct approach: it explicitly outlawed the sharing of food with anyone who looked poor," the group reported in announcing a pending settlement with the city in 2010, after years of litigation.[103] Orlando also banned sharing food with the homeless in 2006.[104] A lawsuit there failed, and the city has since arrested activists who've practiced civil disobedience and continued their charitable work. Dallas's ban, passed in 2005, was challenged by a lawsuit soon after.[105] The law was overturned seven years later.

What kind of a city—*what kind of a human being*—would tell others that they couldn't share food with those in need? Unfortunately, today many cities across the country—including many of the nation's largest cities—have followed the lead of Las Vegas, Orlando, and Dallas, wrongly believing they have both the need and the authority to prevent food Samaritans from aiding those in need. Houston passed a ban in 2012.[106] New York City, under then-mayor Michael Bloomberg, banned many food donations to the homeless there in 2012 "because the city can't assess their salt, fat and fiber content"—as if grams of fiber is a chief concern of hungry people.[107] Philadelphia passed its own ban that same year. In 2014, Birmingham, Alabama barred a local pastor from sharing food with the homeless from a church-owned vehicle because he didn't have a food truck permit.[108] A chef in San Antonio was fined in 2015 for sharing restaurant-quality food with the homeless there without a permit.[109]

I spoke with Jay Hamburger, who's been feeding hundreds of people in Houston every week for more than twenty-five years, about his work and about his city's terrible policies toward sharing food with those in need. Like many people, Hamburger occasionally donated food to those in need over the years. He moved to Thanksgiving feasts, he told me, and eventually "committed to a weekly feast on the streets, quickly growing to cooking for and serving about 200."[110] Today, volunteers drop the food off at Hamburger's home, and he takes it to the streets to those in need.

Hamburger is known on those streets as the "Eggman," a nickname he earned decades ago after he started serving fifteen-dozen hard-boiled eggs each week. In a 2007 profile in the *Houston Chronicle*, Hamburger describes how—for him—sharing food with those in need is about much more than just handing out eggs. "Some people think, it's just an egg," he told the paper.[111] "But to Hamburger it's about the intent, the idea that humans understand the love and care behind a token of affection, the idea that give-and-take is more about the connection forged between two humans than it is about the physical exchange."

Houston's crackdown on sharing food with those in need dates to spring 2012, when Mayor Annise Parker pushed through what Hamburger said was billed as an emergency measure to protect the homeless. Hamburger told me the real emergency was plans "to 'erase' the homeless from civilized areas" at a time when the city was trying to gentrify parts of downtown and open a new soccer stadium.[112] The ordinance, which comes with the prospect of a $2,000 fine and jail time, has had a measurable impact. "There is less food available," he said, "and the homeless suffer increasingly."

Hamburger said he believes he has a legal and ethical duty to continue his work. "No government has a right to interfere with or intercede in my otherwise legal right to express myself through my generosity," he told me. But he's also sensitive to arguments that sharing food with those in need causes litter to be concentrated in a particular area, such as a public park. "I have no defense of littering," he said, "that is unless the government fails to provide proper waste containers and materials where people are expected to gather. This is no different from the area where an outdoor concert is given for the affluent. Humans are wont to litter and the homeless should not be held to a higher standard than we expect of the Inside People," his term for those of us with roofs over our heads.[113]

Hamburger isn't just fighting the city policy on the streets. He's pushing back politically, too. He gathered and submitted 10,000 signatures in 2013 in support of his efforts. When the city balked at taking action, he redoubled his efforts and collected 70,000 new signatures, which he submitted in summer 2015, in an effort to force the city to put the issue before voters. Among his supporters, Hamburger told me, he counts a leading civil rights attorney, a handful of city councilors, members of Food Not Bombs—the group whose members have been arrested for sharing food in Orlando—and a coalition of faith-based organizations and nonprofits. Hamburger also has powerful enemies. Those who support the ban include the mayor and most of the city council, developers, and many groups that also serve the homeless. Hamburger said, disappointedly, that these ban supporters "know that we serve the tattered ends of the population which they fail to reach."[114]

As this chapter has made clear, the broader lesson from *Wickard v. Filburn*—that Americans do not have an inalienable right to grow, make, procure, use, or share their own food—has been repeated and strengthened in the decades since the decision, time and again. Although the *Filburn* case centered on wheat, subsequent rules and court decisions have made clear that the rule holds for all foods you might grow, raise, forage, share, or obtain from the land—including everything from milk to berries to tomatoes. *Even water.*

A 2013 report by the National Conference of State Legislatures found only a dozen states had laws that allowed residents to harvest rainwater on their own property.[115] One of those states, Colorado, had banned the practice until 2009. A *New York Times* piece on the new law highlighted Tom Bartels of southwestern Colorado, who, the paper reported, had "been illegally watering his vegetables and fruit trees from tanks attached to his gutters."[116]

Ultimately, if a person has the interest and passion to seek a more sustainable lifestyle—to opt out of many commercial transactions and to grow, raise, produce, or otherwise obtain food with their own hands, on their own terms—rules still exist that can make that difficult or impossible. If the earlier chapters of this book showed the hardships sustainable producers and consumers face on a daily basis while engaging in food commerce, the present chapter has demonstrated that those who go it on their own often fare even worse. If food-safety rules prevent you from buying raw milk in the marketplace, for example, you're just as likely to find that another set of rules doesn't permit you to raise your own milking goat at home.

Whether at home or in the marketplace, the situation may appear bleak for supporters of sustainable food. But all is not lost. In fact, while there are many terrible food rules on the books, as you've seen, there are also some excellent ones. We need more of them. In the next chapter, you'll learn more about these good food rules—what they do, who they affect, and how they came to be—and see how their bipartisan appeal and recent spread bodes well for the future of food and sustainability alike.

CHAPTER 5

There Are Good Food Rules

ARE THERE GOOD FOOD RULES, as the title of this chapter suggests? Indeed, such rules do exist. For example, early on in this book I endorsed food-safety rules that punish those whose food sickens or kills people. I also endorsed some inspections and testing—to make sure food doesn't do that in the first place. In addition to inspection and testing by agencies such as the FDA and USDA—of the sort, for example, that salumi crafted by Mark DeNittis and Il Mondo Vecchio were subjected to (and passed)—smart rules require employee hand washing. They mandate that food sellers keep potentially hazardous foods—such as raw meat—at temperatures below 40°F. They require warning labels on foods that are more likely to sicken consumers—from raw meat to sprouts to raw milk. Concerns over sustainability play little or no role in such rules. And they shouldn't. Food-safety rules shouldn't care one bit whether or not the guilty party was a sustainable food producer. Leading food-safety lawyer Bill Marler, whom you met in chapter 1, is an equal-opportunity litigator, suing violators of all types and sizes. "To me it is very straightforward," he told me, of every food company's responsibility, regardless of size, to "do everything you can do to produce food that will not kill your customer."[1] I—and readers of this book, I suspect—agree with that statement.

Beyond the importance of rules that prohibit making and selling food that kills people, there's room for rules—good ones—that do take into account and even embrace sustainable food practices. Other good rules, as I describe later in this chapter, prohibit practices that are wholly unsustainable. First, though, let's consider the smart food rules that embrace sustainability. Oftentimes, they are newer ones that permit sustainable practices that were previously banned. Consider rules, such as those in Seattle and San Diego—discussed in chapter 4—that permit residents to keep chickens and goats in their yards. Or federal rules—such as those discussed in chapter 1—that allow brewers to donate or sell spent grains to farmers. What these rules and others like them share is that they are designed to facilitate sustainable practices that people are already engaging in, or are very much inclined to engage in. The rules—as they should—let people choose to live more sustainably. One distinguishing characteristic of these rules, as you'll see in this chapter, is that they frequently enjoy bipartisan support.

Often, these rules seek to rectify many of the issues raised by the bad rules you've read about in this book. In chapter 1, you learned about food-safety rules that needlessly harm sustainable food producers and their customers. In chapter 2, you read about rules that encourage less sustainable food practices, and discourage more sustainable ones. Chapter 3 discussed a host of different rules that promote food waste. And chapter 4 focused on rules that prevent people from using traditional practices to make, obtain, and provide food outside the commercial mainstream.

Examples of food rules that cast an eye to sustainability exist in each of these areas. First, let's look at food safety. In recent years, three different bipartisan efforts around the country—one local, one statewide, and one federal—have sought to push back against decades of increasingly strict food-safety rules that have hit sustainable food producers particularly hard. The first of these rules to pass, part of a movement dubbed "food sovereignty," is now on the books in more than fifteen small towns in Maine.[2] One reason for the growing number of such laws in the state, as NPR reported in 2013, is that a state exemption for poultry producers who sell less than $1,000 per year of chicken contained a host of food-safety requirements that "would cost a poultry farmer some $30,000 to $40,000 to implement."[3] Show me a farmer who spends $30,000 to sell $1,000 worth of food and I'll show you a farmer who's out of business. Food sovereignty ordinances sought to address the absurdities of laws like these.

"We recognize that family farms, sustainable agriculture practices, and food processing by individuals, families and noncorporate entities offers stability to our rural way of life by enhancing the economic, environmental and social wealth of our community," reads the first such law, passed in 2011 in Sedgwick, population 1,196.[4] Food sovereignty laws such as these seek to let farmers sell foods they produced—including raw milk, pasta, and poultry—directly to consumers without subjecting farmers to the usual tangle of federal and state food-safety laws. Although I've argued in support of these laws, I've also recognized that they're more aspirational—akin to when Key West "seceded" from the United States in the early 1980s to form the Conch Republic—than they are binding. Either the FDA or a state such as Maine at any time is free to punish anyone who opts out of any food-safety rules. That happened in 2014, in fact, when Maine's Supreme Court ruled that one town's food-sovereignty ordinance did not protect resident dairy farmer Dan Brown against complying with Maine's food-safety laws.[5] Food sovereignty laws haven't spelled the end of overly burdensome state or FDA food-safety rules. But the visionary Maine rules and their supporters have succeeded in capturing and giving voice to the frustration inherent in many farming communities around the state and the country over draconian food-safety rules.

That voice has resonated across the country. In 2015, Wyoming lawmakers passed the nation's first Food Freedom Act. The new law, which is intended "to encourage the expansion of agricultural sales by farmers markets, ranches, farms" and others, passed with bipartisan support.[6] The law does what Maine's local food-sovereignty ordinances could not: change a state law and legalize many heretofore illegal sustainable food production and sales. Those straight-from-the-farm raw milk, pasta, and poultry sales that are still illegal in Maine, even in the wake of food sovereignty rules, are now legal in Wyoming. That's quite a change in the state. Before the law, Wyoming's local food economy had been one of the most tightly regulated in the nation, reported Wyoming PBS in the wake of passage of the new law.[7]

Wyoming State Rep. Tyler Lindholm (R), who cosponsored the bill with a Democratic colleague, said the Food Freedom Act is meant to foster many goals, including nutrition, support for local foods, and individual freedom. "This legislation is literally a game changer for Agriculture in Wyoming," he told me in 2015.[8] Lindholm and his wife raise beef cattle on their ranch. Thanks to draconian USDA rules for cattle slaughter and beef processing that I discussed in chapter 1 of this book, though, Wyoming's Food Freedom Act doesn't have the power to turn over the regulation of cattle slaughter and processing to the state. That's because, under the U.S. system of government, federal rules usually trump conflicting state rules, just like state rules generally trump conflicting local rules—as you saw in the case of Maine's local food-sovereignty rules failing to survive a challenge from the state. But Lindholm and his Wyoming colleagues still hope to see change soon. "The sale of processed meat, except poultry, is not allowed under the Food Freedom Act," Lindholm told me. "We have to find a workable solution to this issue and you can expect to see legislation in the future dealing with this issue so that ranchers and farmers can also sell beef and pork directly to consumers also. This is just the beginning."[9]

Though Lindholm probably didn't know it at the time, he was right. Food freedom legislation has been introduced in other states, including Utah and Colorado.[10] And just months after Wyoming's Food Freedom Act took effect, bipartisan efforts to rein in the USDA's stranglehold on local meat production began in another legislative body clear across the country. This time, the U.S. Congress has taken up the issue. The Processing Revival and Intrastate Meat Exemption Act, or PRIME Act, would allow states to make their own rules for processing meat that's sold entirely within state borders.[11] The bipartisan bill was introduced by Rep. Thomas Massie (R-KY) and Rep. Chellie Pingree (D-ME) and cosponsored by Reps. Justin Amash (R-MI), John Garamendi (D-CA), Scott Garrett (R-NJ), Jared Huffman (D-CA), and Jared Polis (D-CO). Sen. Rand Paul (R-KY) and Sen. Angus King (I-ME) have introduced a companion bill in the Senate.[12]

Local meat processing used to be the norm. Congress granted the USDA jurisdiction over commercial meat slaughter and processing only in 1967. Since that time, a dramatic consolidation in slaughter and processing has taken place nationwide. "Consolidation toward larger plants led to sharply increased concentration in cattle slaughter and persistent concerns over the future of competition in that industry," reads a USDA report released in 2000.[13] As chapter 1 of this book describes, a shortage of USDA-approved processing facilities and the USDA rule that says only meat processed at USDA-approved slaughterhouses may be sold commercially anywhere in the United States have served to strangle the supply of meat from small farmers at a time when demand for sustainably raised meats has risen dramatically. "USDA regulations effectively force consumers who want to support small-scale, local farmers to buy meat that's been processed in the same large slaughterhouses that larger competitors use," I wrote in 2014.[14] "Consequently, consumers who don't want to support large-scale agriculture have few, if any, ways to opt out of that USDA-supported system." The bill cosponsored by Reps.

Massie, Pingree, Polis, and others in Congress would help states like Wyoming, Maine, Colorado, Kentucky, and others around the country permit their farmers—and you—to opt out. Passage of this law would improve the fabric of America's meat landscape dramatically.

Another set of rules has opened up new markets for sustainable food producers to respond to growing consumer demand in other areas. These rules address the imbalance detailed in chapter 2 of this book, in which food rules tend to favor the largest producers over the smallest ones, and to prevent embryonic food startups from flourishing. This new set of good food rules has begun to level the playing field for many very small food entrepreneurs around the country. These new rules permit home-based food startups to make and sell foods that pose few—if any—food-safety risks to the buying public. Known as "cottage food" laws, they are now found in nearly every state.

Some of the main obstacles faced by food startups are zoning rules, the time and costs of obtaining licenses and permits, and the costs and difficulty of complying with the near-universal requirement that any food prepared for sale must be made in a commercial kitchen. Cottage food laws eliminate the need for commercial kitchen space and reduce some or all of the other barriers. They permit home-based food entrepreneurs to sell low-risk foods such as many baked goods, spice mixtures, teas, and jams. Although state laws vary, states may permit sales from the home, at farmers markets, online, and even to restaurants. Most establish a cap on the dollar amount a seller may make in a given year.[15] Predictably, there are no cottage food giants.

Denver, Colorado recently changed its zoning rules to allow the sale not just of cottage foods but also homegrown produce. "Among the expected benefits of the new regulations are expanded access to affordable foods, particularly in those communities considered 'food deserts,' and community-building through increased neighbor-to-neighbor interactions," read a city 2014 announcement on the new rules.[16] "The change will also help meet the city's sustainability goals by reducing the distance that food travels from farm to table, and will help to create supplemental income opportunities for families seeking greater economic self-sufficiency." Although some cottage food laws are still too strict—for example, setting a cap on the amount of money a seller may earn so low as to discourage their participation in the marketplace—as a whole these rules give sustainably minded food entrepreneurs new ways to provide like-minded consumers with more of the foods they want.

While chapter 2 detailed ways that food rules often favor large producers, in chapter 3 you learned that restaurants, grocers, and convenience stores of all sizes generate nearly 75,000 tons of food waste every year at a time when many Americans are hungry. Offering incentives to restaurants, farms, and others to help feed hungry Americans while also reducing food waste—an approach I proposed to help improve school lunches—seems like a great idea that could earn bipartisan support. In fact, that's just what happened in 2015. A bill in the U.S. Senate, the Good Samaritan Hunger Relief Act of 2015, was cosponsored by Sen. Patrick Leahy (D-VT), Sen. Bob Casey (D-PA), Sen. Thad Cochran (R-MS), Sen. John McCain (R-AZ), Sen. Debbie Stabenow (D-MI), and Sen. Roy Blunt (R-KS). "This bipartisan bill would benefit food banks and hunger charities around the nation," said Sen. McCain, in a statement touting the bill.[17] "At its core, the bill would provide tax incentives for small and medium business who donate food or resources to food banks. This means restaurants, farms, and other food providers can do even more in their local communities to help fight hunger." Many Republican House members also supported a similar bill in that chamber.[18]

Organic Authority lauded what it called a "progressive food waste bill."[19] Feeding America, the nation's largest anti-hunger group, threw its support behind the bill, which would make permanent some temporary, existing tax breaks for food donation.[20] "Because of the uncertainty surrounding the current food-donation tax deduction, some potential donors destroy or dump food, or use it as animal feed, instead of giving it to their local food bank" said Bob Aiken, CEO of Feeding America, in announcing his group's support for the measure. "This is a waste of the nutrient value of the food, as well as the environmental resources invested in its production."[21] Aiken knows of what he speaks. In 2014, Feeding America recovered and used more than two billion pounds of edible food that would have otherwise ended up in landfills or plowed under in fields.

Despite bipartisan support in the Senate, Republican support in the House, and support from anti-hunger and food-waste opponents, Democrats in the House opposed the measure. Rep Jim McGovern (D-MA) said he opposed the bill because it wasn't part of a larger strategy around hunger and because it would add millions to the federal deficit.[22] The White House threatened to veto the bill, issuing a statement that said the Obama administration "strongly opposes" the bill on budgetary grounds.[23] A similar bill had failed to pass the previous year. In fact, this latest attempt represented the *fifth time* in recent years that a similar measure had failed to pass.[24] It's not for a lack of support outside of Washington, D.C. In 2014, for example, more than 850 nonprofit organizations of all ideological stripes wrote to Congress urging passage of the law.[25] "Without an incentive in place and assured, many of the gifts the charitable incentives were intended to promote will simply not take place," the groups wrote.[26]

The bad news is that the Good Samaritan Hunger Relief Act of 2015 never became law. The great news is that another bill—the PATH Act—did become law in 2015.[27] And that bill, which President Obama signed into law in December, effectively did what the Good Samaritan Act was intended to do. After years of failing to encourage food donations and reduce food waste while passing other costly measures that *promote* food waste, Congress finally made the right decision.

Indeed, sometimes Congress *does* get it right. While chapter 3 focused on rules that promote food waste in the commercial sphere, chapter 4 focused on rules that prevent people from making, obtaining, and providing food outside the commercial realm. There, you learned about awful rules that prohibit people from sharing food with those in need. Although terrible local bans on the practice do exist, one excellent federal law stands out for facilitating the efforts of many who wish to share food with those in need. The Bill Emerson Good Samaritan Act, signed into law by President Bill Clinton in 1996, is a bipartisan law that protects charitable individuals against liability for most food donations.[28] The law is named after the late Rep. Bill Emerson (R-MO), a leading anti-hunger advocate in Congress until his death in 1996, shortly before the law's passage.[29] The Emerson Act protects charitable persons, including gleaners—those who take unwanted produce from farms and provide it to those in need—from liability for any illness that donated food might cause. The law rightly protects food donors so long as they were not grossly negligent or did not commit a crime in the process (such as by intentionally tainting food).

Like the PATH Act and the other good food laws discussed so far in this chapter, the Bill Emerson Good Samaritan Act is a smart, bipartisan set of rules that facilitates sustainable food practices that might otherwise be illegal (or needlessly disincentivized) without such laws. All of these good food rules leave people free to engage in more sustainable food practices.

Although concerns over sustainability are at the heart of many of these rules, sometimes good food rules help minimize the environmental impact of food production and sales without any concern for sustainability. Take the example of loosening the regulatory burden on food trucks, as Washington, D.C. has done in recent years. In the nation's capital, long-standing rules required most food trucks to be in constant motion. The particular rule was so antiquated that it was known as the "ice cream truck rule," a reference to the roving ice cream trucks that play jingles as they approach public parks to catch the ear of children in search of a cold Pavlovian treat. The rule stated that trucks could not stop until a line of customers had formed.[30] That may have been fine for ice cream trucks—with their jingles and their frozen treats and their captive audience of park-going kids—but it worked far less well for the new generation of roving food trucks that served high-end lobster rolls and Korean fusion tacos to adults in business suits in the city's downtown. As good as a lobster roll is, it's unlikely that a jingle would attract sufficient numbers of office workers running in suits and dresses to flag down a food truck. What's more—and more important for the purposes of this book—the ice cream truck rule forced many food trucks to drive around aimlessly, wasting fuel while searching for a line of customers.

The problem of the ice cream truck rule found two fixes. The first was technological, as social media helped trucks overcome the ice cream truck rule by telling eager customers to queue at a particular place and time. The second fix was regulatory. The District could not defend the continued existence of the ice cream truck rule, and so—after much wrangling—the rule was repealed. Food truck owners and customers alike were happy. Fuel was saved. Food service was made more sustainable. Everyone was better off, the saying goes, and no one was worse off. In other words, sometimes good food rules can promote sustainability, even if that's not their aim.

Sometimes, a situation calls for rules that prohibit a practice that is wholly unsustainable. I've already endorsed rules barring the destruction of parkland in the name of foraging, rules that prohibit littering while sharing food with the homeless and less fortunate, and rules that restrict some fishing boats from trawling the ocean floor. Other good rules like these exist—both on land and at sea. Take the federal government's current approach to managing shark populations, which appears to be one of the best examples of smart rules that balance consumer demand with necessary sustainability efforts.[31] Both those efforts and that demand are best expressed in this figure: humans kill 100 million sharks each year.[32] Many shark populations are severely threatened as a result. Even those that have rebounded in recent years, such as great white sharks, are still vulnerable. Although some of the shark catch is the result of sportfishing and bycatch, much of it is centered on obtaining shark fins, which are a valuable delicacy in parts of Asia. Often, shark fins are obtained by finning, the practice of catching a shark, cutting off one or more valuable fins while still at sea, and dumping the shark's still-living body back into the ocean.

When a shark is finned, a fisherman keeps just 5 percent of the shark and disposes of the other 95 percent. That means a given boat can hold roughly twenty times as many fins as it can whole sharks. From a sustainability perspective, the practice of shark finning allows certain fishing vessels to seize the valuable part of the shark—its fin—and consequently leave the ocean littered with shark carcasses.

In 2010, recognizing these issues, President Obama signed the Shark Conservation Act (SCA) into law.[33] The SCA bans finning and requires all sharks to reach land with all of their fins attached. The purpose of the SCA is stated very clearly in the law: "to improve the conservation of sharks." Notably, the SCA does *not* ban buying, selling, or eating shark fins. Rather, it simply requires that any shark taken must be brought whole to the shore. This not only ensures that more of the shark must be used—and demand exists for meat and other byproducts, even if they bring a fisherman a smaller return than do fins—it also limits the total catch by making sure ships are full of whole sharks and not just their much smaller fins. The SCA "reflects a balance between addressing the wasteful practice of shark finning and preserving opportunities to land and sell sharks," wrote Alan D. Risenhoover, director of the federal government's Office of Sustainable Fisheries.[34] Bravo.

The benefits of the federal ban on finning are threatened, though, by a new set of state rules that could undermine the federal rules. These laws have alarmed federal officials, including Risenhoover. "Depending on how they are interpreted and implemented, these statutes have the potential to undermine significantly conservation and management of federal shark fisheries," he wrote.[35] One reason is that these conservation-minded state laws actually *require* any shark that's caught and is to be taken back to shore to be finned first.

In 2012, California was the first state to ban the possession, purchase, or sale of any shark fin.[36] What this means in practice is that sharks caught off California and intended to be brought back to shore must first be finned—lest a fisherman be found in possession of a fin and fined. Here it's the shark *fins*, rather than the rest of the shark, that is thrown back into the ocean. Like the example of the futility of punishing ivory poachers and smugglers by destroying ivory—which you read about in chapter 3—laws like that in California reduce the supply of shark fins, drive up their cost, and incentivize the killing of still more sharks for their fins. Thankfully, because the smart *federal* law requires a fisherman to bring the whole intact shark back to shore, the finning-in-reverse resulting from California law is in direct conflict with federal law. A group of shark-fin sellers in California, working with the Asian American Rights Committee of California, sued the state in 2012 to overturn the ban on those grounds.[37] The U.S. Justice Department filed a motion in support of the California fin sellers, rightly arguing that the state's law conflicts with federal law. Still, a federal court upheld the shark-fin ban in 2015.[38] That decision is being appealed.

The court's decision is bad news for sharks. And so is the spread of laws such as California's. Texas, where some sharks are landed, is the latest state to pass such a law.[39] Even states with no shark trade are passing shark-fin bans. Maryland, which passed a law in 2013, doesn't appear to have had a single shark fin pass through the Port of Baltimore in years.[40] These state laws contravene an excellent federal ban on finning and—consequently—violate the Constitution. From the standpoint of sustainability, they also promote shark finning under the guise of preventing it, all to ensure that the 5 percent of the shark most in demand—the fin—will go to waste. That creates more food waste, drives up prices for shark fins, and consequently incentivizes more people to kill more sharks. That's unacceptable—and unsustainable—lawmaking.

I've spent much of this book detailing rules that encourage food waste and other unsustainable practices. You've learned about rules that restrict sustainable and safe food practices under the guise of food safety, such as barring brewers from sharing spent grains with farmers. I've discussed rules that favor large producers over smaller ones, such as standards of identity that sought to force an innovative mayonnaise substitute from calling itself Just Mayo. And you've learned about rules—like bans on gardening—that prohibit people from providing food for themselves and others. In this chapter, I detailed some good food rules. In terms of sustainability, if there are bad food rules and good food rules, what are some guiding principles that can help us distinguish between them? I teased that question in the introduction to this book. In the following chapter, you'll learn the answer to that question and be reminded of some of the people and groups around the country who are turning the answer into action.

CONCLUSION

More Sustainability, Fewer Food Rules

In February 2015, the federal government's Dietary Guidelines Advisory Committee (DGAC), a rotating group of appointed academics that meets every five years to recommend food policies that will promote health, prevent chronic disease, and help people reach and maintain a healthy weight, issued its latest report. Since its inception in 1980, the DGAC has "serve[d] as the cornerstone of all Federal nutrition education and program activities" in the five years after the committee meets. DGAC recommendations are used to set the food policies of many federal agencies, including the FDA and USDA.[1] Those policies include everything from food labeling to the USDA's National School Lunch Program.

For the first time ever, the DGAC addressed the issue of sustainability. Put another way, the cornerstone of all federal nutrition education and programs had never before considered sustainability. The DGAC's sustainability recommendations in the new report included "decreasing meat consumption, choosing seafood from non-threatened stocks, eating more plants and plant-based products, reducing energy intake, and reducing waste."[2] After completing its work, the DGAC concluded "that environmental sustainability adds further dimensions to dietary guidance; not just what we eat but where and how food production, processing, and transportation are managed, and waste is decreased."

Although these recommendations have been controversial for several reasons, some were critical of the committee's nod to sustainability. They argued that sustainability fell outside the DGAC's narrow mission to help every American choose a healthy diet they can abide by. "Sustainable food systems and environmental protection may be important," wrote Jeff Stier of the National Center for Public Policy Research, a conservative think tank, in a *Des Moines Register* op-ed, "but these issues don't belong in discussions of healthy eating."[3] Critics such as Stier were joined by USDA secretary Tom Vilsack, who, the *Wall Street Journal* noted, believes "sustainability issues fall outside the scope of the dietary guidelines."[4] Vilsack hinted he'd disregard the committee's sustainability recommendations.

Both Stier and Secretary Vilsack are correct that sustainability is not part of the DGAC's stated mission. Vilsack's comments to the *Wall Street Journal* that the USDA would steer clear of adopting the DGAC's sustainability recommendations signaled that other federal agencies would, too. Indeed, the word "sustainability" does not appear in the federal dietary guidelines that were issued in January 2016.[5] There's no mention of threatened fish stocks. Neither is there any reference to food waste.

If you've made it this far into this book, then you know the absence of sustainability language in the dietary guidelines is hardly *the thing* that's keeping the USDA from embracing sustainability. The same agency that prohibits the production of safe and sustainable salumi such as that crafted by Mark DeNittis and Il Mondo Vecchio, that bars the humane local slaughter and sale of sustainably raised meat, that promotes food waste with its rigid standards of identity and its National School Lunch

Program, and that rewards farmers with fat subsidies for raising monocultures of GMO corn that's used invariably to feed livestock and to make high fructose corn syrup is not going to become a model of sustainability simply by glad-handing the DGAC's recommendations.

Although sustainability wasn't part of the DGAC's mission and still hasn't made an appearance in the dietary guidelines, two key questions (beyond *why not?*) emerge from the controversy over its inclusion in the DGAC report. First, whether or not the USDA and other federal agencies will listen, were the DGAC's sustainability recommendations any good? *Should* the USDA and others have listened? Second, what if government *did* incorporate sustainability goals into rules moving forward? Where and how might they do it, and do so in a way that's meaningful?

With regard to the first question—whether the DGAC sustainability recommendations are worth their salt—a close look finds them to be woefully lacking. Consider the DGAC's advice to choose seafood from nonthreatened stocks. Although the recommendation is valuable on its face, it rings hollow given that it fails to address the fact that federal rules promote overfishing and cause the loss of thousands of tons of bycatch. The DGAC recommendation ignores a key underlying problem—discussed in chapter 3 of this book—namely, that existing federal rules *contribute to* the problem the DGAC sought to address. The DGAC recommendations fail similarly in other areas. For example, even before the DGAC issued its recommendations, the USDA had already put more plants and plant-based foods into school lunches thanks to the Healthy, Hunger-Free Kids Act, which increased not just vegetables but which also promotes plant-based meat substitutes (such as tofu).[6] As you also learned in chapter 3, food waste—already a problem within the school lunch program before the Healthy, Hunger-Free Kids Act—has only increased since the USDA began enforcing the law. Offering schoolkids more plant-based foods and less meat, as the DGAC recommends, may or may not be more intrinsically sustainable. Recent research by faculty at Carnegie Mellon University has cast some doubt on the long-held belief that fruits and vegetables are inherently more sustainable than meat.[7] Regardless, school lunches are *demonstrably less sustainable* when schoolkids throw away more of the food served in those lunches. Changing the diets of schoolkids so that they simply throw away greater quantities of sustainably raised food is policymaking defeatism at its worst.

Other problems with the DGAC's sustainability recommendations are glaring. The 571-page report, for example, does not mention farm subsidies—a key enemy of sustainability that you learned about in chapter 2—not even once. And while the report refers to the problem of food waste a mere handful of times, it offers no suggestions for how to combat it. In fact, the DGAC's discussion of food waste is so meager that the Environmental Working Group said food waste is "not addressed by the DGAC" report.[8]

These shortcomings point to a key flaw inherent in the DGAC's sustainability recommendations: they suggest the need to achieve different results without addressing the causes and roots of most problems. Tinkering with one element of a deeply flawed system and expecting sustainability to result is absurd. Often, the very premise underlying a program that you've learned about in this book—rather than one particular element of it—is the problem. Consider the FDA's proposed rules for spent grains and the USDA's commodity and marketing programs. These are both rotten to the core. Spraying a little sustainability perfume on them won't eliminate their stench.

With regard to the second question I posed above—how government might incorporate meaningful sustainability goals into rules moving forward—it's worth considering once more what sustainability really means. In 1987, a United Nations agency issued what became known as the Brundtland Commission report.[9] It defined sustainable development—and has come to define sustainability itself—as growth that meets present needs but ensures "the ability of future generations to meet their own needs." The commission's definition speaks of *present* development activities meeting *present* needs. But in speaking of *future* needs, the commission's definition is clear that whatever present development is taking place in the present, we must ensure that future generations can "meet their own needs." A key purpose of development in the present, the commission is rightly saying, is to ensure people in the future are better able to meet their own needs.

My own definition of sustainability, which I offered in the introduction to this book, dovetails nicely with that of the Brundtland Commission. There, I defined sustainability in the food realm as describing foods grown or produced using a set of practices that aspires to maximize the benefits of the food system while minimizing its negative impacts. I've also noted that the benefits of sustainability must contain an inherent economic component. "The practices of sustainable farmers must be able in turn to sustain the farmers," I wrote in a 2011 op-ed.[10] The same holds true for the sustainable fishermen, gardeners, almond milk makers, brewers, foragers, food-waste opponents, and all of the farmers and nonfarmers I've described in this book.

During the course of writing this book, I asked many of the people I spoke with for my research and quoted here to share their own definitions of sustainability. Many very smart people had far more than a few words to say about the term. Christophe Hille, chief financial officer at Fleisher's Craft Butchery, played up the economic component of the term, stating, in part, that to him it embodies "growing a sustainable and fruitful financial relationship . . . by way of responsibly produced food."[11] Iso Rabins, the expert forager and a leader of the successful repeal of California's so-called glove law, defined sustainability in terms of his own activities, in a way that echoes the Brundtland report's determination that sustainability is at once both personal and societal, and is largely centered on the future. "Foraging sustainably for me is knowing what I can take and where without adversely [a]ffecting the future of the resource," Rabins told me.[12] Sustainable food reflects what "the ecosystem is set up to produce," said Greg Van Ullen, founder of OMilk, the almond milk New York State regulators tried to kill off by redefining it as "melloream."[13] Van Ullen's attorney, Jason Foscolo, whose Food Law Firm successfully represented OMilk in that case, offered—no surprises—a more lawyerly view of what sustainability means. "I'm naturally skeptical of product claims of any kind," Foscolo told me, "so when I know I cannot trust a word or descriptor or marketing claim, I seek information."[14] He said online research is invaluable, but so is a healthy dose of skepticism. And not just for lawyers. "If they are going to use the word 'sustainable,' personally—as a consumer, now—I am going to expect them to prove to me they are not bullshitting me," Foscolo said.

Interestingly, these definitions—like the Brundtland Commission's and my own—are not contingent upon the piling up of more rules. Although Hille, Rabins, Van Ullen, Foscolo, and I all support some rules, likely to varying degrees, none of us defines sustainability as an inherent outgrowth of rules. That doesn't mean rules can't help foster sustainability. They can and should, as I've described throughout this book. And rules can and should prevent some unsustainable food practices.

The common thread that runs through this book, then, is that—in innumerable instances—the continued growth of the nation's food rules has not made for a more sustainable food system. Food-safety rules have pushed sustainable food entrepreneurs out of business, weakened others, and discouraged still others from entering the market. In their place, larger food makers have thrived—a lesson that holds with other food rules (such as farm subsidies) that don't pertain to food safety. Rules encourage food waste. And they prohibit people from growing, raising, obtaining, and sharing their own food. By now, I hope you agree that simply piling on more rules is not the answer.

Some rules I've identified—such as basic food-safety rules, fishing quotas, restrictions on trawling, the federal ban on shark finning, and prohibitions on unsustainable foraging—are absolutely necessary. But so many are counterproductive. How do we distinguish between the two—and get to a place in which fewer and better rules promote a more sustainable food system? How we can best identify and foster "good" rules and eliminate "bad" ones? More importantly—returning to the second question I asked above—from this point forward, what are the principles we can use to guide food policy in that direction?

As the introduction to this book identified, there are two simple guiding principles. First, federal, state, and local rules that *promote* unsustainable food system outcomes (such as food waste) should be jettisoned whenever possible. Second, rules that *prohibit* sustainable food system practices (such as those that put Mark DeNittis out of business) should also be eliminated whenever possible. These rules fit nicely into one short proclamation: rules should neither promote unsustainable practices nor prohibit sustainable practices. It's also true—as I've discussed throughout the book—that new and existing rules should stress the importance of achieving good outcomes, rather than adhering to a particular process.

What does that look like in practice? As you learned in chapter 1, food safety rules are important. But their growing focus on adhering to a rigid *process*, rather than on achieving good *outcomes*—requiring costly motorized equipment when inexpensive ice cools at least as well, for example—is leaving many artisanal and sustainable food producers behind. And it's not making our food any safer. In contrast, food-safety rules that focus squarely on the goal of protecting consumers can help food producers of all sizes and types enter and succeed in the market. Requiring good outcomes rather than rigid processes works well in other areas that don't pertain directly to food safety. For example, rules that prohibit raising noisy roosters in urban and suburban yards but permit raising more taciturn hens ensures good outcomes: omelets, rather than noise. Mandating that lunches served in schools contain good food that's tailored to individual student preferences and helps to fight food waste—both good outcomes—requires getting communities involved in school lunchrooms as much as it requires the USDA to get out of those same lunchrooms.

A few other principles must guide food policy going forward. As you learned, rules often favor large producers over small ones. But they should never favor a producer of one size over a producer of another. Receiving government funds to farm, for example, is not a sustainable practice, whether one is growing vegetables on an acre or on thousands of acres. As I described in the introduction to this book, sustainability in the food realm means minimizing environmental impact while maximizing economic returns. If larger food producers are inherently more efficient and competitive because of their large size, good for them. They certainly don't need government help to succeed. Small, sustainable producers, too, must be able to succeed economically to be truly sustainable. Ending farm subsidies and other federal, state, and local rules that favor big food producers over smaller ones means sustainable food producers need fewer rules—not more—to succeed.

Ending farm subsidies is a start. Other rules that promote bad outcomes—such as those that promote food waste—are also suspect. But some of these rules—very few—are ones we must live with. For example, rules that keep cancer-stricken beef out of the food supply, that target dangerous levels of arsenic or lead in foods, or that order the destruction of a packaged food that contains a potentially deadly bacteria or unlabeled allergen do indeed cause some food waste. But their benefits to society are obvious, and easy alternatives to wasting such food are difficult to envision. But good rules such as these that cause food waste are the exception. Oakland's garbage-collection contract, recall, practically forces restaurants in the city to waste food. The USDA National School

Lunch Program forces schools to waste tons of food. And rules for grading fruits, vegetables, meats, and other agricultural products force farmers to waste food. In each case, alternatives exist that would eliminate much of this waste. Oakland restaurateurs would prefer to turn their food waste into compost. They'd continue to do so if the city's garbage contract didn't impede the practice. Families, restaurants, and caterers could reduce their own food waste by turning leftover food into healthy bagged lunches for all schoolchildren, while gradually eliminating all of the tons of school food waste caused by the National School Lunch Program. And, as groups like Fruta Feia are demonstrating, there is a growing market for so-called "ugly" fruits and vegetables that are often kept from the market thanks to grading standards in the European Union and the United States alike. In cases such as these, where alternatives can reduce or eliminate food waste, embracing the status quo is no longer palatable.

Sometimes, as you've learned, rules restrict individuals from making sustainable food choices outside the commercial realm. I spoke with Madeleine Redfern, a Canadian Inuit lawyer who clerked for Canada's Supreme Court before serving as mayor of Iqaluit, Nunavut, where she still lives. Redfern champions the culinary, cultural, environmental, and socioeconomic rights and traditions of her fellow Inuit. She often speaks out against restrictions on hunting. To outsiders, some of the animals she defends eating are controversial. But to her and many in her community, they're the epitome of sustainability. "Our wild foods are seals, fish, walrus, caribou, polar bears, whales, birds, eggs, seaweed, berries, etc.," she told me.[15] Redfern said a local diet necessarily looks far different for her and those around her than it does for many who live in, near, or even within a day's drive of a major city. I asked Redfern who should decide what she and others in her community eat. "Each person in my community should decide what they wish to eat, as elsewhere in the world," she responded. She rattled off a long list of cosmopolitan cities—Berlin, Brussels, Hong Kong, London, Los Angeles, Paris, Rome, and Toronto—and asked why the freedom to choose to eat sustainable foods should be any different for people living in those cities than for her and her fellow Inuit. It shouldn't, of course. We should all enjoy the same rights to feed our families and ourselves and to live as sustainably as we want and can. For those who feed themselves and others, that necessarily means protecting the choice to grow, raise, forage, hunt, scavenge, and eat a wide variety of different foods—whether or not everyone finds such foods palatable.

Truth be told, there are good food rules. What most of these rules have in common is that they all allow people to make more sustainable food choices. That, in a nutshell, is the ultimate goal of this book. Getting there means taking the time to look at existing rules and ones proposed in the future, and seeing if they make sustainable food choices the default option when possible. Conceptually, here's how that looks. If a rule *promotes unsustainable food practices*, it's best to ask whether the rule also truly protects food safety or promotes one of a handful of other absolutely mandatory societal goals. If it does, then ask whether there is another way to achieve the same outcomes without promoting those unsustainable food practices. If there's a way to achieve the same goal without this negative unintended consequence, then we should simply abolish the rule. The same line of inquiry holds true for rules that *prohibit sustainable food practices*. If there's a way to protect food safety or promote some other absolutely mandatory societal goal without restricting sustainable food practices, then we must abolish the rule.

Notably, not one rule that promotes unsustainable food practices or prohibits sustainable food practices that I describe in this book survives this level of scrutiny. There are alternatives—many of which I've described—to all of these problematic rules. Some rules fail almost immediately, like farm subsidies. They promote a host of unsustainable food practices and, likely, obesity and other problems. They're patently indefensible. Eliminate them. Other rules fail because—as in the case of supplanting the USDA National School Lunch Program with my proposal to turn school lunches into a tool for eliminating (rather than promoting) food waste—far better alternatives exist.

But what of the people I alluded to—the legislators and regulators, the public and others—who are needed to make our food system more sustainable? Who are they? Where are they? In fact, you've already read about many of them in this book. Sean Dimin and his colleagues at Sea to Table are fighting the scourge of bycatch and waste in the world's oceans. Jay Hamburger is demonstrating and defending the dignity of sharing food with those in need in Houston. Members of Congress from within and without both major parties, including Rep. Thomas Massie, Rep. Chellie Pingree, Rep. Jared Polis, Sen. Rand Paul, and Sen. Angus King are fighting to allow sustainable beef and dairy farmers to slaughter and sell their products locally. Jason Foscolo and his Food Law Firm—along with nonprofit groups like the Farm-to-Consumer Legal Defense Fund and the Institute for Justice—use the law to help small food entrepreneurs overcome misguided rules, often ones that favor larger food companies. Many of those larger companies aren't the enemy but are, rather, part of the solution. Booming startups such as Hampton Creek and even larger companies such as Unilever, an award-winner for its sustainability efforts, and MillerCoors, the brewery giant that's eliminated its waste from spent grains, are very much a part of the solution. These people and companies, and groups allied with them, are today's and tomorrow's agents of change.

They're helping to build a more sustainable food future. And so are you. If there's a lesson to be learned from many of the rules featured throughout this book, it's that public pressure has sometimes resulted in the defeat of those bad rules. The FDA felt the sting of public outrage over its proposed rules for spent grains and ripening cheese on wooden boards. But other rules remain entrenched. We've piled rules on top of rules for decades—often with disastrous consequences. In some ways—due to rules that erect senseless food-safety barriers for many sustainable producers, promote larger and less sustainable food producers at the expense of smaller competitors, encourage food waste, and trample on a person's right to feed themselves and others—we're further from a sustainable food system than we've ever been. It will take renewed and vocal public indignation to overturn older rules such as USDA farm subsidies and the agency's school lunch programs, and newer ones, such as the problematic elements of the FDA's food-safety rules under FSMA. Whether an existing rule is promoting unsustainable food practices or preventing sustainable ones, it's past time that we abolish it. Importantly, we must also stop passing bad new rules. That means lawmakers and their staff members must consult with experts who understand how food, law, and sustainability can either work together or be at odds, lest they draft new food rules that promote predictably harmful unintended consequences.

We deserve a better food system. It is within reach. If we stop biting the hands that feed us, we will ensure a more sustainable food future for all Americans.

Notes

Preface

1. Paul Shapiro, email message to author, June 17, 2015.

Introduction

1. Mark DeNittis, in discussion with the author, Nov. 8, 2012.
2. Mark DeNittis, email message to author, June 15, 2015.
3. Douglas Brown, In Denver, time-honored techniques feed a growing appetite for old school meats, *Denver Post,* October 26, 2011, www.denverpost.com/food/ci_19184498.
4. Exceptional Newcomer Signature Dish Award Past Recipients, Colorado Restaurant Association, www.coloradorestaurant.com/?page_id=844.
5. Lauren Hendrick, Round 2: Redzikowski, Scott, Wiard, DeNittis, Eater.com, Feb. 13, 2012, denver.eater.com/2012/2/13/6614293/round-2-redzikowski-scott-wiard-denittis.
6. Cure Organic Farm, Our Farm, www.cureorganicfarm.com/index.htm.
7. Baylen Linnekin, How Misguided USDA Regulations Harm Consumers and Restrict Food Freedom, Reason.com, Nov. 10, 2012, https://reason.com/archives/2012/11/10/the-ugliness-of-unmaking-sausages/.
8. Andra Zeppelin, Last Call for Il Mondo Vecchio, Eater, Nov. 16, 2012, denver.eater.com/2012/11/16/6520761/last-call-for-il-mondo-vecchio.

9. Michael Ruhlman, The "No Nitrites Added" Hoax, May 10, 2011, ruhlman.com/2011/05/the-no-nitrites-added-hoax/.
10. Mark DeNittis, in discussion with the author, June 11, 2015.
11. United States Department of Agriculture, Sanitation Standard Operating Procedures (March 26, 2014), www.fsis.usda.gov/wps/wcm/connect/4cafe6fe-e1a3-4fcf-95ab-bd4846d0a968/13a_IM_SSOP.pdf?MOD=AJPERES; United States Department of Agriculture, FSIS Compliance Guideline HACCP Systems Validation 4–5, May 2013, www.fsis.usda.gov/wps/wcm/connect/a70bb780-e1ff-4a35-9a9a-3fb40c8fe584/HACCP_Systems_Validation.pdf?MOD=AJPERES.
12. Lori Midson, Il Mondo Vecchio Will Close at the End of the Month, Ceasing its Salumi and Sausage Production, Nov. 2, 2012, www.westword.com/restaurants/exclusive-il-mondo-vecchio-will-close-at-the-end-of-the-month-ceasing-its-salumi-and-sausage-production-5754983.
13. Paul Cure, in discussion with the author, Nov. 10, 2012.
14. Ken Albala, email discussion with author, Nov. 9, 2012.
15. Farm-to-Consumer Legal Defense Fund v. Wisconsin Dep't. of Agriculture, Trade and Consumer Protection, No. 10-CV-3884, slip op. at 4 (Wis. Cir. Ct., Sep. 9, 2011).
16. Reshma Kirpalani, Woman Faces Jail Time for Growing Vegetable Garden in her Own Front Lawn, ABC News, July 12, 2011, abcnews.go.com/US/vegetable-garden-brings-criminal-charges-oak-park-michigan/story?id=14047214; Martin Comas, After Two-Year Battle with City, Longwood Man Cleans up his Yard, *Orlando Sentinel,* July 30, 2014, articles.orlandosentinel.com/2014-07-30/news/os-longwood-messy-yard-sean-law-20140730_1_sean-law-code-enforcement-fines-longwood-man; Georgia Man Fined for Growing Vegetables, Eat, Drink Better, Sept. 14, 2010, eatdrinkbetter.com/2010/09/14/georgia-man-fined-for-growing-vegetables/.
17. Lori Fullbright, Woman Sues City of Tulsa for Cutting Down her Edible Garden, News on 6, June 15, 2012, www.newson6.com/story/18802728/woman-sues-city-of-tulsa-for-cutting-down-her-edible-garden.
18. Wickard v. Filburn, 317 U.S. 111 (1942).
19. Jim Chen, Filburn's Legacy, 52 *Emory Law Journal* 1719, 1733–34 (2003), papers.ssrn.com/sol3/papers.cfm?abstract_id=901026.

20. U.S. at War: Citizen Roosevelt, Apr. 20, 1942, content.time.com/time/magazine/article/0,9171,790318,00.html.
21. Norma J. Shattuck, During WWII, Victory Gardens Were Practical as well as Patriotic, *San Francisco Chronicle,* Apr. 19, 2003, www.sfgate.com/homeandgarden/article/During-WWII-Victory-Gardens-were-practical-as-2653952.php.
22. U.S. at War: Citizen Roosevelt, Apr. 20, 1942, content.time.com/time/magazine/article/0,9171,790318,00.html.
23. Marian Burros, Obamas to Plant Vegetable Garden at White House, *New York Times,* Mar. 19, 2009, www.nytimes.com/2009/03/20/dining/20garden.html?_r=0.
24. Harvard Food Law and Policy Clinic, hls.harvard.edu/dept/clinical/clinics/food-law-and-policy-clinic-of-the-center-for-health-law-and-policy-innovation/.
25. Nathan Rosenberg & Emily Broad Leib, Pennsylvania's Chapter 57 and its Effects on Farmers Markets, Harvard Food Law and Policy Clinic, Aug. 2012, blogs.law.harvard.edu/foodpolicyinitiative/files/2012/08/PA-FM-FINAL3.pdf.
26. Ibid.
27. Ibid.
28. Michael Pollan & Eric Schlosser, A Stale Food Fight, *New York Times,* Nov. 28, 2010, www.nytimes.com/2010/11/29/opinion/29schlosser.html.
29. Press Release, U.S. Representative Massie Introduces Bipartisan Milk Freedom Legislation, Mar. 27, 2014, massie.house.gov/press-release/press-release-us-representative-massie-introduces-bipartisan-milk-freedom-legislation.

Chapter 1

1. California Assembly Bill 1252, www.leginfo.ca.gov/pub/13-14/bill/asm/ab_1251-1300/ab_1252_cfa_20130821_145449_sen_floor.html.
2. Editorial, Food Safety Glove Law Needs Work, *San Jose Mercury News,* Mar. 31, 2014, www.mercurynews.com/opinion/ci_25460814/mercury-news-editorial-food-safety-glove-law-needs.
3. Betty Hallock, Chefs Hate New Law Requiring Them to Wear Gloves:

"It's Terrible," *Los Angeles Times,* Jan. 11, 2014, www.latimes.com/food/dailydish/la-dd-chefs-gloves-law-20140111-story.html.

4. Petition, Latex in the Bedroom Not in the Kitchen: Repeal the "Glove Law": Section 113961 of AB1252, https://www.change.org/p/state-rep-philip-ting-latex-in-the-bedroom-not-in-the-kitchen-repeal-the-glove-law-section-113961-of-ab1252.
5. Stacey Finz, Lawmakers Pull About-Face on Food Safety "Glove Law," SFGate.com, Mar. 7, 2014, www.sfgate.com/food/article/Lawmakers-pull-about-face-on-food-safety-glove-5295547.php.
6. Iso Rabins, email message to author, Jan. 15, 2014.
7. Aliza Green, The Gloves Can Come Off, as Far as I'm Concerned, *Washington Post,* June 12, 2012, https://www.washingtonpost.com/lifestyle/food/the-gloves-can-come-off-as-far-as-im-concerned/2012/06/11/gJQAR7YuXV_story.html.
8. Megan Hansen, Marin Chefs, Bartenders Pan State Food Safety Glove Law, Marin Independent Journal, Mar. 30, 2014, www.marinij.com/general-news/20140330/marin-chefs-bartenders-pan-state-food-safety-glove-law.
9. Coalition Members, California Retail Food Safety Coalition, www.crfsc.org/about-us/coalition-members.
10. Megan Hansen, Marin Chefs, Bartenders Pan State Food Safety Glove Law, *Marin Independent Journal,* Mar. 30, 2014, www.marinij.com/general-news/20140330/marin-chefs-bartenders-pan-state-food-safety-glove-law.
11. Nina Thorsen, Legislator Washes His Hands of Unpopular Restaurant Glove Law, KQED, Feb. 25, 2014, ww2.kqed.org/news/2014/02/24/author-of-restaurant-glove-law-seeks-to-reverse-measure.
12. Betty Hallock, Governor Signs Repeal of Food-Safety Law Requiring Gloves, *Los Angeles Times*, June 30, 2014, www.latimes.com/food/dailydish/la-dd-california-jerry-brown-repeal-food-safety-law-gloves-20140630-story.html.
13. Steve Cuozzo, Health Department Deserves an "F You" Rating for Stupid Sushi Glove Rule, *New York Post,* Nov. 1, 2015, nypost.com/2015/11/01/health-department-has-a-vendetta-against-city-restaurants/.
14. Public Law 111-353, 124 Stat. 3885, Jan. 4, 2011.

15. FDA, Background on the FDA Food Safety Modernization Act (FSMA), www.fda.gov/Food/GuidanceRegulation/FSMA/ucm239907.htm.
16. Michael Pollan & Eric Schlosser, A Stale Food Fight, *New York Times,* Nov. 29, 2010.
17. FDA, Fact Sheets on the Subparts of the Original FSMA Proposed Rule for Produce Safety, Jan. 2013, www.fda.gov/Food/GuidanceRegulation/FSMA/ucm334552.htm.
18. FDA, Standards for the Growing, Harvesting, Packing, and Holding of Produce for Human Consumption, Proposed Rule; Supplemental Notice Of Proposed Rulemaking, Fed. Reg., Sept. 29, 2014, https://www.federalregister.gov/articles/2014/09/29/2014-22447/standards-for-the-growing-harvesting-packing-and-holding-of-produce-for-human-consumption.
19. Rising Sun Farms, www.risingsunfarms.com/.
20. Comments of Elizabeth Fujas, Public Hearing, FDA Food Safety Modernization Act, Mar. 28, 2013, www.fda.gov/downloads/Food/GuidanceRegulation/FSMA/UCM357247.zip.
21. Mason Walker, See Where the Fastest-Growing Companies Rank, *Portland Business Journal,* June 20, 2013, www.bizjournals.com/portland/blog/2013/06/pbj100-see-where-the-fastest-growing.html.
22. Rising Sun Farms, www.risingsunfarms.com/.
23. Comments of Elizabeth Fujas, Public Hearing, FDA Food Safety Modernization Act, Mar. 28, 2013, www.fda.gov/downloads/Food/GuidanceRegulation/FSMA/UCM357247.zip.
24. Ibid.
25. Ibid.
26. Michael Shepherd, Maine's Farmers Wary of New Food Safety Rules, *Portland Press Herald,* Aug. 19, 2013, www.pressherald.com/2013/08/19/maines-farmers-wary-of-new-food-safety-rules_2013-08-20/.
27. Meghan Pierce, Farmers Say New Food Safety Regulations Hurt Small NH Farms, *Manchester Union-Leader,* Aug. 20, 2013, www.unionleader.com/apps/pbcs.dll/article?AID=%2F20130821%2FNEWHAMPSHIRE07%2F130829917&template=printart.
28. Food Safety Modernization Act, Rulemaking Materials and Comments, www.regulations.gov/#!searchResults;rpp=25;po=0;s=fsma;dct=FR%252BPR%252BN%252BO%252BPS%252BSR (last visited Feb. 10, 2016).

29. Standards for the Growing, Harvesting, Packing, and Holding of Produce for Human Consumption, Docket Folder, FDA-2011-N-0921, FDA, www.regulations.gov/#!docketDetail;D=FDA-2011-N-0921.
30. Sen. Jon Tester, The Government's Role in Food Safety, *Food Safety News,* Sept. 29, 2015, www.foodsafetynews.com/2015/09/the-governments-role-in-food-safety/#.Vrt3Z8fMyqA.
31. Press Release, Sen. Jon Tester, Senate Overwhelmingly Passes Food Safety Bill with Tester's Amendment, Nov. 30, 2010, www.tester.senate.gov/?p=press_release&id=1078.
32. Ibid.
33. CDC, Estimates of Foodborne Illness in the United States, May 8, 2014, www.cdc.gov/foodborneburden/trends-in-foodborne-illness.html.
34. FDA, Final Rule, Standards for the Growing, Harvesting, Packing, and Holding of Produce for Human Consumption, 21 C.F.R. Pts. 11, 16, & 112, Nov. 27, 2015, https://s3.amazonaws.com/public-inspection.federalregister.gov/2015-28159.pdf.
35. FDA, Final Rule, Current Good Manufaturing Practice, Hazard Analysis, and Risk-Based Preventive Controls for Human Food, 21 C.F.R. Pt. 1 et seq., Sept. 7, 2015, https://www.federalregister.gov/articles/2015/09/17/2015-21920/current-good-manufacturing-practice-hazard-analysis-and-risk-based-preventive-controls-for-human.
36. Painter, J.A., et al. Attribution of foodborne illnesses, hospitalizations, and deaths to food commodities by using outbreak data, United States, 1998–2008. *Emerg. Infect. Dis.,* Mar. 2013, wwwnc.cdc.gov/eid/article/19/3/11-1866_article.
37. CDC, Attribution of Foodborne Illness, 1998–2008 - Images, Contribution of Different Food Commodities (Categories) to Estimated Domestically Acquired Illnesses and Deaths, 1998–2008, Last Updated Jan. 29, 2013, www.cdc.gov/foodborneburden/attribution-image.html.
38. FDA, FSMA Facts, Background on the FDA Food Safety Modernization Act (FSMA), July 11, 2011, www.fda.gov/downloads/Food/GuidanceRegulation/UCM263773.pdf.
39. FDA, Inspection & Compliance, May 7, 2015, www.fda.gov/Food/GuidanceRegulation/FSMA/ucm257978.htm.
40. FDA, FDA's Draft Approach for Designating High-Risk Foods as Re-

quired by Section 204 of FSMA, Feb. 2014, www.fda.gov/downloads/Food/GuidanceRegulation/FSMA/UCM380212.pdf.

41. Barry Estabrook, Why Isn't the FDA Stopping the Epidemic of Food-borne Illness?, *Mother Jones,* Dec. 5, 2012, www.motherjones.com/environment/2012/11/fda-out-lunch.
42. FDA, Final Rule, Current Good Manufacturing Practice, Hazard Analysis, and Risk-Based Preventive Controls for Human Food, Sept. 17, 2015, www.regulations.gov/#!documentDetail;D=FDA-2011-N-0920-1979; FDA, Standards for the Growing, Harvesting, Packing, and Holding of Produce for Human Consumption, Final Rule, Fed. Reg., Nov. 27, 2015, https://www.federalregister.gov/articles/2015/11/27/2015-28159/standards-for-the-growing-harvesting-packing-and-holding-of-produce-for-human-consumption#h-10.
43. FDA, Standards for the Growing, Harvesting, Packing, and Holding of Produce for Human Consumption, Final Rule, Fed. Reg., Nov. 27, 2015, https://www.federalregister.gov/articles/2015/11/27/2015-28159/standards-for-the-growing-harvesting-packing-and-holding-of-produce-for-human-consumption.
44. Baylen Linnekin, The FDA Looks to Crack Down on Manure (Again), Reason.com, Mar. 12, 2016, https://reason.com/archives/2016/03/12/the-fda-looks-to-crack-down-on-manure-ag/singlepage.
45. Bill Marler, email message to author, July 5, 2015.
46. Baylen Linnekin, Craft Brewers Face Regulatory Challenges, Reason.com, Mar. 30, 2013, http://reason.com/archives/2013/03/30/booming-craft-beer-faces-regulatory-hurd/singlepage.
47. *The Eclectic Medical Journal,* 3rd ed., John M. Scudder, M.D., ed. (1878).
48. Comments of the Beer Institute & The American Malting Barley Association, Proposed Rule - Current Good Manufacturing Practice and Hazard Analysis and Risk-Based Preventive Controls for Human Food [Docket No.: FDA-2011-N-0920] RIN:0910-AG36, Nov. 22, 2013.
49. Robin Wilkey, New FDA Regulation Could Cripple Ranchers, Beer Brewers, Huffington Post Green, Apr. 11, 2014, www.huffingtonpost.com/2014/04/11/food-safety-modernization_n_5135629.html.
50. Paul Gatza, Brewers Association, Docket No. FDA-2011-N-0922: Proposed Rule Regarding Current Good Manufacturing Practice and Hazard

Analysis and Risk-Based Preventive Controls for Food for Animals, Mar. 28, 2014.

51. Lynne Terry, Beer Prices Could Go Up Under FDA Rule that Angers Farmers, Brewers, *The Oregonian,* Apr. 20, 2014, www.oregonlive.com/health/index.ssf/2014/04/fda_rule_would_increase_cost_o.html.
52. Ibid.
53. M.L. Johnson, FDA Backs Off Animal Feed Rule Affecting Brewers, Associated Press, Apr. 24, 2014, wivb.com/2014/04/24/schumer-fda-will-back-off-spent-grain-proposal/.
54. KGW Staff, "Spent Grain Rule" could boost beer, food prices, KGW.com, Apr. 15, 2014, www.kgw.com/story/news/2014/07/26/12626494/.
55. Robin Wilkey, New FDA Regulation Could Cripple Ranchers, Beer Brewers, Huffington Post Green, Apr. 11, 2014, www.huffingtonpost.com/2014/04/11/food-safety-modernization_n_5135629.html.
56. Hopworks Urban Brewery, Keeping it Green, hopworksbeer.com/do-good/environment/; KGW Staff, "Spent Grain Rule" could boost beer, food prices, KGW.com, Apr. 15, 2014, legacy.kgw.com/story/news/2014/07/26/12626494/.
57. Press Release, FDA Issues Updated Spent Grain Rules, Beer Institute, Sept. 9, 2014, www.beerinstitute.org/news-media/press-releases/fda-issues-updated-spent-grain-rules.
58. MillerCoors, From Grain to Glass, 2009, www.millercoors.com/sites/millercoors/files/2009-MillerCoors-Sustainability-Report.pdf; MillerCoors, Great Beer, Great Responsibility, MillerCoors 2015 Sustainability Report, www.millercoors.com/sites/millercoors/files/2015-MillerCoors-Sustainability-Report.pdf.
59. Oregon Natural Meats, The "Brew Beef" Story, www.naturalbrewbeef.com/ninkasi.
60. Donna Pacheo, email message to author, Aug. 4, 2015.
61. Michael R. Taylor, Getting it Right on Spent Grains, FDA Voice, Apr. 24, 2015, blogs.fda.gov/fdavoice/index.php/2014/04/getting-it-right-on-spent-grains.
62. Sara Nelson, email message to author, Aug. 4, 2015.
63. FDA, Letter on Use of Wooden Shelves for Cheese Aging, 2014, avail-

able at www.foodsafetynews.com/files/2014/06/Use-of-wooden-shelves-for-cheese-aging.pdf.

64. Sally Pollak, Cheesemakers Cheer Wood Shelves, *Burlington Free Press,* June 16, 2014, www.burlingtonfreepress.com/story/news/local/vermont/2014/06/16/fda-wood-shelves-cheesemaking/10503777/.
65. Jeanne Carpenter, Game Changer: FDA Rules No Wooden Boards in Cheese Aging, Cheese Underground, June 7, 2014, www.cheeseunderground.blogspot.com/2014/06/game-changer-fda-rules-no-wooden-boards.html.
66. Sally Pollak, Cheesemakers Cheer Wood Shelves, *Burlington Free Press,* June 16, 2014, www.burlingtonfreepress.com/story/news/local/vermont/2014/06/16/fda-wood-shelves-cheesemaking/10503777/.
67. Samantha Christmann, FDA's letter opposing wooden aging shelves for cheese making brings sharp industry retort, *Buffalo News,* June 11, 2014, www.buffalonews.com/business/fdas-letter-opposing-wooden-aging-shelves-for-cheese-making-brings-sharp-industry-retort-20140611.
68. Gordon Severson, Cheesemakers concerned after FDA cracks down on wood-aged cheese, WKOW.com, June 24, 2014, www.wkow.com/story/25732850/2014/06/09/cheesemakers-concerned-after-fda-cracks-down-on-wood-aged-cheese.
69. FDA, Press Release, United States enters consent decree with New York cheese producer due to Listeria contamination, Apr. 29, 2014, www.fda.gov/NewsEvents/Newsroom/PressAnnouncements/ucm395339.htm.
70. Stephanie Strom & Kim Severson, F.D.A. Rule May Alter Cheese-Aging Process, *New York Times,* June 10, 2014, www.nytimes.com/2014/06/11/business/us-rule-may-alter-cheese-aging-process.html.
71. Sally Pollak, Cheesemakers Cheer Wood Shelves, *Burlington Free Press,* June 16, 2014, www.burlingtonfreepress.com/story/news/local/vermont/2014/06/16/fda-wood-shelves-cheesemaking/10503777/.
72. Ibid.
73. Donna Pacheco, email message to author, Aug. 4, 2015.
74. FDA, Clarification on Using Wood Shelving in Artisanal Cheesemaking, June 11, 2014, www.fda.gov/Food/NewsEvents/ConstituentUpdates/ucm400808.htm.

75. Ibid.
76. Press Release, Rep. Peter Welch, Rep. Welch Reacts to FDA "Clarification" on Use of Wood Shelves to Age Cheese, June 12, 2014, https://welch.house.gov/media-center/press-releases/rep-welch-reacts-fda-clarification-use-wood-shelves-age-cheese.
77. https://twitter.com/hashtag/saveourcheese.
78. Charles Abbott, USDA Admits Skipped Meat Plant Checks for 30 Years, Reuters, Mar. 29, 2007, www.reuters.com/article/us-usa-meat-usda-idUSN2930654720070329.
79. Stacy Finz & Carolyn Lochhead, Slaughterhouse accused of selling meat from cows with cancer, *San Francisco Chronicle,* Feb. 26, 2014, www.sfgate.com/health/article/Slaughterhouse-accused-of-selling-meat-from-cows-5267836.php#photo-5939827.
80. Ibid.
81. Livestock Slaughter, 2014 Summary, USDA, Apr. 2015 www.usda.gov/nass/PUBS/TODAYRPT/lsan0415.pdf.
82. High Sierra Resource Conservation & Development Council, Next Steps: Implementation of Small and Very Small Niche Meat Harvesting and Cut-and-Wrap Facilities in California, Nov. 30, 2012, ucanr.edu/sites/placernevadasmallfarms/files/164099.pdf.
83. Becky Kramer, Frustrated by Regulations, Ranchers Build Slaughterhouse Co-Op, *The Spokesman-Review,* Sept. 15, 2013, www.spokesman.com/stories/2013/sep/15/taking-control/
84. U.S. Rep. Thomas Massie, in discussion with the author, July 29, 2015.
85. Lyndsey Layton, As Demand Grows for Locally Raised Meat, Farmers Turn to Mobile Slaughterhouses, *Washington Post,* June 20, 2010, www.washingtonpost.com/wp-dyn/content/article/2010/06/18/AR2010061803509.html.
86. Karen Miltner, Slaughterhouse Options Shrink for Small Farmers, *USA Today,* May 27, 2010, usatoday30.usatoday.com/money/industries/food/2010-05-27-slaughterhouses27_ST_N.htm.
87. Sam Anderson, On-Farm Poultry Processing, Beginning Farmer Network's Blog, bfnmass.org/blog/farm-poultry-processing (last visited Apr. 16, 2016).
88. Stacy Finz & Carolyn Lochhead, Slaughterhouse Accused of Selling Meat

from Cows with Cancer, *San Francisco Chronicle,* Feb. 26, 2014, www.sfgate.com/health/article/Slaughterhouse-accused-of-selling-meat-from-cows-5267836.php#photo-5939827.

89. Ibid.
90. Nicolette Hahn Niman, Support Your Local Slaughterhouse, *New York Times,* Mar. 1, 2014, www.nytimes.com/2014/03/02/opinion/sunday/support-your-local-slaughterhouse.html.
91. Lynda Simkins, in discussion with the author, June 30, 2015.
92. Natick Community Organic Farm, www.natickfarm.org.
93. Lynda Simkins, in discussion with the author, June 30, 2015.
94. Newton Farmers' Market Rules & Regulations, 2015.
95. Mass. Dept. of Public Health, Food Protection Program Policies, Procedures and Guidelines, Issue: Farmer's Markets, Revised Apr. 30, 2013, www.mass.gov/eohhs/docs/dph/environmental/foodsafety/farmer-market-guidelines.pdf.
96. Trish Umbrell, email message to author, July 7, 2015.
97. Jenny Miller, New Regulations Mean Greenmarket Vendors Can No Longer Cut Their Cheese, Grub Street, June 22, 2011, www.grubstreet.com/2011/06/deparment_of_ag_says_no_to_cut.html.
98. New York State Dept. of Agriculture & Markets, Art. 20-C, Licensing of Food Processing Establishments, www.agriculture.ny.gov/FS/industry/04circs/Art20CLicofFooCIR951.pdf.
99. Amy Zimmer, Greenmarket Vendors Say Cheese Slicing Ban Stinks, DNAInfo, June 27, 2011, https://www.dnainfo.com/new-york/20110627/murray-hill-gramercy/union-square-greenmarket-vendors-say-cheese-slicing-ban-stinks.
100. Baylen Linnekin, Stop Cutting the Cheese, NY Tells Farmers' Markets, Reason's Hit & Run, June 27, 2011, https://reason.com/blog/2011/06/27/stop-cutting-the-cheese-ny-tel.
101. New York Dept. of Agriculture & Markets, 2754.6. Exemptions. (d) Slicing and packaging of cheese at farmers' markets. https://govt.westlaw.com/nycrr/Document/I0fad5fcac22211dda8b4a344a7766531?viewType=FullText&originationContext=documenttoc&transitionType=CategoryPageItem&contextData=(sc.Default).
102. Marion Renault, Minnesota Farmers Markets Can Start Offering Sam-

ples, *Minneapolis Star Tribune,* Apr. 23, 2014, www.startribune.com /minnesota-farmers-markets-can-start-offering-samples/256215931/.

103. Jeremy Roebuck, Stricter Food Law in Pa. Frustrates Farmers' Markets, *Philadelphia Inquirer,* May 1, 2011, articles.philly.com/2011-05-01/news /29493407_1_market-vendors-food-safety-new-rules.
104. Nathan Rosenberg & Emily Broad Leib, Pennsylvania's Chapter 57 and Its Effects on Farmers Markets, Harvard Food Law & Policy Clinic, Aug. 2012, www.chlpi.org/wp-content/uploads/2013/12/PA-FM-FINAL3.pdf.
105. Ibid.
106. USDA Food Safety & Inspection Service, "Danger Zone" (40 °F - 140 °F), www.fsis.usda.gov/wps/portal/fsis/topics/food-safety-education/get -answers/food-safety-fact-sheets/safe-food-handling/danger-zone-40-f -140-f/CT_Index (last visited Jun. 13, 2013).
107. Nathan Rosenberg & Emily Broad Leib, Pennsylvania's Chapter 57 and Its Effects on Farmers Markets, Harvard Food Law & Policy Clinic, Aug. 2012, www.chlpi.org/wp-content/uploads/2013/12/PA-FM-FINAL3.pdf.
108. Mississippi Retail Sale of Fresh and Frozen Fish, Meat, Poultry and any Other Potentially Hazardous Foods, with the Exclusion of Seafood and Frozen Desserts, from Mobile Vehicles, Mississippi Dept. of Agriculture & Commerce, www.mdac.ms.gov/wp-content/uploads/SalesMeatPoultry .pdf.
109. Growing Mississippi, MS Dept. of Agriculture's Focus on Consumer Protection Heightened This Holiday Season, Nov. 11, 2013, growingms .com/news/2013/11/ms-dept-agricultures-focus-consumer-protection -heightened-holiday-season/.
110. Square Market Rules, www.batesvillemainstreet.com/wp-content/uploads /2015/04/2015VendorPack.pdf.
111. Becky Gillette, State Cracking Down on Side-of-the-Road Sellers, *Mississippi Business Journal,* Oct. 11, 1999, msbusiness.com/1999/10/state -cracking-down-on-sideoftheroad-sellers/.
112. Nathan Rosenberg, email message to author, July 11, 2015.
113. Meeting Minutes, Mississippi Food Policy Council, Apr. 10, 2012, https:// mississippifoodpolicycouncil.com/minutes-and-reports/april-2013/.
114. Ibid.
115. Bob Segall, FDA proposes new food transportation rule to prevent "hot

trucks," WTHR.com Apr. 2, 2014, www.wthr.com/story/25147107/2014/04/02/fda-proposes-new-food-transportation-rule-to-prevent-hot-trucks.

116. Press Release, Sen. Sherrod Brown, Following A Series Of Investigative Reports Of Food Safety Violations On Refrigerated Trucks, Brown Urges FDA To Take Action To Ensure Safety Of Food Supply Chain, Apr. 3, 2014, www.brown.senate.gov/newsroom/press/release/following-a-series-of-investigative-reports-of-food-safety-violations-on-refrigerated-trucks-brown-urges-fda-to-take-action-to-ensure-safety-of-food-supply-chain.
117. Nathan Rosenberg, email message to author, July 11, 2015.
118. Local Food Directories: National Farmers Market Directory, USDA, search.ams.usda.gov/farmersmarkets/.
119. Farm Flavor, Mississippi Cow Country, farmflavor.com/us-ag/mississippi/animals-livestock-mississippi/mississippi-cow-country/.
120. Ken Meter & Megan Phillips Goldberg, An Overview of the Mississippi Farm and Food Economy, May 15, 2014, www.crcworks.org/msfood.pdf.
121. Delta Directions, Where's the Meat?, www.deltadirections.com/wheres-the-meat/.
122. Small Farms Manitoba, Harborside Farms, https://www.smallfarmsmanitoba.com/farms/56/harborside-farms.
123. Canadian Agricultural Human Resource Council, About Harborside Farms, 2011, www.cahrc-ccrha.ca/sites/default/files/files/publications/Farm-Profiles/Harborside%20Farms%20Profile.pdf.
124. Mike Green, Happy heritage hogs make for prize-winning prosciutto, CBC, May 5, 2013, www.cbc.ca/manitoba/scene/food/2013/05/05/happy-heritage-hogs-make-for-prize-winning-prosciutto/.
125. Ibid.
126. Ibid.
127. CBC News, Manitoba inspectors seize farm's award-winning meats, Aug. 30, 2013, www.cbc.ca/news/canada/manitoba/manitoba-inspectors-seize-farm-s-award-winning-meats-1.1359057.
128. Lorraine Stevenson, Pilot Mound farm's prize-winning meat product seized by health inspectors, *Manitoba Co-Operator*, Sept. 6, 2013, www.manitobacooperator.ca/2013/09/06/pilot-mound-farms-prize-winning-meat-product-seized-by-health-inspectors/.

129. Bill Redekop, Farmers No Longer Face Charges, *Winnipeg Free Press,* May 14, 2014, www.winnipegfreepress.com/local/farmers-no-longer-face-charges-259179021.html.
130. Ibid.
131. Sheldon Birnie, Regulatory Snarls for Small-scale Farmers, *Briarpatch,* May 25, 2015, briarpatchmagazine.com/articles/view/regulatory-snarls-for-small-scale-farmers.
132. Helena Bottemiller, Q&A: Nestle on Food Safety Politics, *Food Safety News,* Sept. 21, 2009, www.foodsafetynews.com/2009/09/qa-marion-nestle-on-food-safety-politics/#.VfhzPLSZ571.
133. Sarah Klein and David Plunkett, FDA's New Posture Is Promising, Not Pathetic, *Food Safety News,* Feb. 6, 2013, www.foodsafetynews.com/2013/02/fdas-new-posture-is-promising-not-pathetic/#.VfhzjbSZ571.
134. Editorial, "Food Safety" and the GOP, *Wall Street Journal,* Dec. 2, 2010, www.wsj.com/articles/SB10001424052748704594804575649121695684294.

Chapter 2

1. Marion Burros, U.S. Imposes Standards for Organic-Food Labeling, *New York Times,* Dec. 21, 2000, www.nytimes.com/2000/12/21/us/us-imposes-standards-for-organic-food-labeling.html.
2. Molly O'Neill, Organic Industry Faces an Ethics Question, *New York Times,* May 17, 1995, www.nytimes.com/1995/05/17/garden/organic-industry-faces-an-ethics-question.html.
3. Peter Whoriskey, Sure, that food has the government's organic label. But that doesn't mean it was made without man-made chemicals, *Washington Post*'s Wonkblog, Apr. 28, 2015, www.washingtonpost.com/news/wonkblog/wp/2015/04/28/sure-that-food-has-the-governments-organic-label-but-that-doesnt-mean-it-was-made-without-chemicals/.
4. Amanda Onion, Dispute: What Makes Milk Organic?, ABC News, Mar. 14, 2005, abcnews.go.com/Technology/print?id=572069.
5. Kimberly Kindy & Lyndsey Layton, Integrity of Federal "Organic" Label Questioned, *Washington Post,* July 3, 2009, www.washingtonpost.com/wp-dyn/content/article/2009/07/02/AR2009070203365.html.

6. The Cornucopia Institute, FDA/USDA Collude to Eliminate True Organic Egg Production, July 23, 2013, www.cornucopia.org/2013/07/fda usda-collude-to-eliminate-true-organic-egg-production/; About Us, Cornucopia Institute, www.cornucopia.org/about-us/.
7. The Cornucopia Institute, Who Owns Organic, www.cornucopia.org/who -owns-organic/.
8. Marion Nestle, The endless controversy over organics, Food Politics, Feb. 16, 2012, www.foodpolitics.com/2012/02/the-endless-controversy-over -organics/.
9. U.S. Government Accountability Office, Farm Programs, www.gao.gov /key_issues/farm_programs/issue_summary.
10. Baylen J. Linnekin, End Farm Subsidies and Make Agriculture Sustainable, *Baltimore Sun*, May 18, 2011, www.baltimoresun.com/news/opinion /oped/bs-ed-farm-subsidies-20110518-story.html.
11. Alan Bjerga, Record Farm Profit Amid Drought Raises Questions of Aid, Bloomberg Business, Aug. 29, 2012, www.bloomberg.com/news/arti cles/2012-08-29/record-farm-profit-amid-drought-raises-questions-of -aid.
12. Environmental Working Group, EWG Farm Subsidies, https://farm.ewg .org/region.php?fips=00000&progcode=total&yr=2012.
13. Joan McCoy, Should Rich Farmers Get Subsidies?, *Arkansas Leader*, June 20, 2006, www.arkansasleader.com/2006/06/top-story-should-rich-farmers -get.html.
14. Paul Krugman, True Blue Americans, *New York Times*, May 7, 2002, www.nytimes.com/2002/05/07/opinion/true-blue-americans.html.
15. Brian M. Reidl, How Farm Subsidies Harm Taxpayers, Consumers, and Farmers, Too, The Heritage Foundation, June 20, 2007, www.heritage .org/research/reports/2007/06/how-farm-subsidies-harm-taxpayers-con sumers-and-farmers-too.
16. Ron Nixon, Billionaires Received U.S. Farm Subsidies, Report Finds, *New York Times*, Nov. 7, 2013, www.nytimes.com/2013/11/07/us/billion aires-received-us-farm-subsidies-report-finds.html?_r=0.
17. S.A. Miller, Bon Jovi, Bruce Springsteen Cash in on Farm Aid, *New York Post*, Nov. 15, 2011, nypost.com/2011/11/15/farm-aid-for-bruce-bon -jovi/.

18. Brian M. Riedl & John E. Frydenlund, At the Federal Trough: Farm Subsidies for the Rich and Famous, The Heritage Foundation, Nov. 26, 2001, www.heritage.org/research/reports/2001/11/at-the-federal-trough-farm-subsidies-for-the-rich-and-famous.
19. Glenn Thrush, Anti-socialist Bachmann got $250K in federal farm subsidies, Politico, Dec. 22, 2009, www.politico.com/blogs/on-congress/2009/12/anti-socialist-bachmann-got-250k-in-federal-farm-subsidies-023679.
20. Joan McCoy, Should Rich Farmers Get Subsidies?, *Arkansas Leader,* June 20, 2006, www.arkansasleader.com/2006/06/top-story-should-rich-farmers-get.html.
21. Environmental Working Group, EWG Farm Subsidies, https://farm.ewg.org/region.php?fips=00000 https://www.farm.ewg.org/region.php?fips=00000&progcode=total&yr=2012.
22. Editorial, Congress should rein in crop insurance, *Minneapolis Star Tribune,* May 8, 2012, www.startribune.com/editorial-congress-should-rein-in-crop-insurance/150245775/.
23. Frank Morris, Most Agree "Welfare for Farmers" Has To Go, NPR, Sept. 23, 2013, www.npr.org/2013/09/23/225303958/farmers-question-subsidies.
24. Lauren Servin, How Government Incentivizes the Overproduction of Junk Food, Roosevelt Institute, rooseveltinstitute.org/new-guardhow-our-government-incentivizes-overproduction-junk-food/.
25. Ramsey Cox & Erik Wasson, Senate votes 75–22 to end debate on farm bill, The Hill's Floor Action, June 6, 2013, www.thehill.com/blogs/floor-action/senate/303863-senate-votes-75-22-to-end-debate-on-farm-bill.
26. Press Release, Sen. Thad Cochran, Cochran, USDA Organize Farm Bill & Crop Insurance Listening Sessions, Oct. 15, 2014, www.cochran.senate.gov/public/index.cfm/news-releases?ID=1122b007-e869-4a33-9848-37179fdaf410; Press Release, U.S. Senate Committee on Agriculture, Nutrition, & Forestry, Cochran: Reach Farm Bill Agreement As Soon As Possible, Oct. 30, 2013, www.cochran.senate.gov/public/index.cfm/news-releases?ID=f301fa86-8d27-474b-9efe-8338271202b2.
27. Ramsey Cox & Erik Wasson, Senate votes 75–22 to end debate on farm bill, The Hill's Floor Action, June 6, 2013, www.thehill.com/blogs/floor-action/senate/303863-senate-votes-75-22-to-end-debate-on-farm-bill.

28. Baylen J. Linnekin, End Farm Subsidies and Make Agriculture Sustainable, *Baltimore Sun,* May 18, 2011, www.baltimoresun.com/news/opinion/oped/bs-ed-farm-subsidies-20110518-story.html.
29. Anne Weir, Taxpayers' Bill for Farm Subsidies: $30 Billion by 2018, EWG's Agmag, July 10, 2015, www.ewg.org/agmag/2015/07/taxpayers-bill-farm-subsidies-30-billion-2018.
30. Baylen Linnekin, This Farm Bill Stinks, Reason.com, Feb. 1, 2014, https://reason.com/archives/2014/02/01/this-farm-bill-stinks/singlepage.
31. James McDonald, Cropland Consolidation and the Future of Family Farms, USDA Economic Research Service, Sept. 3, 2013, www.ers.usda.gov/amber-waves/2013-september/cropland-consolidation-and-the-future-of-family-farms.aspx#.Vfl1MLSZ570.
32. James M. McDonald, Why Are Farms Getting Larger? The Case of the U.S., USDA Economic Research Service, 2011, ageconsearch.umn.edu/bitstream/115361/2/MacDonald.pdf.
33. Ferd Hoefner, The New Farm Bill: The Good, The Bad, and the Wait-and-See, Civil Eats, Jan. 31, 2014, www.civileats.com/2014/01/31/the-new-farm-bill-the-good-the-bad-and-the-wait-and-see/.
34. USDA pulls plug on some farm subsidy data, The Center for Public Integrity, May 21, 2010, www.publicintegrity.org/2010/05/21/2668/usda-pulls-plug-some-farm-subsidy-data.
35. Nancy Watzman, Farm bill allows Congress to keep crop subsidies secret, Sunlight Foundation, Feb. 7, 2014, https://sunlightfoundation.com/blog/2014/02/07/farm-bill-allows-congress-to-keep-crop-subsidies-secret/.
36. Jeffrey T. LaFrance, Jay P. Shimshack, & Steven Wu, The Environmental Impacts of Subsidized Crop Insurance: Crop Insurance & the Extensive Margin, 2001, econweb.ucsd.edu/~carsonvs/papers/830.pdf.
37. Ruben N. Lubowski et al., Environmental Effects of Policy-Induced Land-Use Changes, Environmental Effects of Agricultural Land-Use Changes, USDA Economic Research Service, Aug. 2006, www.ers.usda.gov/media/469928/err25_1_.pdf.
38. Miguel A. Altieri, The Ecological Role of Biodiversity in Ecosystems, *Agriculture, Ecosystems & Environment* 19, 1999, is.muni.cz/el/1423/jaro2014/HEN437/um/Altieri_Ecological_role.pdf.
39. Suzy Friedman, Let's Focus on a Farm's Performance, Not Its Size, Environ-

mental Defense Fund's Growing Returns blog, Mar. 17, 2015, blogs.edf.org/growingreturns/2015/03/17/lets-focus-on-a-farms-performance-not-its-size/.

40. Mary Angelo, Jason Czarnezki, & Bill Eubanks, Food, Agriculture, and Environmental Law (2013).
41. Environmental Working Group, EWG Farm Subsidies, https://farm.ewg.org/.
42. Timothy A. Wise, Identifying the Real Winners from U.S. Agricultural Policies, Global Development & Environment Institute Working Paper No. 05–07, Dec. 2005, www.ase.tufts.edu/gdae/Pubs/wp/05-07RealWinnersUSAg.pdf.
43. National Family Farm Coalition, The Facts Behind King Corn, www.nffc.net/Learn/Fact%20Sheets/King%20Corn%20Fact%20Sheet.pdf.
44. Dawn Brighid, High Fructose Corn Syrup: If This Doesn't Convince You, Nothing Will, The Sustainable Table, www.sustainabletable.org/704/high-fructose-corn-syrup-if-this-doesn-t-convince-you-nothing-wil.
45. Joel Salatin, email message to author, Apr. 30, 2012.
46. Veronique Dupont, GMO Corn, Soybeans Dominate US Market, Phys.org, June 4, 2013, www.phys.org/news/2013-06-gmo-corn-soybeans-dominate.html.
47. Mike Russo & Dan Smith, Apples to Twinkies 2013, U.S. PIRG, July 2013, www.uspirg.org/sites/pirg/files/reports/Apples_to_Twinkies_2013_USPIRG.pdf.
48. Joel Salatin, email message to author, Apr. 30, 2012.
49. Editorial, For a Healthier Country, Overhaul Farm Subsidies, *Scientific American,* May 1, 2012, www.scientificamerican.com/article/fresh-fruit-hold-the-insulin/.
50. National Sustainable Agriculture Coalition, Most Want Real Farm Subsidy Reform, But Mega-Farms Want More Taxpayer Money, June 11, 2015, www.sustainableagriculture.net/blog/payment-limit-rule-comments/.
51. Baylen J. Linnekin, End farm subsidies and make agriculture sustainable, *Baltimore Sun,* May 18, 2011, www.baltimoresun.com/news/opinion/oped/bs-ed-farm-subsidies-20110518-story.html.
52. USDA Commodity Purchase Program for Raisin Processors/Packers, California Raisin Marketing Board, Jan. 22, 2015, www.calraisins.org

/about/instructions-on-usda-commodity-purchase-program-for-raisin-processorspackers/.

53. David A. Fahrenthold, One Grower's Grapes of Wrath, *Washington Post,* July 7, 2013, www.washingtonpost.com/lifestyle/style/one-growers-grapes-of-wrath/2013/07/07/ebebcfd8-e380-11e2-80eb-3145e2994a55_story.html.
54. Confirmation of Regulations, California Raisin Marketing Order; Section 610 Review, Federal Register, Jan. 30, 2006, www.federalregister.gov/articles/2006/01/30/06-821/california-raisin-marketing-order-section-610-review#h-10.
55. David A. Fahrenthold, One Grower's Grapes of Wrath, *Washington Post,* July 7, 2013, www.washingtonpost.com/lifestyle/style/one-growers-grapes-of-wrath/2013/07/07/ebebcfd8-e380-11e2-80eb-3145e2994a55_story.html.
56. Ibid.
57. David G. Savage, High court rules against raisin board in dispute over setting aside crops to prop up prices, *Los Angeles Times,* June 22, 2015, www.latimes.com/business/la-fi-court-california-raisins-20150623-story.html.
58. Brief of Sun-Maid Growers of California and the Raisin Marketing Association as Amici Curiae in Support of Respondent, Horne v. U.S. Dept. of Agriculture, April 8, 2015, No. 14–275, www.americanbar.org/content/dam/aba/publications/supreme_court_preview/BriefsV5/14-275_amicus_resp_sunmaidgrowers.authcheckdam.pdf.
59. About Sun Maid Raisins, America's Greatest Brands, www.americasgreatestbrands.com/volume7/assets/AGB%20pdfs/AGB%20SunMaid.pdf.
60. Brief of Sun-Maid Growers of California and the Raisin Marketing Association as Amici Curiae in Support of Respondent, Horne v. U.S. Dept. of Agriculture, April 8, 2015, No. 14–275, www.americanbar.org/content/dam/aba/publications/supreme_court_preview/BriefsV5/14-275_amicus_resp_sunmaidgrowers.authcheckdam.pdf.
61. Ibid.
62. Timothy Taylor, Raisins: When Insiders Set the Rules, Conversable Economist, June 24, 2015, www.conversableeconomist.blogspot.com/2015/06/raisins-when-insiders-set-rules.html.

63. *Horne v. U.S. Dept. of Agriculture*, 576 U. S. ____ (2015), www.supremecourt.gov/opinions/14pdf/14-275_c0n2.pdf.
64. USDA, Marketing Order Regulating the Handling of Spearmint Oil Produced in the Far West; Revision of the Salable Quantity and Allotment Percentage for Class 3 (Native) Spearmint Oil for the 2014–2015 Marketing Year, Aug. 21, 2015, www.ams.usda.gov/rules-regulations/marketing-order-regulating-handling-spearmint-oil-produced-far-west-revision.
65. Madilynne Clark, Big Picture — Marketing Orders Have Grower Support, *Capital Press,* May 28, 2015, www.capitalpress.com/Opinion/Columns/20150528/big-picture-x2014-marketing-orders-have-grower-support.
66. Siddhartha Mahanta, Big Beef, *Washington Monthly,* Jan./Feb. 2014, www.washingtonmonthly.com/magazine/january_february_2014/features/big_beef048356.php?page=all.
67. Bill Tomson, U.S. Makes Special Purchase of $40 Million of Chicken Products, *Wall Street Journal,* Aug. 15, 2011, www.wsj.com/articles/SB10001424053111903392904576510863093422074.
68. Jeffrey Kluger, Pork Gets a Swine Flu Bailout, *Time,* Sept. 11, 2009, www.content.time.com/time/health/article/0,8599,1921649,00.html.
69. Brad Plumer, How the U.S. government spends millions to get people to eat more pizza, *Washington Post*'s Wonkblog, Feb. 10, 2014, www.washingtonpost.com/news/wonkblog/wp/2014/02/10/13-percent-of-americans-are-eating-pizza-on-any-given-day/.
70. Physicians Committee for Responsible Medicine, Government Support for Unhealthful Foods, https://www.pcrm.org/health/reports/agriculture-and-health-policies-unhealthful-foods.
71. Paul Shapiro, email message to author, June 17, 2015.
72. Parke Wilde, USDA reports on pizza consumption and on dairy checkoff program initiatives to increase pizza demand, US Food Policy blog, Feb. 7, 2014, usfoodpolicy.blogspot.com/2014/02/usda-reports-on-pizza-consumption-and.html.
73. John Newton & Todd Kuethe, Could the Bird Flu Become a 100-Million-Bushel Corn Problem?, AgWeb, June 18, 2015, www.agweb.com/article/could-the-bird-flu-become-a-100-million-bushel-corn-problem-NAA-university-news-release/.

74. Morgan Brennan, Inside Sunrise Farms' avian flu chicken slaughter, CNBC, Apr. 24, 2015, www.cnbc.com/2015/04/24/inside-sunrise-farms-avian-flu-chicken-slaughter.html.
75. Don Carr, email message to author, July 14, 2015.
76. H.R. 933, Consolidated and Further Continuing Appropriations Act of 2013, www.gpo.gov/fdsys/pkg/BILLS-113hr933enr/pdf/BILLS-113hr933enr.pdf.
77. H.R. 933, § 735, Farmer Assurance Provision, Consolidated and Further Continuing Appropriations Act of 2013.
78. Monsanto, Monsanto Statement Regarding Farmer Assurance Provision in H.R. 933, Mar. 28, 2013, www.monsanto.com/newsviews/pages/statement-regarding-farmers-assurance-provisions.aspx.
79. American Soybean Association, ASA Joins Fellow Ag Groups to Urge Practical Biotech Policy in FY2013 Appropriations Bill, June 14, 2012, https://soygrowers.com/asa-joins-fellow-ag-groups-to-urge-practical-biotech-policy-in-fy2013-appropriations-bill/.
80. H.R. 933, Consolidated and Further Continuing Appropriations Act of 2013, www.gpo.gov/fdsys/pkg/BILLS-113hr933enr/pdf/BILLS-113hr933enr.pdf.
81. 5 U.S. 137 (1803).
82. Baylen Linnekin, A Constitutional Argument Against the So-Called "Monsanto Protection Act," Reason.com, Apr. 6, 2013, https://reason.com/archives/2013/04/06/why-i-oppose-the-so-called-monsanto-prot/singlepage.
83. David Rogers, Big Agriculture flexes its muscle, Politico, Mar. 25, 2013, www.politico.com/story/2013/03/big-agriculture-tom-vilsack-monsanto-089268.
84. USDA, Food Standards and Labeling Policy Book, Aug. 2005, www.fsis.usda.gov/OPPDE/larc/Policies/Labeling_Policy_Book_082005.pdf.
85. 9 C.F.R. § 319.180, Frankfurter, frank, furter, hotdog, weiner, vienna, bologna, garlic bologna, knockwurst, and similar products, https://www.gpo.gov/fdsys/pkg/CFR-2011-title9-vol2/pdf/CFR-2011-title9-vol2-sec319-180.pdf.
86. National Milk Producers Federation, Imitation Dairy Products FAQ, www.nmpf.org/washington_watch/standardsandsafety/imitation_dairy/FAQ.

87. USDA, Food Standards and Labeling Policy Book, Aug. 2005, www.fsis.usda.gov/OPPDE/larc/Policies/Labeling_Policy_Book_082005.pdf.
88. 21 C.F.R. § 163.124 White chocolate, https://www.gpo.gov/fdsys/pkg/CFR-2011-title21-vol2/pdf/CFR-2011-title21-vol2-sec163-124.pdf.
89. Terence Chea, Food-tech firms use plant products to crack the egg market, NBC News, Dec. 8, 2013, www.nbcnews.com/business/food-tech-firms-use-plant-products-crack-egg-market-2D11708741.
90. Josh Tetrick, email message to author, May 29, 2015.
91. Stephanie Strom, Hellmann's Maker Sues Company Over Its Just Mayo Substitute Mayonnaise, *New York Times,* Nov. 10, 2014, www.nytimes.com/2014/11/11/business/unilever-sues-a-start-up-over-mayonnaise-like-product.html?_r=0.
92. Michele Simon, email message to author, Nov. 20, 2014.
93. GlobeScan, The 2014 Sustainability Leaders, May 14, 2014, www.globescan.com/component/edocman/?view=document&id=103&Itemid=591
94. Stephanie Strom, Hellmann's Maker Sues Company Over Its Just Mayo Substitute Mayonnaise, *New York Times,* Nov. 10, 2014, www.nytimes.com/2014/11/11/business/unilever-sues-a-start-up-over-mayonnaise-like-product.html?_r=0.
95. Press Release, Unilever Withdraws Lawsuit Against Hampton Creek, Unilever, Dec. 18, 2014, https://www.unileverusa.com/news/press-releases/2014/unilever-withdraws-lawsuit-against-hampton-creek.html?criteria=year%3d2014Bad.
96. Stephanie Strom, Just Mayo Spread Violates Mayonnaise and Label Rules, F.D.A. Says, *New York Times,* Aug. 25, 2015, www.nytimes.com/2015/08/26/business/fda-says-eggless-spread-violates-mayonnaise-and-label-rules.html.
97. Anni Gasparro, Just Mayo Reaches Agreement with FDA to Keep Name, Change Label, *Wall Street Journal,* Dec. 17, 2015, www.wsj.com/articles/just-mayo-reaches-agreement-with-fda-to-keep-name-change-label-1450394163.
98. N.Y. A.G.M. Law § 50-g, NY Code, Section 50-G, Licenses to manufacturers of melloream.
99. Craig Claiborne, The 1960's: Haute Cuisine in America, *New York Times,* Jan. 1, 1970, query.nytimes.com/mem/archive/pdf?res=940CE7DE1739E63BBC4953DFB766838B669EDE.

100. Dairy Group Would Curb Melloream, *The Saratogian,* Jan. 8, 1968, www.fultonhistory.com/Newspapers%2021/Saratoga%20Springs%20NY%20Saratogian/Saratoga%20Springs%20NY%20Saratogian%201968/Saratoga%20Springs%20NY%20Saratogian%201968%20-%200094.pdf.
101. N.Y. A.G.M. Law § 50-g, NY Code, Section 50-G, Licenses to manufacturers of melloream.
102. Greg Van Ullen, email message to author, Aug. 18, 2015.
103. Jason Foscolo, email message to author, July 30, 2015.
104. National Milk Producers Federation, NMPF Asks FDA to Restrict Soy Beverage Labeling, Feb. 14, 2000, www.nmpf.org/washington_watch/standards/soy.
105. Milk, 9 *Webster's Dictionary* 754, 1999.
106. Travis Pillow, Ocheesee Creamery Devoted to Producing All Natural Dairy Products, Tallahassee Democrat, May 15, 2013, webcache.googleusercontent.com/search?q=cache:lr7VfOlN-lgJ:archive.tallahassee.com/article/20130515/LIVING03/305150028/Ocheesee-Creamery-devoted-producing-all-natural-dairy-products.
107. Michele Hatton, Local Spotlight—Ocheesee Creamery, New Leaf Market Co-Op's Natural Times, Jan./Feb./Mar. 2012, www.newleafmarket.coop/newsroom/newsletter/janfebmar-2012/local-spotlight-ocheesee-creamery.
108. Kendra Smith-Howard, *Pure & Modern Milk,* Oxford University Press, 2013.
109. Kayla Stirzel, Supplementing Your Health, The Villages Daily Sun, Aug. 13, 2013, www.health.usf.edu/nocms/villages/articles/Supplementing_your_Health_081313.pdf.
110. Justin Pearson, in discussion with the author, Aug. 25, 2015.
111. Press Release, Shira Rawlinson, Federal Court Keeps Florida Creamery Censored, Institute for Justice, Mar. 31, 2016, ij.org/press-release/federal-court-keeps-florida-creamery-censored/.
112. Justin Pearson, in discussion with the author, Apr. 7, 2016.
113. National Milk Producers Federation, NMPF Asks FDA to Restrict Soy Beverage Labeling, Feb. 14, 2000, www.nmpf.org/washington_watch/standards/soy.
114. 572 U.S. ___ (2014).
115. Marian Burros, F.D.A. Imposing Stricter Rules on Food Labels, *New York*

Times, May 5, 1994, www.nytimes.com/1994/05/05/us/fda-imposing-stricter-rules-on-food-labels.html.

116. Clif Bar, chocolate chip, www.clifbar.com/products/clif-bar/clifbar/chocolate-chip#nutrition.
117. Snickers, Snickers Bar, www.snickers.com/nutritional-info.
118. Helena Bottemiller, USDA Bought 21 Million Pounds of Beef Last Year from Slaughterhouse Now Closed for Animal Abuse, *Food Safety News,* Aug. 22, 2012, www.foodsafetynews.com/2012/08/usda-bought-21-million-pounds-of-beef-from-central-valley-meat-last-year/#.VfnCOrSZ573.
119. Robert Rodriguez, Hanford's Valley Meat Co. reopens after fixing "unsanitary conditions," *The Fresno Bee,* Feb. 19, 2014, www.fresnobee.com/news/business/article19518639.html.
120. Iowa H.F. 589, An Act Relating to An Offense Involving Agricultural Operations, and Providing Penalties, and Including Effective Date Provisions, Mar. 2, 2012, coolice.legis.iowa.gov/Cool-ICE/default.asp?Category=billinfo&Service=Billbook&menu=false&ga=84&hbill=HF589.
121. Kansas 47–1827, Prohibited acts; criminal penalties, 2014, www.kslegislature.org/li_2014/b2013_14/statute/047_000_0000_chapter/047_018_0000_article/047_018_0027_section/047_018_0027_k/.
122. Lee Davidson, Animal rights groups seek veto of Utah's "ag-gag" bill, *The Salt Lake Tribune,* Mar. 9, 2012, www.sltrib.com/sltrib/politics/53684910-90/activists-animal-bill-farm.html.csp.
123. Wes, Taking a Stand Against Silence, National Young Farmers Coalition, Apr. 8, 2013, www.youngfarmers.org/taking-a-stand-against-silence/.
124. Lake Runyon, Judge Strikes Down Idaho "Ag-Gag" Law, Raising Questions for Other States, NPR's The Salt blog, Aug. 4, 2015, www.npr.org/sections/thesalt/2015/08/04/429345939/idaho-strikes-down-ag-gag-law-raising-questions-for-other-states.

Chapter 3

1. Press Release, "Oakland Recycles" Launches Major New Trash, Compost and Recycling Services, City of Oakland, Calif., June 25, 2015.
2. Morvarid Bagherzadeh, Mitsuhiro Inamura, & Hyunchul Jeong, Food Waste Along the Food Chain, OECD Food, Agriculture and Fisheries

Papers, Dec. 22, 2014, www.oecd-ilibrary.org/agriculture-and-food/food-waste-along-the-food-chain_5jxrcmftzj36-en.

3. Sam Levin, Oakland's Trash Program Promotes Waste, *East Bay Express,* July 15, 2015, www.eastbayexpress.com/oakland/oaklands-trash-program-promotes-waste/Content?oid=4412694.
4. Mike Blasky, Oakland restaurant owners outraged over dramatic compost collection rates, *East Bay Times,* July 9, 2015, www.eastbaytimes.com/breaking-news/ci_28460943/oakland-restaurant-owners-outraged-over-dramatic-compost-collection.
5. Seung Y. Lee, Oakland restaurants protest sharp compost fee hike, Berkeleyside's Nosh, July 14, 2015, www.berkeleyside.com/2015/07/14/oakland-restaurants-protest-sharp-compost-fee-hike/.
6. Chip Johnson, Oakland's high composting fees rotten, *San Francisco Chronicle,* July 13, 2015, www.sfchronicle.com/bayarea/johnson/article/Oakland-s-high-composting-fees-rotten-6382846.php.
7. Robert Gammon, Enough with Environmentally Regressive Policies, *East Bay Express,* July 15, 2015, www.eastbayexpress.com/oakland/enough-with-the-environmentally-regressive-policies/Content?oid=4412711.
8. Chip Johnson, Oakland City Council was arrogant in awarding garbage contract, SFGate, Sept. 23, 2014, www.sfgate.com/bayarea/article/Oakland-City-Council-was-arrogant-in-awarding-5773253.php.
9. Dana Gunders, Wasted: How America Is Losing Up to 40 Percent of Its Food from Farm to Fork to Landfill, NRDC, Aug. 2012, www.nrdc.org/food/files/wasted-food-IP.pdf.
10. Food Waste Reduction Alliance, About the Food Waste Reduction Alliance, www.foodwastealliance.org/about-us-page-2/.
11. Jean C. Buzby, Hodan Farah Wells, & Jeffrey Hyman, The Estimated Amount, Value, and Calories of Postharvest Food Losses at the Retail and Consumer Levels in the United States, USDA Economic Information Bulletin No. (EIB-121), Feb. 2014, www.ers.usda.gov/publications/eib-economic-information-bulletin/eib121.aspx?mkt_tok=3RkMMJWWfF9wsRonuKjOZKXonjHpfsX56%2BwqXaC%2FlMI%2F0ER3fOvrPUfGjI4ATsthI%2BSLDwEYGJlv6SgFT7DGMaNny7gNUxI%3D#.Uw5ZRc6tbTr.
12. Jean C. Buzby & Jeffrey Hyman, Total and per capita value of food loss in

the United States, Food Policy, July 20, 2012, ucce.ucdavis.edu/files/data store/234-2425.pdf.

13. George Webster, Moldy matters: How wasted food is destroying the environment, CNN, June 27, 2012, www.cnn.com/2012/06/27/world/europe/food-waste-emissions-pichler/.
14. United Nations Food & Agriculture Organization, Food wastage footprint, Impacts on natural resources, 2013, www.fao.org/docrep/018/i3347e/i3347e.pdf.
15. Ibid.
16. Ruben N. Lubowski et al., Major Uses of Land in the United States, 2002, USDA Economic Information Bulletin No. (EIB-14), May 2006, www.ers.usda.gov/publications/eib-economic-information-bulletin/eib14.aspx.
17. United Nations Food & Agriculture Organization, Food wastage footprint, Impacts on natural resources, 2013, www.fao.org/docrep/018/i3347e/i3347e.pdf.
18. School Food Focus, School Food 101, School Food Focus & C.S. Mott Group for Sustainable Food Systems at Michigan State University, www.foodsystems.msu.edu/uploads/files/cost-of-school-lunch.pdf.
19. USDA, FY 2010 Budget Summary & Annual Performance Plan, www.obpa.usda.gov/budsum/FY10budsum.pdf.
20. Barry Yeoman, Unhappy Meals, *Mother Jones,* Jan./Feb. 2003, www.motherjones.com/politics/2003/01/unhappy-meals.
21. Gordon W. Gunderson, National School Lunch Act, USDA Food & Nutrition Service, Aug. 26, 2015, www.fns.usda.gov/nslp/history_5#28; Gordon W. Gunderson, National School Lunch Program (NSLP), USDA Food & Nutrition Service, June 17, 2014, www.fns.usda.gov/nslp/history_4.
22. Regina Weiss, Should School Lunch Be Free for All? Janet Poppendieck Thinks So, Huffington Post, May 25, 2015, www.huffingtonpost.com/regina-weiss/should-school-lunch-be-fr_b_791425.html.
23. USDA, School Meals, Healthy Hunger-Free Kids Act, Mar. 3, 2014, www.fns.usda.gov/school-meals/healthy-hunger-free-kids-act.
24. Juliana F.W. Cohen et al., Impact of the New U.S. Department of Agriculture School Meal Standards on Food Selection, Consumption, and Waste, *Am. J. Prev. Med.,* Apr. 2014, www.ncbi.nlm.nih.gov/pmc/articles/PMC3994463/pdf/nihms569417.pdf.

25. Amy Hubbard, USDA school lunch rules "best ever"—though pizza is still a "vegetable," *Los Angeles Times,* Nation Now, Jan. 25, 2012,
26. Marion Nestle, The USDA's New School Nutrition Standards Are Worth Celebrating, *The Atlantic,* Jan. 26, 2012, www.theatlantic.com/health/archive/2012/01/the-usdas-new-school-nutrition-standards-are-worth-celebrating/252038/.
27. Healthy, Hunger-Free Kids Act of 2010, Public Law 11-296, Dec. 13, 2010, www.gpo.gov/fdsys/pkg/PLAW-111publ296/pdf/PLAW-111publ296.pdf.
28. Elementary Menu, Montgomery County (Md.) Public Schools, Feb. 2014 (on file with author).
29. National School Lunch Program: Participation & Lunches Served, USDA Food & Nutrition Service, Sept. 4, 2015, www.fns.usda.gov/sites/default/files/pd/slsummar.pdf.
30. J.N. Kish, U.S. Population 1776 to Present, Annual United States population growth numbers from 1776 to Present Day, Aug. 3, 2010, https://www.google.com/fusiontables/DataSource?dsrcid=225439#rows:id=1.
31. National School Lunch Program: Participation & Lunches Served, USDA Food & Nutrition Service, Sept. 4, 2015, www.fns.usda.gov/sites/default/files/pd/slsummar.pdf.
32. Jim McLaughlin, Students strike against new federal school lunch rules, *Milwaukee Journal Sentinel,* Sept. 12, 2012, www.jsonline.com/news/education/students-strike-against-new-federal-school-lunch-rules-t96t7sp-170124676.html.
33. Jared Liotta, Sandwiches bulked up at Staples after student complaints, *Westport News,* Sept. 14, 2012, www.westport-news.com/news/article/Sandwiches-bulked-up-at-Staples-after-student-3866290.php.
34. Randi Weiner, A change in school snacks: Healthy only, Lohud, July 7, 2014, www.lohud.com/story/news/education/hall-monitor/2014/07/07/change-school-snacks-healthy/12284263/.
35. Teresa Watanabe, Solutions sought to reduce food waste at schools, *Los Angeles Times,* Apr. 1, 2014, www.latimes.com/local/la-me-lausd-waste-20140402-story.html#page=1.
36. Editorial, To curb school lunch waste, ease the fruit and vegetable rules, *Los Angeles Times,* Apr. 8, 2014, www.latimes.com/opinion/editorials/la-ed-school-lunch-20140408-story.html.
37. Ron Regan, Millions wasted in federal school lunch program, WEWS,

Sept. 16, 2014, www.newsnet5.com/news/local-news/investigations/mil lions-wasted-in-federal-school-lunch-program.

38. School Nutrition Association, School Nutrition Trends Survey 2014, Aug. 2014, https://schoolnutrition.org/uploadedFiles/Resources_and_Re search/Research/SNA2014TrendsSurvey.pdf.
39. Michael Marcenelle & Carmen Byker, Food Waste Among Elementary School Children: Opportunities & Challenges, https://schoolnutrition .org/uploadedFiles/Presentations/ANC_2012_-_Denver(1)/2._Nutri tion/071314%20at%2012%20-%20Food%20Waste%20Among%20 Elementary%20School%20Children%20Challenges%20%20Opportu nities.pdf.
40. David Just & Joseph Price, Default options, incentives and food choices, *Public Health Nutrition*, Dec. 2013, https://veggieproject.byu.edu/Dr %20Prices%20Papers/default%20options.pdf.
41. U.S. Government Accountability Office, Implementing Nutrition Changes Was Challenging and Clarification of Oversight Requirements Is Needed, Jan. 2014, www.gao.gov/assets/670/660427.pdf.
42. Juliana Cohen, et al., School Lunch Waste among Middle School Students: Implications for Nutrients Consumed and Food Waste Costs, *Am. J. Prev. Med.,* Feb. 2013, www.ncbi.nlm.nih.gov/pmc/articles/PMC 3788640/.
43. Juliana F.W. Cohen et al., Impact of the New U.S. Department of Agriculture School Meal Standards on Food Selection, Consumption, and Waste, *Am. J. Prev. Med.,* Apr. 2014, www.ncbi.nlm.nih.gov/pmc/articles /PMC3994463/pdf/nihms569417.pdf.
44. Juliana Cohen, email message to author, Jan. 6, 2016.
45. USDA Food & Nutrition Service, Offer Versus Serve, School Year 2014–2015, www.fns.usda.gov/sites/default/files/SP57-2014a.pdf.
46. Juliana Cohen, email message to author, Jan. 6, 2016.
47. Teresa Watanabe, Solutions sought to reduce food waste at schools, *Los Angeles Times,* Apr. 1, 2014, www.latimes.com/local/la-me-lausd-waste-20 140402-story.html#page=1.
48. Mark Wheeler, Love at first bite? Not for L.A. school kids and their vegetables, UCLA Newsroom, May 22, 2014, www.newsroom.ucla.edu/re leases/love-at-first-bite.

49. William J. McCarthy, email message to author, Dec. 9, 2015.
50. Janet Poppendieck, *Free for All,* 2009, University of California Press, Berkeley.
51. Chef Ann Cooper, The Future of School Food Means the Future Health of the Nation's Children, *U.S. News & World Report,* July 7, 2014, www.health.usnews.com/health-news/blogs/eat-run/2014/07/07/the-future-of-school-food-means-the-future-health-of-the-nations-children.
52. Timothy W. Jones, Using Contemporary Archaeology and Applied Anthropology to Understand Food Loss in the American Food System, Report to the USDA Economic Research Service, 2004, www.ce.cmu.edu/~gdrg/readings/2006/12/19/Jones_UsingContemporaryArchaeologyAndAppliedAnthropologyToUnderstandFoodLossInAmericanFoodSystem.pdf.
53. Eliza Barclay, For Restaurants, Food Waste Is Seen as Low Priority, NPR's The Salt, Nov. 27, 2012, www.npr.org/sections/thesalt/2012/11/27/165907972/for-restaurants-food-waste-is-seen-as-low-priority.
54. Can Government Control Obesity?, KCRW's To the Point, Oct. 3, 2012, www.kcrw.com/news-culture/shows/to-the-point/can-government-control-obesity.
55. USDA, USDA Grade Standards for Food: How They Are Developed and Used (1973), https://books.google.com/books?id=a3svAAAAYAAJ&dq=only+sell+usda+graded+fruits+and+vegetables&q=okra#v=onepage&q=okra&f=false.
56. Rogers Orchards, Buy Apples, www.rogersorchards.com/buy_apples.asp.
57. Debbie Roos, Selling Eggs, Meat, and Poultry in North Carolina: What Farmers Need to Know, NC State University Cooperative Extension, Feb. 26, 2011, https://growingsmallfarms.ces.ncsu.edu/growingsmallfarms-meatandeggs/.
58. Rochelle Billow, Are the Beauty Standards for Fruits & Vegetables Unfair?, *Bon Appetit,* July 29, 2014, www.bonappetit.com/entertaining-style/trends-news/article/fruit-vegetable-beauty-standards.
59. Perspectives on Federal Retail Food Grading, Office of Technology Assessment, June 1977, https://www.princeton.edu/~ota/disk3/1977/7707/7707.PDF.
60. See, for example, United States Standards for Grades of Swiss Cheese,

Emmentaler Cheese, USDA, 66 Fed. Reg. 7458, Jan. 23, 2001, https://www.federalregister.gov/articles/2001/01/23/01-2017/united-states-standards-for-grades-of-swiss-cheese-emmentaler-cheese.

61. USDA, Produce Quality and Condition Script, 2012, www.nfsmi.org/documentlibraryfiles/PDF/20120821025227.pdf.
62. Dana Gunders, NRDC's Switchboard, Jan. 16, 2013, https://www.nrdc.org/experts/dana-gunders/breaking-grade-barrier-grocery-store-pioneers.
63. Larry Meadows, What's Your Beef—Prime, Choice or Select?, USDA's blog, Jan. 28, 2013, www.blogs.usda.gov/2013/01/28/what's-your-beef---prime-choice-or-select/.
64. Penn State Extension, Telling the Grass-Fed Beef Story, www.extension.psu.edu/animals/beef/grass-fed-beef/articles/telling-the-grass-fed-beef-story.
65. USDA, USDA Grade Standards for Food: How They Are Developed and Used10(1973).https://books.google.com/books?id=a3svAAAAYAAJ&pg=PA10&lpg=PA10&dq=Requests+for+standards+may+come+from+trade+%0Aor+consumer+groups&source=bl&ots=FmnDyua7gQ&sig=AhAnXLRXYzoAOa2SmaPnbt-BQpQ&hl=en&sa=X&ved=0ahUKEwi3ocDHpuHKAhXMcD4KHTFgCCkQ6AEIHTAA#v=onepage&q=Requests%20for %20standards%20may%20come%20from%20trade.
66. USDA Marketing & Regulatory Programs, Agriculture Fact Book 2001–02, www.usda.gov/factbook/chapter12.htm.
67. USDA, Bunched Carrots Grades & Standards, www.ams.usda.gov/grades-standards/bunched-carrots-grades-and-standards.
68. John Oliver, *Last Week Tonight,* July 30, 2015, https://www.youtube.com/watch?v=yIgDy95VcQc.
69. NRDC, Left-Out: An Investigation of the Causes & Quantities of Crop Shrink, https://www.nrdc.org/resources/left-out-investigation-fruit-and-vegetable-losses-farm.
70. Lynda Simkins, in discussion with the author, June 30, 2015.
71. USDA, United States Standards for Grades of Maple Syrup, Mar. 2, 2015, https://www.ams.usda.gov/sites/default/files/media/MapleSyrupStandards.pdf.
72. Jimmy Nguyen, Supermarkets and Restaurants Are Fighting Food Waste & Saving Money, USDA blog, Sept. 17, 2014, www.blogs.usda

.gov/2014/09/17/supermarkets-and-restaurants-are-fighting-food-waste-saving-money/.

73. Linda Scott Kantor et al., Estimating and Addressing America's Food Losses, *FoodReview,* Jan.-Apr. 1997, www.endhunger.org/PDFs/USDA-Jan97a.pdf.
74. Dana Gunders, NRDC's Switchboard, Jan. 16, 2013, https://www.nrdc.org/experts/dana-gunders/breaking-grade-barrier-grocery-store-pioneers.
75. David Mas Masumoto, Learning to live with imperfection, *Merced Sun Star,* June 30, 2012, www.mercedsunstar.com/opinion/opn-columns-blogs/article3268546.html.
76. Raphael Minder, Tempting Europe with Ugly Fruit, *New York Times,* May 24, 2014, www.nytimes.com/2014/05/25/world/europe/tempting-europe-with-ugly-fruit.html?_r=0.
77. Regulations, Commission Regulation (EC) No 1221/2008, *Official Journal of the European Union,* Dec. 5, 2008, www.eur-lex.europa.eu/LexUriServ/LexUriServ.do?uri=OJ:L:2008:336:0001:0080:en:PDF.
78. Maria Canelhas, email message to author, July 10, 2014.
79. Maria Canelhas, in discussion with the author, July 31, 2014.
80. Maria Canelhas, email message to author, June 26, 2015.
81. Maria Canelhas, email message to author, July 18, 2014.
82. Raphael Minder, Tempting Europe with Ugly Fruit, *New York Times,* May 24, 2014, www.nytimes.com/2014/05/25/world/europe/tempting-europe-with-ugly-fruit.html?_r=0.
83. Maria Canelhas, email message to author, July 26, 2015.
84. Ibid.
85. Maria Canelhas, email message to author, July 18, 2015.
86. Maria Canelhas, email message to author, July 26, 2015.
87. Jochen Faget, Dodgy stats understate Portugal's unemployment rate, Deutsche Welle, Apr. 28, 2015, www.dw.com/en/dodgy-stats-understate-portugals-unemployment-rate/a-18414326.
88. Awards, Fruta Feia, frutafeia.pt/en/thanks (last visited Apr. 17, 2016).
89. Bob Granleese et al., The OFM 50: the 50 hottest places, people and trends in food, *The Guardian,* Mar. 15, 2015, www.theguardian.com/lifeandstyle/2015/mar/15/ofm-50-hottest-trends-people-places-in-food-for-2015.
90. Maria Canelhas, email message to author, June 26, 2015.

91. Raphael Minder, Tempting Europe with Ugly Fruit, *New York Times,* May 24, 2014, www.nytimes.com/2014/05/25/world/europe/tempting-europe-with-ugly-fruit.html?_r=0.
92. Steve Holt, How Buying Smaller Fruit Could Save California's Drought-Stricken Family Farms, Civil Eats, June 22, 2015, www.civileats.com/2015/06/22/how-buying-smaller-fruit-could-save-californias-drought-stricken-family-farms/.
93. Meagan McGinnes & Jean Nagy, America's most local food market opens in Boston, *Boston Globe,* July 29, 2015, www.boston.com/news/local/massachusetts/2015/07/29/america-most-local-food-market-opens-boston/A73Ob1hhjveJyR0PO4gm3I/story.html?p1=well_ICYMI_subheadline_hp.
94. The Safina Center, Bycatch, www.safinacenter.org/issues/fish-as-food/bycatch/.
95. Monterey Bay Aquarium, Seafood Watch, Wild Seafood, www.seafoodwatch.org/ocean-issues/wild-seafood/bycatch.
96. Amanda Keledjian et al., Wasted Catch, Oceana, Mar. 2014, www.oceana.org/sites/default/files/reports/Bycatch_Report_FINAL.pdf.
97. The Pew Charitable Trusts, Waste Not, Want Not, Feb. 2015, www.pewtrusts.org/~/media/Assets/2015/03/EBFMWasteNotWantNot.pdf.
98. NOAA Fisheries, Magnuson-Stevens Fishery Conservation and Management Act, www.fisheries.noaa.gov/sfa/laws_policies/msa/index.html.
99. Alastair Bland, Why 500 Million U.S. Seafood Meals Get Dumped In The Sea, NPR's The Salt, Mar. 21, 2014, www.npr.org/sections/thesalt/2014/03/21/292094853/why-500-million-u-s-seafood-meals-get-dumped-in-the-sea.
100. FAO, Discards in the World's Marine Fisheries, 2005, www.fao.org/docrep/008/y5936e/y5936e0b.htm.
101. Brian J. Rothschild, Testimony on Improving the Magnuson Stevens Act, U.S. Senate Committee on Commerce, Science, & Transportation, Nov. 3, 2013, www.centerforsustainablefisheries.org/wp-content/uploads/IMPROVING-THE-MAGNUSON-STEVENS-ACT.-B.Rothschild-Testimony.pdf.
102. Brian Rothschild, Time to overhaul U.S. fisheries oversight, Center for Sustainable Fisheries, Aug. 10, 2011, www.centerforsustainablefisheries.org

/2011/08/my-view-brian-rothschild-time-to-overhaul-u-s-fisheries-oversight/.

103. The Nature Conservancy, California: Central Coast Groundfish Project, www.nature.org/ourinitiatives/regions/northamerica/unitedstates/california/howwework/central-coast-groundfish-project.xml.
104. Leslie Kaufman, Partnership Preserves Livelihoods and Fish Stocks, *New York Times,* Nov. 27, 2011, www.nytimes.com/2011/11/28/science/earth/nature-conservancy-partners-with-california-fishermen.html?_r=3&adxnnl=1&pagewanted=1&adxnnlx=1322504624-wN4j5DZ+HY15aG+8fk2j+Q.
105. Sean Dimin, email message to author, July 31, 2015.
106. Finished Works, Waste at Sea-Striped Bass North Carolina, YouTube, Jan. 20, 2011, https://www.youtube.com/watch?v=VGnqSD9V8Pg.
107. Lacey Act, 18 U.S.C. 42-43 (2004) www.fws.gov/le/pdffiles/Lacey.pdf.
108. Press Release, U.S. Department of Justice, Thirteen Commercial Fishermen Charged in North Carolina with Illegally Harvesting and Selling Atlantic Striped Bass, Jan. 21, 2015, www.justice.gov/opa/pr/thirteen-commercial-fishermen-charged-north-carolina-illegally-harvesting-and-selling.
109. Ibid.
110. Sean Dimin, email message to author, July 31, 2015.
111. Ibid.
112. Mwangi S. Kimenyi, The dilemma of destroying ivory as an anti-poaching strategy, Brookings's Africa in Focus, Mar. 6, 2015, www.brookings.edu/blogs/africa-in-focus/posts/2015/03/06-destroying-ivory-anti-poaching-strategy-kimenyi.
113. Leslie Kaufman, Partnership Preserves Livelihoods and Fish Stocks, *New York Times,* Nov. 27, 2011, http://www.nytimes.com/2011/11/28/science/earth/nature-conservancy-partners-with-california-fishermen.html.
114. Baylen Linnekin, The Lobster Underground, Reason, Apr. 2011, https://reason.com/archives/2011/03/10/the-lobster-underground/single page.
115. Ben Sargent, email message to author, June 16, 2015.
116. Ibid.
117. Travis Riggs, in discussion with the author, July 31, 2015.

118. Andrew Knowlton, How Houston Restaurants Are Making "Bycatch" a Buzzword, *Bon Appetit,* Sept. 11, 2012, www.bonappetit.com/columns/the-foodist/article/how-houston-restaurants-are-making-bycatch-a-buzzword.

Chapter 4

1. Jim Chen, Filburn's Legacy, 52 *Emory Law Journal* 1719, 1759 (2003) http://papers.ssrn.com/sol3/papers.cfm?abstract_id=901026.
2. Michael Pollan, *The Omnivore's Dilemma,* Penguin, 2006.
3. Public Law 95–258, An Act to Amend the Internal Revenue Code of 1954, Oct. 14, 1978, https://www.gpo.gov/fdsys/pkg/STATUTE-92/pdf/STATUTE-92-Pg1255.pdf.
4. Bruce Butterfield, The Impact of Home and Community Gardening in America, National Gardening Association, 2009, www.gardenresearch.com/files/2009-Impact-of-Gardening-in-America-White-Paper.pdf.
5. Press Release, Food Gardening in the U.S. at the Highest Levels in More Than a Decade According to New Report by the National Gardening Association, National Gardening Association, Apr. 2, 2014, http://www.garden.org/articles/articles.php?q=show&id=3819.
6. Steven Kurutz, The Battlefront in the Front Yard, *New York Times,* Dec. 19, 2012, http://www.nytimes.com/2012/12/20/garden/gardeners-fight-with-neighbors-and-city-hall-over-their-lawns.html.
7. Ibid.
8. Lori Fullbright, Woman Sues City of Tulsa for Cutting Down Her Edible Garden, News on 6, June 21, 2012, www.newson6.com/story/18802728/woman-sues-city-of-tulsa-for-cutting-down-her-edible-garden.
9. Order & Judgment, Denise Morrison v. Kevin Cox & Gretchen Mugoda (10th Cir. 2013) ca10.washburnlaw.edu/cases/2013/11/13-5034.pdf.
10. Lori Fullbright, Woman Sues City of Tulsa for Cutting Down Her Edible Garden, News on 6, June 21, 2012, www.newson6.com/story/18802728/woman-sues-city-of-tulsa-for-cutting-down-her-edible-garden.
11. Glenda Lewis, Oak Park battles city over vegetable garden in their front yard, WXYZ, June 30, 2011, https://web.archive.org/web/20110704221845/http://www.wxyz.com/dpp/news/region/oakland_county/oak-park-battles-city-over-vegetable-garden-in-their-front-yard.
12. Webster's Ninth New Collegiate Dictionary, 1983.

13. Steven Hoffer, Oak Park Drops Gardening Charges Against Julie Bass, Goes After Her Dogs, Huffington Post, Sept. 14, 2011, www.huffington post.com/2011/07/15/julie-bass-front-yard-gar_n_899723.html.
14. Deirdre Fernandes, Newton officials call tomato display illegal, *Boston Globe,* May 22, 2012, www.bostonglobe.com/metro/2012/05/21/how-does-his-garden-grow-pretty-high/mruxiZwkuJIvyDAoCUTzaK/story.html?camp=pm.
15. Deirdre Fernandes, Newton hanging tomato garden finds a new home—at theological school, *Boston Globe,* June 1, 2012, www.boston.com/yourtown/news/newton/2012/06/newton_hanging_tomato_garden_f.html.
16. Marybel Rodriguez, Miami Shores Couple Sues Village Over Veggies, CBS4, Nov. 19, 2013, http://miami.cbslocal.com/2013/11/19/miami-shores-sues-village-over-veggies/.
17. Mark Schlueb, Front-yard gardeners win a round in city battle, *Orlando Sentinel,* Jan. 15, 2013, http://articles.orlandosentinel.com/2013-01-15/news/os-front-yard-gardens-20130115_1_front-yard-garden-jason-helvenston.
18. Leslie A. Gordon, Legal battles over gardens are sprouting up across the country, ABA Journal, Apr. 1, 2013, www.abajournal.com/magazine/article/legal_battles_over_gardens_are_sprouting_up_across_the_country/.
19. Casey Miner, Urban Farms vs. Urban Zoning, Ecology Center's blog, Mar. 3, 2010, www.ecologycenter.org/terrainmagazine/spring-2010/urban-farms-vs-urban-zoning/.
20. Press Release, Seattle City Council approves urban farm and community garden legislation improving access to locally grown food, Seattle City Council, Aug. 16, 2010, http://www.seattle.gov/news/detail.asp?ID=10996&Dept=28.
21. Denver Water, Vegetable and Flower Gardens, www.denverwater.org/Conservation/TipsTools/Outdoor/VegetableGarden/; Urban Plantations, Water Conservation: Fruit and Vegetable Gardens vs. Lawns, www.urbanplantations.com/newsletter/water-conservation-fruit-and-vegetable-gardens-vs-lawns.
22. USDA, Urban Chicken Ownership in Four U.S. Cities, National Animal Monitoring System, Apr. 2013, https://www.aphis.usda.gov/animal_health/nahms/poultry/downloads/poultry10/Poultry10_dr_Urban_Chicken_Four.pdf.

23. John Harrison et al., Backyard Chicken Keeping: Myths and Facts, Report Submitted to the Dunwoody Planning Commission, Feb. 2, 2010, www.jkheneghan.com/city/meetings/2010/Feb/02092010_Planning_Backyard%20Chicken%20Keeping%20-%20Myths%20and%20Facts.pdf.
24. BackyardChickens.com, About Us, July 14, 2014, www.backyardchickens.com/a/about-us (last visited Apr. 17, 2016).
25. Salt Lake City, SLC Green - Raising Chickens in Salt Lake City, www.slcgov.com/slc-green/chickens.
26. USDA, Urban Chicken Ownership in Four U.S. Cities, National Animal Monitoring System, Apr. 2013, https://www.aphis.usda.gov/animal_health/nahms/poultry/downloads/poultry10/Poultry10_dr_Urban_Chicken_Four.pdf.
27. Todd Cooper, Backyard chickens go to court; feuding neighbors told not to squawk, Omaha.com, Aug. 14, 2015, www.omaha.com/news/metro/backyard-chickens-go-to-court-feuding-neighbors-told-not-to/article_fe217614-41dc-11e5-a6ec-930560a9f4f8.html.
28. Diane Gale Andreassi, South Lyon Keeps Its Ban on Backyard Chickens, *Hometown Life,* Aug. 13, 2015, www.hometownlife.com/story/news/local/south-lyon/2015/08/13/mayor-swing-vote-nixing-backyard-chicken-ordinance/31466165/; John Turk, Springfield Twp. Family Fighting Against Backyard Chicken Ordinance After Being Cited by Officials, *The Oakland Press,* Aug. 5, 2015, www.theoaklandpress.com/general-news/20150804/springfield-twp-family-fighting-against-backyard-chicken-ordinance-after-being-cited-by-officials; Dan Moran, Backyard Chicken Proposal Fails in Waukegan, *Chicago Tribune,* Aug. 18, 2015, www.chicagotribune.com/suburbs/lake-county-news-sun/news/ct-lns-waukegan-no-chickens-st-0819-20150818-story.html.
29. CIPRoud.com, Tazewell County Woman Pushing for Change in Land Ordinance, June 15, 2012, www.centralillinoisproud.com/news/top-local-news/tazewell-county-woman-pushing-for-change-in-land-ordinance.
30. Baylen Linnekin, I Say Tomato, You Say No, Reason.com, June 23, 2012, http://reason.com/archives/2012/06/23/i-say-tomato-you-say-no/singlepage.
31. CIPRoud.com, Tazewell County Woman Pushing for Change in Land Ordinance, June 15, 2012, www.centralillinoisproud.com/news/top-local-news/tazewell-county-woman-pushing-for-change-in-land-ordinance.

32. USDA Center for Emerging Issues, The Goat Industry: Structure, Concentration, Demand and Growth, 2005, https://www.aphis.usda.gov/animal_health/emergingissues/downloads/goatreport090805.pdf.
33. USDA Agricultural Research Service, Nigerian Dwarf Cluster Analysis Summary, Sept. 2014, www.ars.usda.gov/SP2UserFiles/Place/30120505/animal/Nigerian%20Dwarf%20clusters09242014.pdf.
34. City of San Diego, Keeping Goats in the City of San Diego, www.sandiego.gov/development-services/pdf/news/keepinggoats.pdf.
35. Jill Richardson, Why Goats Are Coming to an Urban Backyard Near You, AlterNet, May 2, 2014, http://www.alternet.org/culture/why-goats-are-coming-next-urban-backyard-near-you.
36. Alma McCarty, Harlem leaders deny miniature goat exception to livestock ordinance, News 12, Aug. 24, 2015, www.wrdw.com/home/headlines/Harlem-leaders-to-vote-on-allowing-miniature-goats-on-smaller-properties-322743881.html.
37. Newcott, Zachary, Visalia Times Delta Local Top 5, *Visalia Times Delta,* www.visaliatimesdelta.com/story/news/local/2015/05/17/visalia-times-delta-local-top/27508473/.
38. Susan Walsh, email message to author, May 19, 2015.
39. San Joaquin Valley Agriculture, University of California Cooperative Extension, http://vric.ucdavis.edu/virtual_tour/sanjoq.htm.
40. Museum Description, Visit Visalia, www.visitvisalia.org/member/tulare-county-museum-of-farm-labor-and-agriculture/515780/.
41. Zachary Newcott, Visalia Times Delta Local Top 5, *Visalia Times-Delta,* May 17, 2015, www.visaliatimesdelta.com/story/news/local/2015/05/17/visalia-times-delta-local-top/27508473/.
42. Susan Walsh, email message to author, May 19, 2015.
43. Ibid.
44. Jerrold Jensen, Make Sure You Get Full Story on Visalia Chickens, Goats, *Visalia Times-Delta,* Aug. 7, 2015, www.visaliatimesdelta.com/story/opinion/2015/08/06/make-sure-get-full-story-visalia-chickens-goats/31251039/.
45. Susan Walsh, email message to author, May 19, 2015.
46. KSEE News, Visalia Leaders Vote Down Chicken Ordinance, YourCentralValley.com, June 1, 2015, www.yourcentralvalley.com/news/kgpe-local-news/visalia-leaders-vote-down-chicken-ordinance.

47. Lewis Griswold, Visalia Goat Owner Circulates Ballot Proposal, *The Fresno Bee,* Aug. 15, 2015, www.fresnobee.com/news/local/news-columns-blogs/lewis-griswold/article31220048.html.
48. Farm-to-Consumer Legal Defense Fund v. Wisconsin Dept. of Agriculture, Decision & Order on Zinniker Plaintiffs' Clarification Motion, Sept. 9, 2011, Case No. 09-CV-6313, http://farmtoconsumer.org/docs/zinniker-order-09-09-11-on-mot-4-clarification.pdf.
49. Zinniker Family Farm, About Us, www.zinnikerfarm.com/about-us.html.
50. Kate Galbraith, The Great Cow-Sharing Debate, *New York Times*, Green blog, Jan. 28, 2009, www.green.blogs.nytimes.com/2009/01/28/the-great-cow-sharing-debate/.
51. Farm-to-Consumer Legal Defense Fund, Raw Milk Nation—Interactive Map, www.farmtoconsumer.org/raw-milk-nation-interactive-map/.
52. Rick Barrett, Doyle Vetoes Raw Milk Bill, *Milwaukee Journal Sentinel,* May 19, 2010, www.jsonline.com/business/94272169.html.
53. Wisconsin Department of Agriculture, Trade and Consumer Protection, Raw Milk FAQs, http://datcp.wi.gov/Food/Raw_Milk/FAQs/?AspxAutoDetectCookieSupport=1.
54. Ibid.
55. Zinniker Family Farm, About Us, www.zinnikerfarm.com/about-us.html.
56. Farm-to-Consumer Legal Defense Fund v. Wisconsin Dept. of Agriculture, Decision & Order, Aug. 12, 2011, Case No. 09-CV-6313.
57. Farm-to-Consumer Legal Defense Fund v. Wisconsin Dept. of Agriculture, Zinniker Plaintiffs' Motion for Clarification & Memorandum in Support, Aug. 25, 2011, Case No. 09-CV-6313, http://farmtoconsumer.org/docs/mot-2-clarify-rule-56-zinniker-ps.pdf.
58. Farm-to-Consumer Legal Defense Fund v. Wisconsin Dept. of Agriculture, Decision & Order on Zinniker Plaintiffs' Clarification Motion, Sept. 9, 2011, Case No. 09-CV-6313, http://www.farmtoconsumer.org/docs/zinniker-order-09-09-11-on-mot-4-clarification.pdf.
59. Ibid.
60. Eldorado National Forest, Welcome to the Eldorado National Forest, www.fs.usda.gov/Internet/FSE_DOCUMENTS/fsbdev7_018898.pdf.
61. Montgomery Parks, Rules & Regulations, Chapter V: Regulation of General Conduct and Personal Behavior (Code of Conduct), www.montgomeryparks.org/rules/rules_regs_ch5.shtm.

62. Greg Visscher, email messages to author, July-Dec. 2015.
63. Ibid.
64. Ibid.
65. Ibid.
66. Rick Pelicano, email message to author, Aug. 27, 2015.
67. John Kass, Crime Fighters Try a New Way to Uproot Thugs and Punks—Weed Out the Flower Pickers, *Chicago Tribune,* June 28, 2013, http://articles.chicagotribune.com/2013-06-28/news/ct-met-kass-0628-20130628_1_dandelions-crime-fighters-joanna.
68. Lisa W. Foderaro, Enjoy Park Greenery, City Says, but Not as Salad, *New York Times,* July 29, 2011, http://www.nytimes.com/2011/07/30/nyregion/new-york-moves-to-stop-foraging-in-citys-parks.html.
69. Alastair Bland, Mushroom Foraging: When The Fun(gi) Hunt Gets Out of Hand, NPR's The Salt, Dec. 4, 2013, www.npr.org/sections/thesalt/2013/12/03/248582278/mushroom-foraging-when-the-fun-gi-hunt-gets-out-of-hand.
70. Karl Jacoby, *Crimes against Nature: Squatters, Poachers, Thieves, and the Hidden History of American Conservation,* University of California Press, Berkeley, 2014.
71. Ibid.
72. Iso Rabins, email message to author, July 9, 2015.
73. Ibid.
74. San Francisco Bay Guardian, Local Heroes 2010, www.sfbg.com/specials/best-bay-2010-local-heroes.
75. Krislyn Placide, Q&A: Iso Rabins, Gourmet Hunter-Gatherer, Sierra Club's Greenlife, June 22, 2012, www.sierraclub.typepad.com/greenlife/2012/06/foraging-qa-iso-rabins-the-gourmet-hunter-gatherer.html.
76. Peter Jamison, Out of the Wild, SF Weekly, Mar. 18, 2009, www.sfweekly.com/sanfrancisco/out-of-the-wild/Content?oid=2171797.
77. Scott James, Dining Experiences, All Illicit, That Extend Beyond the Palate, *New York Times,* Jan. 6, 2011, www.nytimes.com/2011/01/07/us/07bcjames.html?_r=0.
78. Peter Jamison, Out of the Wild, SF Weekly, Mar. 18, 2009, www.sfweekly.com/sanfrancisco/out-of-the-wild/Content?oid=2171797.
79. Iso Rabins, email message to author, July 9, 2015.
80. Ibid.

81. Greg Visscher, email messages to author, July-Dec. 2015.
82. Daily News, Lottery for berry picking permits open, July 28, 2015, www.newburyportnews.com/news/local_news/lottery-for-berry-picking-permits-open/article_58332e4a-b346-5cfd-ba00-923cde770437.html.
83. Greg Visscher, email messages to author, July-Dec. 2015.
84. Elizabeth S. Barron & Marla R. Emery, Natural Resource Technical Report NPS/NCR/NCRO/NRTR—2009/002, Protecting Resources: Assessing Visitor Harvesting of Wild Morel Mushrooms in Two National Capital Region Parks, Aug. 2009, National Park Service, www.nps.gov/cue/publications/NCRO_Morel_socsci_GTR_ESB10Mar10_Web_Version.pdf%20.
85. Michael S. Rosenwald, Maryland bans wild ginseng harvest on state land, upsetting diggers, *Washington Post,* June 22, 2013, https://www.washingtonpost.com/local/maryland-bans-wild-ginseng-harvest-on-state-land-upsetting-diggers/2013/06/22/eb02d00c-d9d6-11e2-a9f2-42ee3912ae0e_story.html.
86. Elizabeth S. Barron & Marla R. Emery, Natural Resource Technical Report NPS/NCR/NCRO/NRTR—2009/002, Protecting Resources: Assessing Visitor Harvesting of Wild Morel Mushrooms in Two National Capital Region Parks, Aug. 2009, National Park Service, www.nps.gov/cue/publications/NCRO_Morel_socsci_GTR_ESB10Mar10_Web_Version.pdf%20.
87. Ibid.
88. Greg Visscher, email to the author, Dec. 5, 2015.
89. Jordan Carlton Schaul, Road Deaths May Be the No. 1 Threat to U.S. Wildlife, National Geographic's Voices, Apr. 25, 2011, www.voices.nationalgeographic.com/2011/04/25/roadkill-threat-to-wildlife/.
90. Ben Martin, Roadkill: Sickening or sustainable?, The Ecologist's Green Living, Feb. 20, 2012, www.theecologist.org/green_green_living/food_and_drink/1249525/roadkill_sickening_or_sustainable.html.
91. PETA, Is it OK to eat roadkill?, www.peta.org/about-peta/faq/is-it-ok-to-eat-roadkill/.
92. Jane Eastoe, *Wild Food,* National Trust, 2013.
93. Mike Michael, Roadkill: Between Humans, Nonhuman Animals, and Technologies, Animals & Society, 2004, https://www.animalsandsociety.org/assets/library/542_s1241.pdf.

94. Associated Press, Illinois Law Lets Motorists Salvage Fur, Food from Roadkill, *USA Today,* Jan. 7, 2012, www.usatoday30.usatoday.com/news/nation/story/2012-01-07/furbearer-retrieving-roadkill/52434074/1.
95. Mark Robison, Dining on roadkill becoming legal in more states, not Nevada, RGJ.com, Mostly Dogs, Apr. 23, 2013, www.blogs.rgj.com/mostlydogs/2013/04/23/dining-on-roadkill-becoming-legal-in-more-states-not-nevada/.
96. Eric Nicholson, Finally, a Texas Politician Is Calling for an End to the State's Roadkill-Eating Ban, *Dallas Observer,* Feb. 21, 2014, www.dallasobserver.com/news/finally-a-texas-politician-is-calling-for-an-end-to-the-states-roadkill-eating-ban-7141085.
97. Catherine Price, Does This Rabbit Taste Like Tires?, Slate, Feb. 2, 2011, www.slate.com/articles/life/food/2011/02/does_this_rabbit_taste_like_tires.single.html.
98. Brianna Loper, Roadkill Salvage Law a Success in Its First Year, *The Daily Inter Lake,* Nov. 17, 2014, www.dailyinterlake.com/members/roadkill-salvage-law-a-success-in-its-first-year/article_e09e6aec-6ebb-11e4-91d7-6f587db7cfd9.html.
99. Andy Kulie, New law may lighten the load of roadkill on road commissions, ABC 10 News, July 1, 2014, www.abc10up.com/new-law-may-lighten-the-load-of-roadkill-on-road-commissions/.
100. Max Gorden, Change in road kill law, WKOW.com, Aug. 2, 2015, www.wkow.com/story/29691653/2015/08/02/change-in-road-kill-law.
101. Jennifer Oldham, Roadkill: Increasingly, It's What for Dinner, Associated Press, Mar. 6, 2013, www.northjersey.com/news/roadkill-increasingly-it-s-what-for-dinner-1.539890?page=all.
102. Matt Pearce, Homeless Feeding Bans: Well-Meaning Policy or War on the Poor?, *Los Angeles Times,* June 11, 2012, www.articles.latimes.com/2012/jun/11/nation/la-na-nn-homeless-feeding-bans-20120611.
103. Phil Hooper, Putting the "Public" back in Public Parks, ACLU of Nevada's The Torch, June 15, 2010, www.aclunv.org/blog/sacco.
104. Sarah Anne Hughes, Food Not Bombs Group Arrested for Feeding Homeless, Violating Orlando Ordinance, *Washington Post,* June 3, 2011, www.washingtonpost.com/blogs/blogpost/post/food-not-bombs-group-arrested-for-feeding-homeless-violating-orlando-ordinance/2011/06/03/AGufUBIH_blog.html.

105. Robert Wilonsky, Federal judge rules that Dallas' homeless feeding ordinance violates ministries' religious freedoms, The Dallas News's City Hall Blog, Mar. 28, 2013, www.cityhallblog.dallasnews.com/2013/03/federal-judge-rules-that-dallas-homeless-feeding-ordinance-violates-ministries-religious-freedoms.html/.
106. Clare Leschin-Hoar, Who Needs a Training Course to Feed the Homeless?, TakePart, Mar. 8, 2012, www.takepart.com/article/2012/03/07/who-needs-training-course-feed-homeless.
107. CBS New York, Bloomberg Strikes Again: NYC Bans Food Donations to the Homeless, Mar. 19, 2012, www.newyork.cbslocal.com/2012/03/19/bloomberg-strikes-again-nyc-bans-food-donations-to-the-homeless/.
108. Baylen Linnekin, Bans on Sharing Food with Homeless Persist, Reason.com, Apr. 19, 2014, https://reason.com/archives/2014/04/19/bans-on-sharing-food-with-homeless-persi.
109. Baylen Linnekin, Another Infuriating Crackdown on Sharing Food With the Homeless, Reason.com, Apr. 18, 2015, https://reason.com/archives/2015/04/18/another-infuriating-crackdown-on-sharing.
110. Jay Hamburger, email message to author, Aug. 1, 2015.
111. Eyder Peralta, "Eggman" Found His True Calling Helping to Feed Homeless, *Houston Chronicle,* Dec. 14, 2007, www.chron.com/life/holidays/article/Eggman-found-his-true-calling-helping-to-feed-1623649.php.
112. Jay Hamburger, email message to author, Aug. 1, 2015.
113. Ibid.
114. Ibid.
115. National Conference of State Legislatures, State Rainwater: Graywater Harvesting Law & Legislation, Sept. 1, 2013, www.ncsl.org/research/environment-and-natural-resources/rainwater-harvesting.aspx.
116. Kirk Johnson, It's Now Legal to Catch a Raindrop in Colorado, *New York Times,* June 28, 2009, www.nytimes.com/2009/06/29/us/29rain.html?_r=0.

Chapter 5

1. Bill Marler, email message to author, July 5, 2015.
2. Press Release, Farm-to-Consumer Legal Defense Fund, Sixteenth Maine Town Passes Food Sovereignty Ordinance, July 10, 2015, www.farmto

consumer.org/blog/2015/07/10/sixteenth-maine-town-passes-food-sovereignty-ordinance/.

3. Maria Godoy, Farm Free or Die! Maine Towns Rebel Against Food Rules, NPR's The Salt, June 21, 2013, www.npr.org/sections/thesalt/2013/05/28/186955163/farm-free-or-die-maine-towns-rebel-against-food-rules.
4. Town of Sedgwick, Maine, Local Food & Community Self-Governance Ordinance, www.sedgwickmaine.org/images/stories/local-food-ordinance.pdf.
5. State of Maine v. Dan Brown, Maine Supreme Judicial Court, Han-13–345, June 17, 2014, www.courts.maine.gov/opinions_orders/supreme/lawcourt/2014/14me79br.pdf.
6. State of Wyoming, Wyoming Food Freedom Act, July 1, 2015, http://legisweb.state.wy.us/2015/Engross/HB0056.pdf.
7. Video, Farm to Fork Wyoming - Food Freedom Part 2, Wyoming PBS, July 15, 2015, http://video.wyomingpbs.org/video/2365528446/.
8. Wyoming State Rep. Tyler Lindholm, email message to author, Mar. 13, 2015.
9. Ibid.
10. Baylen Linnekin, Food Freedom Spreading Across States, Reason.com, Dec. 12, 2015, reason.com/archives/2015/12/12/food-freedom-spreading-across-states.
11. Baylen Linnekin, PRIME Act Would Steer Meat Processing in the Right Direction, Reason.com, Aug. 1, 2015, reason.com/archives/2015/08/01/prime-act-would-steer-meat-processing-in/singlepage.
12. Press Release, Sen. Rand Paul, Sens. Paul, King Introduce Legislation to Support Local Meat Processing, Mar. 8, 2016, https://www.paul.senate.gov/news/press/king-paul-introduce-legislation-to-support-local-meat-processing.
13. James M. McDonald, Consolidation in U.S. Meatpacking, USDA Economic Research Service, Feb. 2000, www.ers.usda.gov/media/493235/aer785_1_.pdf.
14. Baylen Linnekin, Breaking the USDA's Slaughterhouse Stranglehold, Reason.com, Mar. 8, 2014, reason.com/archives/2014/03/08/breaking-the-usdas-slaughterhouse-strang/singlepage.

15. Sam Stall, Law change allows entrepreneurs to market homemade food, Indianapolis Business Journal, Apr. 21, 2012, www.ibj.com/articles/33968-law-change-allows-entrepreneurs-to-market-homemade-food.
16. City of Denver, Office of Sustainability, City Council Approves At-Home Sales of Fresh Produce and Cottage Foods to Expand Access to Healthy, Affordable Food in Denver, July 15, 2014, https://www.denvergov.org/content/denvergov/en/office-of-sustainability/news-events/2014/city-council-approves-at-home-sales-of-fresh-produce-and-cottage.html.
17. Press Release, Statement by Sen. John McCain on Introducing the Good Samaritan Hunger Relief Tax Incentive Act of 2015, Sen. John McCain, Apr. 15, 2015, www.mccain.senate.gov/public/index.cfm/2015/4/statement-by-senator-john-mccain-on-introducing-the-good-samaritan-hunger-relief-tax-incentive-act-of-2015.
18. Emma Dumain, House GOP Touts Tax Breaks to Help Feed the Hungry, Roll Call's 218, Feb. 10, 2015, http://www.rollcall.com/218/gop-tax-breaks-to-feed-hungry.
19. Jill Ettinger, Progressive Food Waste Bill Headed to Congress, Organic Authority, Feb. 10, 2015, www.organicauthority.com/progressive-food-waste-bill-headed-to-congress/.
20. Feeding America, Feeding America Leads the Nation in Recovering Food to Feed the Hungry; Yet Billions of Additional Pounds of Food Go to Waste, Apr. 17, 2015, www.feedingamerica.org/hunger-in-america/news-and-updates/press-room/press-releases/feeding-america-leads-food-recovery.html.
21. Ibid.
22. Willy Blackmore, What's Wrong With a Bill That Helps the Hungry and Reduces Food Waste?, TakePart, Feb. 9, 2015, www.takepart.com/article/2015/02/09/food-waste-anti-hunger-bill.
23. Executive Office of the President, Statement of Administration Policy H.R. 644—Fighting Hunger Incentive Act of 2015, Feb. 10, 2015, https://www.whitehouse.gov/sites/default/files/omb/legislative/sap/114/saphr644r_20150210.pdf.
24. Kellie Meyer, Reed Fighting Hunger Incentive Act, WENY, May 27, 2014, www.weny.com/news/All/reed-fighting-hunger-incentive-act052714.
25. Feeding America, Coalition Urges House to Pass America Gives More

Act of 2015, Feb. 11, 2015, www.feedingamerica.org/hunger-in-america/news-and-updates/press-room/press-releases/coalition-urges-house-to-pass-Act.html.

26. Congressional Record, Statement of Rep. Dave Camp on the Fighting Hunger Incentive Act of 2014, July 17, 2014, https://www.congress.gov/congressional-record/2014/7/17/house-section/article/h6364-3.
27. Press Release, Independent Sector, Charitable Community Applauds Congress's Historic Deal on Tax Incentives for Charitable Giving, Dec. 18, 2015, www.independentsector.org/2015-joint-release-tax-deal.
28. Model Good Samaritan Food Donation Act, Public Law 104—210, Oct. 1, 1996, www.gpo.gov/fdsys/pkgPLAW-104publ210/pdf/PLAW-104publ210.pdf.
29. Congressional Hunger Center, Bill Emerson, www.hungercenter.org/about/emerson/.
30. Washington, D.C., Dept. of Consumer & Regulatory Affairs, Mobile Food Truck Licensing Information, dcra.dc.gov/service/mobile-food-truck-licensing-information.
31. Xander Landen, Great white shark population on the rise after years of decline, PBS Newshour, June 22, 2014, www.pbs.org/newshour/rundown/great-white-shark-population-rise-years-decline/.
32. Smithsonian National Museum of Natural History, Ocean Portal, Shark Finning: Sharks Turned Prey, www.ocean.si.edu/ocean-news/shark-finning-sharks-turned-prey.
33. Proposed Rule, Magnuson-Stevens Act Provisions; Implementation of the Shark Conservation Act of 2010, May 2, 2013, https://www.federalregister.gov/articles/2013/05/02/2013-10439/magnuson-stevens-act-provisions-implementation-of-the-shark-conservation-act-of-2010.
34. Alan D. Risenhoover, Magnuson-Stevens Act Provisions; Implementation of the Shark Conservation Act of 2010, Proposed rule; request for comments, 78 Fed. Reg. 25,685 (May 2, 2013) https://www.gpo.gov/fdsys/pkg/FR-2013-05-02/html/2013-10439.htm.
35. Ibid.
36. Cal. Assembly Bill 376, Shark Fins, Feb. 14, 2011, www.leginfo.ca.gov/pub/11-12/bill/asm/ab_0351-0400/ab_376_bill_20111007_chaptered.html.

37. Chinatown Neighborhood Association v. Edmund G. Brown, Case No. 13–15188, U.S. Dist. Ct. of App. (9th Cir.), July 22, 2013, www.defenders.org/publications/amicus-brief-shark-finning-CA.pdf.
38. Danny Clemens, Federal Court Upholds California Shark Fin Ban, Discovery, July 28, 2015, www.discovery.com/tv-shows/shark-week/shark-feed/federal-court-upholds-california-shark-fin-ban/.
39. Texas House Bill 1579, Relating to the sale and purchase of shark fins or products derived from shark fins; creating a criminal offense, June 20, 2015, www.txlege.texastribune.org/84/bills/HB1579/.
40. Press Release, Maryland Becomes First State on East Coast to Ban Shark Fin Trade, Humane Society of the United States, May 2, 2013, www.humanesociety.org/news/press_releases/2013/05/maryland-bans-shark-fin-trade-050213.html?credit=web_id448985267; National Marine Fisheries Service, Fisheries Statistics and Economics Division, Imports, 2011, July 2015, www.st.nmfs.noaa.gov/pls/webpls/trade_alldstrct_compare.data_in?qtype=IMP&qmnth=12&qyear=2011&qproduct=SHARK&qsort=DISTRICT&qoutput=TABLE.

Conclusion

1. Dietary Guidelines, USDA Center for Nutrition Policy & Promotion, www.cnpp.usda.gov/dietaryguidelines.
2. Scientific Report of the 2015 Dietary Guidelines Advisory Committee (Advisory Report), Part D. Chapter 5: Food Sustainability and Safety, Feb. 2015, http://health.gov/dietaryguidelines/2015-scientific-report/.
3. Jeff Stier, Iowan's USDA Appointment Raises Concern, *The Des Moines Register,* July 18, 2014, www.desmoinesregister.com/story/opinion/columnists/2014/07/18/iowans-usda-appointment-raises-concern/12820451/.
4. Tennille Tracy, Vilsack: Dietary Guidelines Are About Health, Not Environment, *Wall Street Journal's* Washington Wire, Mar. 11, 2015, http://blogs.wsj.com/washwire/2015/03/11/vilsack-dietary-guidelines-are-about-health-not-environment/.
5. Dietary Guidelines for Americans, 2015–2020, U.S. Dept. of Health & Human Services & U.S. Dept. of Agriculture, Jan. 2016, health.gov/dietaryguidelines/2015/guidelines/full/.

6. Final Rule, Nutrition Standards in the National School Lunch and School Breakfast Programs, U.S. Dept. of Agriculture, Federal Register, Jan. 26, 2012, www.fns.usda.gov/sites/default/files/01-26-12_CND.pdf.
7. Michelle S. Tom et al., Energy use, blue water footprint, and greenhouse gas emissions for current food consumption patterns and dietary recommendations in the US, *Env. Sys. & Decisions* 1, Nov. 24, 2015, link .springer.com/article/10.1007/s10669-015-9577-y.
8. Environmental Working Group, Scientific Report of the 2015 Dietary Guidelines Advisory Committee, Apr. 15, 2015, www.ewg.org/testimony -official-correspondence/scientific-report-2015-dietary-guidelines-advi sory-committee.
9. Report of the World Commission on Environment and Development: Our Common Future, United Nations, Mar. 1987, www.un-documents .net/our-common-future.pdf.
10. Baylen J. Linnekin, End farm subsidies and make agriculture sustainable, Chicago Tribune, May 18, 2011, www.chicagotribune.com/bs-ed-farm -subsidies-20110518-story.html.
11. Christophe Hille, email message to author, July 12, 2015.
12. Iso Rabins, email message to author, July 9, 2015.
13. Greg Van Ullen, email message to author, Aug. 18, 2015.
14. Jason Foscolo, email message to author, July 30, 2015.
15. Madeleine Redfern, email message to author, July 2, 2015.

Index

Island Press | Board of Directors